FINDING ANSWERS IN

U.S.
CENSUS
RECORDS

FINDING ANSWERS IN
U.S.
CENSUS
RECORDS

Loretto Dennis Szucs
& Matthew Wright

Ancestry

Library of Congress Cataloging-in-Publication Data

Szucs, Loretto Dennis.
    Finding answers in U.S. census records / Loretto Dennis Szucs.
        p. cm.
Includes bibliographical references and index.
    ISBN 0-916489-98-1 (pbk. : alk. paper)
    1. United States—Genealogy—Handbooks, manuals, etc. 2. United
States—Census—Handbooks, manuals, etc. I. Wright, Matthew, 1972-
II.
Title.
    CS49 .S984 2001
    929'.1'072073--dc21

                                                2001003238

Published by Ancestry® Publishing, an
imprint of MyFamily.com, Inc.

P.O. Box 990
Orem, Utah 84059
www.ancestry.com

First Printing 2001
10 9 8 7 6 5 4 3 2

Printed in the United States of America

TABLE OF CONTENTS

INTRODUCTION

When the Founding Fathers of the United States convened the Constitutional Convention in 1787 they had no idea that they would, in the course of their deliberations, create the means to an end for generations of American family history researchers. While Article I, Section 2 of the Constitution does not directly mention preserving vital personal information for future generations, it does instruct the government to conduct a decennial census in an effort to fairly apportion the number of federal representatives from each state as well as to decide on the amount of direct taxes to be levied. That effort to take stock of the U.S. population every ten years has produced, as a natural by-product, the greatest source of genealogical information available to U.S. researchers.

Because they contain such important information about individuals, families, and communities, U.S. Census records are the most frequently used records created by the federal government. Recognizing their value to researchers, the National Archives began to microfilm federal census records in 1941 and with microfilming came the ability to make duplicate copies, then to digitize them. Because of technological developments, federal census records can now be researched from a home computer or via the Internet at the nearest archives or library.

Beyond the records resulting from the population head counts conducted by the federal government, there are a number of other census schedules that should not be overlooked by researchers. Agricultural, industry and manufacturing, mortality, slave, and other special census schedules created by the federal government are also worth exploring, as are state and local censuses. Special censuses reveal a great deal about American territories, and some provide hard-to-find details about Native Americans. While the latter vary greatly in content and availability, information not available elsewhere can often be found in them.

ABOUT THIS BOOK

This book is a guide to help researchers effectively locate and use the abundant and valuable U.S. Census records, whether it is the population schedules, state and local census schedules, or special census schedules. After a brief history of the origin of the census, the book discusses each type of census and explores what specific points a researcher needs to keep in mind when working with them. Beginning and advanced researchers will find useful information that has been culled from authoritative sources and documented accordingly in an extensive bibliography.

The larger part of this book is based on "Research in Census Records," a chapter that originally appeared in *The Source: A Guidebook of American Genealogy* (Salt Lake City, Ancestry. Szucs and Luebking, eds., 1997). The extraordinary developments in technology and vastly increased accessibility to census records in the past several years have made it clear that a freestanding and updated guide to using these historical treasures was necessary. Because most of the basic record descriptions and the methodology outlined in the original chapter have not changed, we elected to reproduce them as they originally appeared, however, updates were made wherever necessary (To include information on the 1930 U.S. Federal census, for example). In this new version you will also find an abundance of new artwork, including illustrative copies of actual census records.

In addition, three appendixes have been added to aid census researchers. The first contains a listing of the major online and/or electronic sources for U.S. Census research. The second is a directory of important libraries and archives with microfilm repositories where family historians can view, rent, create, or buy microfilm copies of their census records of interest. The third appendix contains census extraction forms for all the available census years from 1790 to 1930, a chart summarizing what questions were asked for each census, an official census information request form.

WHY THE CENSUS IS AS IMPORTANT AS EVER

Census records contain the basic documentation for the study of U.S. history, biography, demography, immigration, migration, ethnicity, occupations, economics, social anthropology, medical history, local history, and family history. Social historians, journalists, the media, and government agencies have come to rely on the census as a reliable source for fascinating and valuable pieces of information.

Certain research topics have lent themselves well to the use of the U.S. Census. Occupational data and property values noted in some census years have been the basis for economic studies, and inquiries regarding Revolutionary War pensioners (1840) and Civil War veterans (1890 and 1910) can aid military research. Reconstruction of historic sites in Philadelphia; an examination of foreign-born farmers, women, and blacks in nineteenth-century Concord, Massachusetts; and regional studies, such as that of Dickinson County, Kansas, have sought support from a combination of records—notably the census. The 1860 census provided particulars on the domestics in their place of employment, while making possible the reconstitution of their families of origin residing on surrounding farmlands. More recent census records have been used by medical researchers to track families and to study hereditary and communicable disease patterns.

The most popular use of the census, however, is to trace family history. No other source matches the census record's ability to place people in a certain place at a certain time, or to provide such a detailed picture of lives and lifestyles at given intervals. The promise of that picture, and of seeing it clearly, keeps researchers going against all odds. It is with an awareness of that promise that we have written this book. If we have done our job right, you are well on your way to important findings in the quest to bring your family history to life.

Loretto Dennis Szucs
Matthew Wright

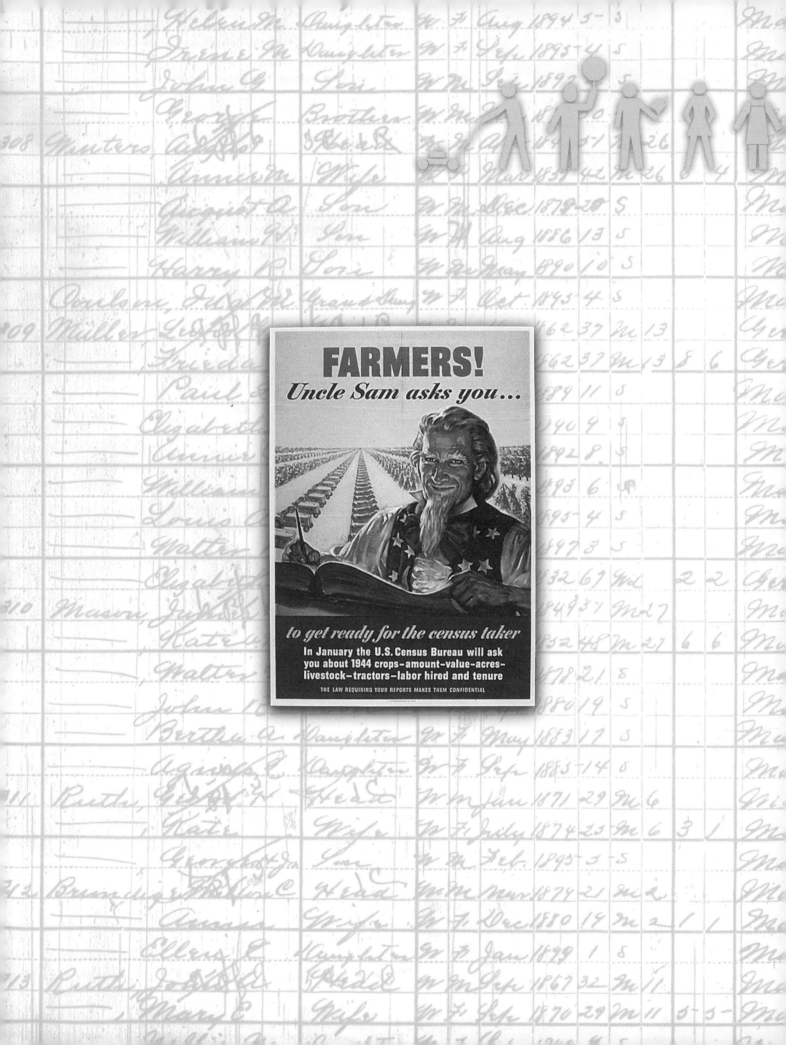

Understanding the U.S. Census

What is the name, age, sex, color, occupation, and birthplace of each person residing in this house? Which of these individuals attended school or was married within the year? Who among them is deaf and dumb, blind, insane, "idiotic," a pauper, or a convict? Is there anyone in the household over twenty years of age who cannot read and write? What is the name of the slave owner? How many slaves belong to the owner? What is the tribe of this Indian? What were the places of birth of the person's parents? In what year did this person immigrate to the United States and, if naturalized, what was the year of naturalization?

For answers to these and other questions, researchers look to census records. While not all of these inquiries were made in every census year, each of the decennial (occurring every ten years) enumerations of the inhabitants of the United States has its own potential for solving mysteries of the past. Few, if any, records shed as much light on individuals, families, or communities as do population census schedules. From the first federal census of 1790 to the 1930 census (the most recent census available to the public), the records present a vast resource that is rich in personal information and is very accessible.

This book will provide a brief history of the U.S. federal population censuses from 1790 to 1930, including a section describing "General Strengths and Limitations of Census Records." Suggestions in the General Strengths and Limitations section will be useful not only for searching federal schedules but also for searching special and state censuses described later in the book. The contents and special features of each federal decennial census are also described in chronological order, followed by a section on related census indexes. Where and how to use census records is discussed in the last part of this book. The impact and availability of electronic or digital census resources is discussed throughout, where appropriate, as well as in Appendix I.

HISTORICAL BACKGROUND

The actual records of civilization's first population counts have apparently not survived, but it is known that in early Babylonia, Egypt, and China the inhabitants were counted on a regular basis. There are ancient written accounts of the Greeks and Romans having taken censuses, but those tallies, too, seem to have been lost over the centuries. On the North American continent, the Spaniards led the way in census-taking, counting heads in 1577 in what was then Mexico.

Since 1790, the U.S. government has taken a nationwide population count every ten years. Though never intended for genealogical purposes, the federal censuses are among the most frequently used records for those looking for links with the past. Unique in scope and often surprisingly detailed, the census population schedules created from 1790 to 1930 are among the most used of federally created records. Over the course of two centuries, the United States has changed significantly, and so has the census. From the six basic questions asked in the 1790 census, the scope and categories of information have changed and expanded dramatically.

> Representatives and direct Taxes shall be apportioned among the several States which may be included within this Union, according to their respective Numbers... The actual Enumeration shall be made within three Years after the first Meeting of the Congress of the United States, and within every subsequent Term of ten Years, in such Manner as they shall by Law direct.
>
> —Article I, Section 2, of the United States Constitution

Article I, Section 2, of the U.S. Constitution required that an enumeration of the people be made within three years after the first meeting of the Congress. In March 1790, after President Washington signed the first census act, Secretary of State Thomas Jefferson sent a copy of the law to each of the seventeen U.S. marshals and instructed them to appoint as many assistants as they needed to take the census.

From 1790 to 1880, census districts were aligned with existing civil divisions. The district marshals were authorized to subdivide each district into reasonable geographical segments to facilitate supervision of the enumeration. Enumeration districts were limited in size to 10,000 individuals by the Census Act of 1850, but final tallies show that the number was usually less than 6,000. In 1880, the Census Office appointed supervisors to further subdivide the districts. In that year, the average population of each of the 28,000 enumeration districts was less than 2,000.[1]

Early censuses were essentially basic counts of inhabitants, but as the nation grew, so did the need for statistics that would reflect the characteristics of the people and the conditions under which they were living. The logical means for obtaining a clearer picture of the American populace was to solicit more information about individuals. In 1850, the focus of the census was radically broadened. Going far beyond the vague questions previously asked of heads of households, the 1850 census enumerators were instructed to ask the age, sex, color, occupation, birthplace, and other questions regarding every individual

Each decade enumerators have used different modes of travel to take them from interview to interview.
(Source: U.S. Census Bureau, Public Information Office.)

in every household. Succeeding enumerations solicited more information; by 1930, census enumerators asked thirty questions of every head of household and almost as many questions of everyone else in the residence. As W.S. Rossiter, chief clerk of the Bureau of the Census around the first part of the twentieth century, stated, "The modern census is thus the result of evolution."[2]

THE CENSUS BUREAU

Although the Constitution, ratified in 1787, called for a census every ten years, there was no special government agency to conduct and tabulate the results of this massive survey. Until 1840, federal marshals managed the process as best they could. In 1850, the first Census Office was opened in Washington, D.C. However, it was disbanded after the 1850 census and only reestablished in time to take the census and tally the results in 1860, 1870, 1880, 1890, and 1900.

Not until 1902 was the Bureau of the Census established as a permanent bureau in the Department of the Interior. In 1903 the bureau was transferred to the Department of Commerce. The Bureau of the Census is responsible for providing statistics about the population and economy of the nation and for collecting, tabulating, and publishing a wide variety of statistical data for government and private users.[3]

STRENGTHS AND LIMITATIONS OF CENSUS RECORDS

Few, if any, records reveal as many details about individuals and families as do the U.S. federal censuses. The population schedules are successive "snapshots" of Americans that depict where and how they were living at particular periods in the past. Census records since 1850 suggest dates and places of birth, relationships, family origins, changes in residence, schooling, occupations, economic and citizenship status, and more.

Once home sources have been exhausted, the census is often the best starting point for U.S. genealogical research. The availability of statewide indexes for almost every census year makes them logical tools to locate individuals whose precise residence is unknown. While some inaccuracies are to be expected in census records, they still provide some of the most fascinating and useful pieces of personal history to be found in any source. If nothing else, census records are important sources for placing individuals in specific places at specific times. Additionally, information found in the census will often point to other sources critical to complete research, such as court, land, military, immigration, naturalization, and vital records.

The importance of census records does not diminish over time in any given research project. It is always wise to return to these records as discoveries are made in other sources because, as new evidence about individuals is found, some data that seemed unrelated or unimportant in a first look at the census may take on new importance.

When family, vital, or religious records are missing, census records may be the only means of documenting the events of a person's life. Vital registration did not begin until around 1920 in many areas of the United States, and fires, floods, and other disasters have destroyed some official government records. When other documentation is missing, census records are frequently used by individuals who must prove their age or citizenship status (or that of their parents) for Social Security benefits, insurance, passports, and other important reasons.

PROBLEMS CREATED AT THE TIME THE CENSUS WAS TAKEN

When evaluating any source, it is always wise to consider how, when, and under what conditions the record was made. By understanding some of the difficulties encountered by enumerators, it becomes easier to understand why some individuals cannot be found in the census schedules or in the indexes to them.

From the first enumeration in 1790 to the most recent in 2000, the government has experienced difficulties in gathering the precise information it desired for a number of reasons. At least one of the problems experienced in extracting information from individuals for the first census continues to vex officials today: There were and still are many people who simply do not trust the government's motives. Many citizens have worried that their answers to census questions might be used against them, particularly regarding issues related to taxation, military service, and immigration. Some have simply refused to answer enumerators' questions; others have lied.

BOUNDARIES

In the days before regular mail service, government representatives conducted door-to-door canvasses of their appointed districts. Supervisors subdivided districts using existing local boundaries. The town, township, military district, ward, and precinct most often constituted one or more enumeration districts.[4] Boundaries of towns and other minor civil divisions, and in some cases of counties, were ill defined, so enumerators were frequently uncertain whether a family resided in their district or in an adjoining district. For this reason, it is not unusual to find individuals and families listed twice in the census and others missed entirely. Robert C. Anderson, et al., provide excellent examples and an analysis of this rather common problem in "Duplicate Census Enumerations," *The American Genealogist* 62 (2) (April 1987): 97–105; 62 (3) (July 1987): 173–81; 62 (4) (October 1987): 241–44.

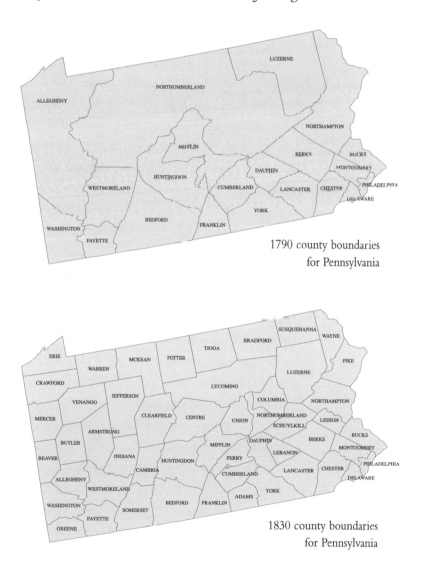

1790 county boundaries
for Pennsylvania

Over the years, state, county, township, and city ward boundaries have changed. Any census search can be thrown off by these changes and inconsistencies. For a thorough discussion of boundaries with detailed maps, see William Thorndale and William Dollarhide, *Map Guide to the U.S. Federal Censuses, 1790–1920* (Baltimore: Genealogical Publishing Co., 1987). The introduction to this useful work includes a discussion of duplication in census records.

1830 county boundaries
for Pennsylvania

HISTORICAL PERSPECTIVE

For a better sense of how census takers carried out their duties in a given year, it is useful to imagine the landscape and the modes of travel available in the specific time period. In the earliest census years, travel was obviously more difficult and sometimes very dangerous—conditions that did not improve for decades in the more rural states and territories of the "Wild West."

To complicate the situation further, a large portion of the young nation's population lived in small villages and isolated farms that were dispersed over a large area. It was not uncommon for a census enumerator to make a long trip to a remote farm, only to find no one at home. In these instances, he was left to make a decision—whether to try again on another day, or question farm or household help, neighbors, or even young children. The latter appears to have been an option taken by many. In some situations, enumerators probably found it easier to guess themselves.

But obtaining answers directly from the head of household or an adult in the house was no guarantee of accuracy either. For a number of reasons, ages are always suspect in census records. Many people tend to be secretive about their age; women may have been particularly sensitive about revealing the truth. One woman tracked in the census taken in New York from 1850 to 1880 claimed to have aged only twelve years in the thirty-year period. According to the 1850 and 1860 censuses of Springfield, Illinois, Mary, wife of Abraham Lincoln, aged only seven years in the ten-year period (figure 1). She, or someone reporting for her, claimed that she was twenty-eight in 1850 and only thirty-five in 1860. Dozens of cases have been similarly noted; undoubtedly, some honestly could not remember how old they were. If a person's age was not exactly known, it was frequently rounded off to the closest decade, making ages reported as thirty, forty, fifty, and so on somewhat suspect. Therefore, unless an age reported in the census can be corroborated with another source, it should not be considered totally reliable.

When questions were answered by someone other than the subject of the inquiry, the likelihood of error increased. A husband or wife might not always know the birthplaces of a spouse's parents. A child being quizzed might easily be unsure of the birthplaces of his or her parents. Census schedules do not tell us who may have answered the enumerator's questions.

An important point to remember is that enumerators simply wrote down the responses given to them. They were not authorized to request any kind of proof, such as birth, marriage, or property ownership records. However, every individual contacted by a government representative was required by law to answer truthfully. Anyone refusing to answer or willfully providing false information was guilty of a misdemeanor and subject to a fine. As early as 1790, offenders were fined twenty dollars,

Figure 1. 1850 (top) and 1860 (bottom) federal census entries for the household of Abraham Lincoln, Springfield, Sangamon County, Illinois. The entries appear on pages 120 and 130, respectively.

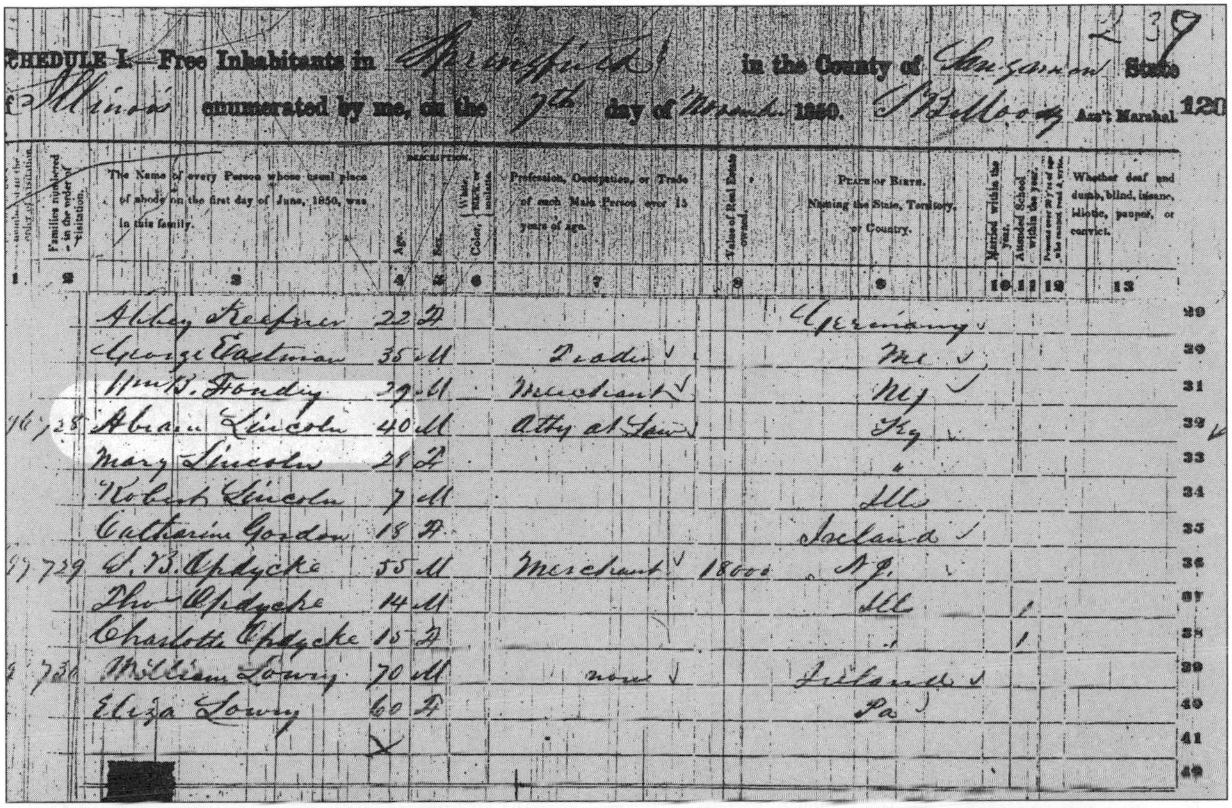

SCHEDULE I.—Free Inhabitants in Springfield in the County of Sangamon State of Illinois enumerated by me, on the 7th day of November 1850. J. B. Moody Ass't Marshal. 120

Dwelling-houses numbered in the order of visitation	Families numbered in the order of visitation	The Name of every Person whose usual place of abode on the first day of June, 1850, was in this family.	Age	Sex	Color, White, black, or mulatto	Profession, Occupation, or Trade of each Male Person over 15 years of age.	Value of Real Estate owned.	Place of Birth, Naming the State, Territory, or Country.	Married within the year.	Attended School within the year.	Persons over 20 y'rs of age who cannot read & write.	Whether deaf and dumb, blind, insane, idiotic, pauper, or convict.	
1	2	3	4	5	6	7	8	9	10	11	12	13	
		Abbey Keefner	22	F				Germany					29
		George Eastman	35	M		Trader		Me					30
		Wm B. Fondey	29	M		Merchant		NY					31
96	728	Abram Lincoln	40	M		Atty at Law		Ky					32
		Mary Lincoln	28	F				"					33
		Robert Lincoln	7	M				Ills					34
		Catharine Gordon	18	F				Ireland					35
97	729	S. B. Opdycke	55	M		Merchant	1800	NJ					36
		Thos Opdycke	14	M				Ill		1			37
		Charlotte Opdycke	15	F				"		1			38
[illegible]	730	William Lowry	70	M		none		Ireland					39
		Eliza Lowry	60	F				Pa					40
			X										41
													42

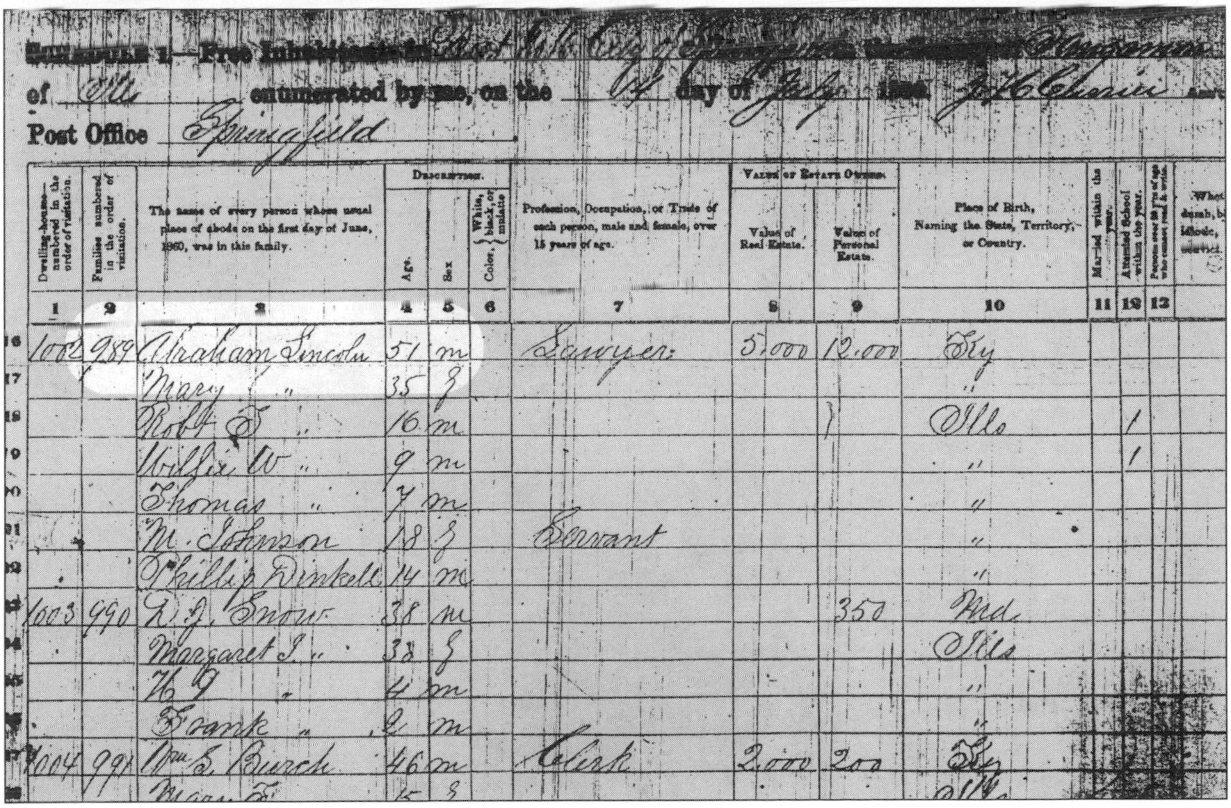

SCHEDULE 1.—Free Inhabitants in [illegible] in the County of Sangamon State of Ills enumerated by me, on the 04 day of July 1860. [illegible] Ass't Marshal.

Post Office Springfield

	Dwelling-houses—numbered in the order of visitation.	Families numbered in the order of visitation.	The name of every person whose usual place of abode on the first day of June, 1860, was in this family.	Age.	Sex.	Color, White, black, or mulatto	Profession, Occupation, or Trade of each person, male and female, over 15 years of age.	Value of Real Estate.	Value of Personal Estate.	Place of Birth, Naming the State, Territory, or Country.	Married within the year.	Attended School within the year.	Persons over 20 y'rs of age who cannot read & write.
	1	2	3	4	5	6	7	8	9	10	11	12	13
16	1002	989	Abraham Lincoln	51	m		Lawyer	5,000	12,000	Ky			
17			Mary "	35	f					"			
18			Robt T. "	16	m					Ills		1	
19			Willie W. "	9	m					"		1	
20			Thomas "	7	m					"			
21			M. Johnson	18	f		Servant			"			
22			Phillip Dinkell	14	m					"			
23	1003	990	D. J. Snow	38	m				350	Ind.			
24			Margaret J. "	38	f					Ills			
25			H. J. "	4	m					"			
26			Frank "	2	m					"			
27	1004	991	Wm S. Burch	46	m		Clerk	2,000	200	Ky			
28			Mary E.	15	f					Ills			

to be split between the marshals' assistants and the government. But relatively few individuals were hauled into court for refusing to answer or for not answering truthfully. It would have been an impossible task for the government to follow through and to investigate everyone's answers.

It was not until 1830 that the census office supplied printed questionnaires or "schedules." The enumerators of the 1790, 1800, 1810, and 1820 censuses returned the results of their canvassing on whatever paper they had. Each also had to post copies of their censuses in two public places in their assigned areas. Presumably, people who could read would see discrepancies or omissions and call them to the attention of officials. Unfortunately few, if any, of these duplicates have survived.

Another factor that comes into play in the accuracy of every census record is the competency of the enumerator who recorded the information. Individuals were not necessarily well-educated or qualified for the job, and anyone who has studied census records knows that good penmanship was not a requirement. Census takers were political appointees who were frequently chosen because they were of the correct political affiliation in a particular time and place, or just knew the right people.

Wages were definitely not an incentive for would-be census takers. In 1790, even the highest pay rate, one dollar for fifty persons, barely covered an enumerator's expenses. In 1920, payment was on a per-capita or per-diem basis—sometimes a combination of the two. An enumerator was paid between one and four cents per person, depending on the urban or rural setting of the district to be counted.

The United States has always been home to a large number of immigrants, and those who did not speak English well presented still another problem for the census taker. Often, enumerators could hardly understand the information given to them by people with foreign accents. Names were frequently misunderstood and misspelled by enumerators to the extent that they may not even begin with the correct letters, making them hard to find in census schedules and almost impossible to find in indexes. The German name Pfeiffer could easily be heard and committed to paper as Fifer, for example. An Irish census taker in Cleveland recorded the Polish name Menkalski as McKalsky in the 1920 census. Places of birth may have been equally difficult to translate into English.

Whether recording information from a foreign-born or American-born individual, some enumerators took the quickest way to get the job done. Some used initials rather than given names, some used nicknames, and some omitted places of birth, value of real estate, occupations, and other details. In boarding houses, hotels, and clusters of workers' cottages, enumerators could easily overlook entire families.

While enumerators were given basic instructions as early as 1820, it was not until 1850 that the Census Office printed uniform instructions for the enumerators, explaining their responsibilities, procedures, the specifics of completing the schedules, and the intent of each question asked. In 1850, the Census Office also provided enumerators with a large portfolio to accommodate the oversize forms (which measured twelve by eighteen inches; this book (opened) by comparison is eleven by seventeen inches), pens, a portable ink stand, ink, and blotting paper. Enumerators were instructed not to fold the pages and not to allow anyone to "meddle with [their] papers." Pages were numbered consecutively as they were completed. Each page was dated on the day it was begun, even if it was not completed until another day. Every page was to include the enumerator's signature, the name of the civil division, county, and state and, after 1870, the local post office.

According to the 1850 census instructions, the enumerator, on completing the entry for each family, farm, or shop, was to read the information back to the person interrogated so that errors could be corrected immediately. But if an informant was unclear or incorrect in giving information in the first place, this procedure did little to correct errors. A significant portion of the American population could not read or write in the 19th Century, so if an enumerator misspelled the family surname it could easily have stayed that way, whether or not it was repeated by the enumerator.

As the enumeration of each subdistrict was completed, the enumerator was to make two copies that were to be carefully compared to the original for accuracy. Hand copying, of course, brings the very strong possibility of mistakes that are often unknown to the creator of the copy. Experience with the various copies of the census shows that most copies were not error free. It was cumbersome and tedious to copy names and endless columns of personal information. It is unlikely that enumerators envisioned the copies ever being read again once the statistical tabulations were completed, so it is easy to believe that many became careless as the job wore on.

As the process was completed, the enumerator was to sign each page of the census and, at the end of each set of copies, to certify that the census had been taken and copied according to instructions. One set was to be filed with the clerk of the county court, and the other two were to be forwarded to the supervisor. As the supervisor received the completed schedules, it was his or her duty to see that every part of the district had been visited and that the copies were in good order. One set was then sent to the state or territory, and the other was forwarded to the U.S. Census Office for statistical analysis. Unfortunately, it is almost impossible to distinguish the original census taken by the enumerator—the one likely to be most accurate—from the copies, which were prone to additional inaccuracies due to mistakes in the copying process. While it is usually not possible to know if the original census or a copy was sent, it is relatively easy to recognize the census that was sent to the Census Office. "Researchers can distinguish the latter set from the other two because the Census

Office made tabulations directly on the schedules; consequently, the central office copy bears pencil, crayon, and red ink markings on virtually every page."[5]

In 1880, the procedure of making three sets of returns was abandoned. Enumerators forwarded the originals to the Census Office and did not make copies. In an attempt to correct errors, however, the Census Act of 1880 called for "public exhibition of the population returns," and for this purpose it authorized enumerators to make a list of names with age, sex, and color of all persons enumerated in the district, to be filed with the clerk of the county court. If any of these lists have survived, they will be found at the county level.

In most enumerations, census takers were instructed to number each dwelling consecutively in the order of visit, though it was not always clear how the instructions may have changed or been interpreted from year to year. It should be emphasized that there was no connection between the household numbers (usually the number listed in the first column to the left of the census page) and the locality or address.

Census instructions defined a dwelling as any structure in which a person was living, including a room above a store, warehouse, or a factory or a wigwam on the outskirts of a settlement. Institutions, such as hospitals, orphanages, poorhouses, garrisons, asylums, and jails, were counted as single-dwelling houses. It was not until the 1880 census that the character and name of the institution were required to be written in the margin. The 1880 census was also the first to include street addresses in cities.

In most years, census instructions stated that all persons temporarily absent on a journey or visit were to be counted with the rest of their family in their usual abode. However, children away at school and living near the school or college were to be enumerated with that family or institution. According to the instructions, "seafaring men" were to be reported at their homes on land, no matter how long their absence, if they were believed to be still alive. Sailors residing in boarding houses were not to be counted there but rather at their permanent residences, if they had any. Expressmen, canalmen, railroad employees, and others engaged in transportation were to be enumerated with their families if they returned to their homes at regular intervals.

Census instructions were quite specific as to how enumerators were to map out and proceed through their assigned areas so that no one would be missed. The 1920 instructions, for example, stated:

> 68. *Method of canvassing a city block - If your district is in a city or town having a system of house numbers canvass one block or square at a time. Do not go back and forth across the street. Begin each block at one corner, keep to the right, turn the corner, and go*

in and out of any court, alley, or passageway that may be included in it until the point of starting is reached. Be sure you have gone around and through the entire block before you leave it.

69. The arrows in the following diagram indicate the manner in which a block containing an interior court or place is to be canvassed:

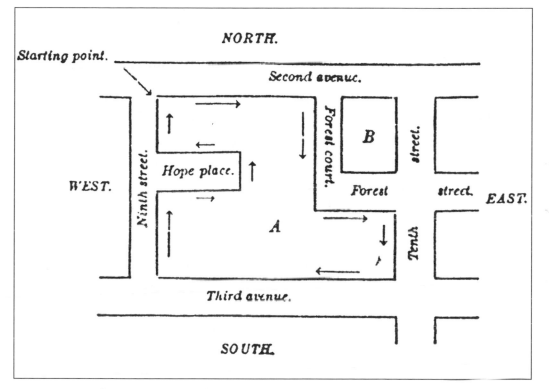

Department of Commerce, Bureau of the Census, Fourteenth Census of the United States. January 1, 1920: Instructions to Enumerators (Washington, D.C.: Government Printing Office, 1919).

MISSING CENSUSES

According to most authorities, the 1790 census schedules for Delaware, Georgia, Kentucky, New Jersey, Tennessee, and Virginia were burned during the War of 1812. Some records, such as the 1790 records for Virginia, have been reconstructed from state enumerations and tax lists. In later enumerations, city blocks, neighborhoods, townships and sections of townships, and even entire counties are known to be missing from the census schedules, simply because no census was taken in the particular area in a given year or because they were lost before they reached Washington, D.C.

Probably the most noted loss of the federal enumerations is that of the 1890 census. Most of the 1890 schedules were destroyed in a fire in the Commerce Department in 1921.

FALSE CENSUS ENTRIES

Another confusing situation can arise in census research when names show up in a district where they do not belong—sometimes more than once! According to Arlene Eakle, Ph.D., "padding the totes," or adjusting the census for political reasons, was not uncommon. "Frontier areas, anxious for statehood, often added bogus names. In 1857, seven counties in Minnesota had wild population totals, complete with fake names on the schedules. Jurisdictions facing increased taxes might also understate their populations to keep overall per capita taxes lower. The 1880 Utah census juggled households to disguise polygamy at a time when federal officials were seeking evidence for the prosecution of those convicted of unlawful cohabitation."[6]

MISSING PERSONS

Bogus entries may have been a frustration in some times and places, but a far greater problem in every census year has been that of undercounting. Whether families or individuals were not counted because they lived in remote areas or because they would not tolerate an enumerator's personal questions, millions have been missed since official government census-taking began. The Census Bureau has acknowledged "that the 1990 census, which put the U.S. population at 248.7 million, missed an estimated 5 million people—ranging from 1.7 percent of whites to 5.2 percent of Hispanics" (*Chicago Tribune*, Tuesday, 17 March 1992, sec. 2, page 4). While no stone should remain unturned in the search for an individual in the census, the unfortunate truth is that a significant portion of the population has been missed entirely.

An example of damaged microfilm.

LEGIBILITY

Probably no other factor causes more frustration for a researcher than finding the general area in which an individual or family should be found in the census and then not being able to read the page or pages of interest. Often, worn and torn pages, faded or smeared ink, and the disintegrating paper of the original census are to blame. Most frequently, however, poor microfilming techniques caused unfocused and blurred sections, overexposed and underexposed pages, and words to be obscured because of tightly bound volumes or mending tape.

Microfilming of federal census records took place in the 1940s, when the technology was in its infancy and techniques had not yet been perfected. Because of the poor

Suggestions For Microfilm Searches

Courtesy of
Arlene Eakle

Because most census searches are still made on microfilm, below are some suggestions to make research easier.

1. Become familiar with the surnames in your area so that you can recognize them with only half of their letters distinct. Study a county history, a tax list, or a landowner's atlas.

2. Create a "pony" from the actual entries in the census. How does the writer make a, h, s, p, j, and other letters which could be misinterpreted? Draft an alphabet with uppercase and lowercase letters for comparison. An easy way is to slip a piece of plain paper onto the viewing surface and trace the letters from the page.

3. Use a reader in a darkened room, with a strong light to project the image. Slip a colored piece of paper—pink, yellow, and green are effective—onto the viewing surface.

4. Copy the microfilmed page, enlarging or reducing the image to make it clearer and sharper. Many microfilm copiers have interchangeable lenses.

5. Review the whole schedule so you don't miss important entries that appear out of place. Record all columns for each entry, even if the information seems unimportant, and record all members of the household whether they are familiar or not. In multiple-family dwellings, record all family units living in the building. These families are often related, especially in immigrant settlement areas.

6. Copy the data exactly as it appears in the record. If the given name is abbreviated, copy the abbreviated form. Do not expand it. If the entry is crossed through or changed, copy the entry, the cross-through line, and the changes. Note carefully the last entry on each page. Family units may be split between two pages without a repeat of the surname.

7. Use finding tools and indexes to get into the census quickly, then search the census carefully to get all the data it contains (see the bibliography). If all the data is available, it is possible to block out the pedigree for several generations from this source alone. Then, proof can be sought in other records to ensure that names in the pedigree really belong there. If you are researching a common name like Brown or Jones, the censuses can help eliminate those that do not fit, making searches in other sources less time-consuming.

quality of the original microfilming, some of the 1850, 1860, and 1870 schedules were microfilmed a second time. The versions can be distinguished because the earlier microfilming included two pages to a frame, the newer having only one census page per frame. Unfortunately, the original census schedules for 1900, 1910, and 1920 were destroyed in 1946 (with the approval of the Archivist of the United States and Congress), so records that are not legible cannot be re-microfilmed.

The quality of microfilms may vary from one copy to another. Generally, the original microfilm will be better than later generations of the same. Census microfilms have been duplicated a number of times in order to make the records available to as many researchers as possible. In some cases, the National Archives in Washington, D.C., may have the best copy.

Digitization of microfilmed records offers a second chance to capture these images the right way. A proprietary process used by Ancestry.com, for example, has been used to scan a second generation copy of the microfilm in 256 shades of gray (as opposed to black and white) and then to optimize it using software filters. The resultant images are often easier to read than the original.

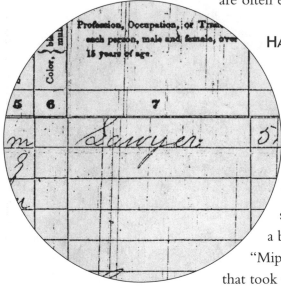

A difficult handwriting style.

HANDWRITING

Poor penmanship, archaic handwriting styles, and symbols are other leading causes of researchers' inability to find or read specific names or information in census records. Many letters can be misinterpreted unless a study is made of the enumerator's handwriting style. For example, uppercase letters L and S are frequently difficult to distinguish. In one district of the 1850 census, the word "lawyer" looks more like "sawyer." Likewise, a birthplace of Missouri might look more like "Mifouri" or "Mipouri" to someone unfamiliar with the long 's' character that took the place of a double 's' in some manuscripts.

Despite the many imperfections of the census, it should again be emphasized that census records are one of the first sources used in almost every genealogical project. They are invaluable for placing an individual in a particular time and place and for connecting the individual to other sources. The foregoing descriptions make it fairly easy to see why census records are not perfect or entirely reliable. But, as noted author Val Greenwood suggests, "no research on an American genealogical problem after the beginning of census is complete until all pertinent census schedules have been searched."[7]

Courtesy of
Juliana Szucs Smith

Suggestions For Online Searches

Increasingly, census records can be accessed using electronic media. Below are some tips for searching electronic census indexes.

1. **ADVANCED SEARCH TOOLS** Most electronic indexes provide users with various options for more effective searching. In cases where you are dealing with common surnames in large cities, it is often helpful to specify more information to narrow down your search. In addition, when an ancestor cannot be located using basic searches, sometimes they can be located by entering different combinations of information, such as first name and township/county/state or other keywords that may be available in the database.

2. **KEYWORDS** When searching a database, users are typically given the choice of searching by surname, given name, locality, and keyword. If the user begins by using only the surname and state, the resulting matches will likely be too broad. While it is sometimes impossible to include a given name or locality, try narrowing down the search results using keywords. For example, suppose you are searching for an ancestor named John Brown from Mississippi. After putting those details in the search you could also add any other information you know about him in the keyword field, e.g. the township, a country of origin, a language, a date, etc.

3. **SOMETIMES LESS IS MORE** Keep in mind that databases will only give hits on exact matches. When too much information in included in a search, you run the risk of eliminating a possible hit in cases where names have been abbreviated or misspelled, where variations exist, or when information is missing. (A more detailed article on this topic is available online at: <http://www.ancestry.com/library/view/columns/compass/1170.asp>.)

4. **GIVEN NAMES** If you specify a given name, be sure to also look for variations, misspellings, or abbreviations of that name. Sometimes only an initial or abbreviation is used, such as Chas. for Charles or Thos. for Thomas. Also look for variations and different spellings—Eliza, Beth, Liz, Liza, for Elizabeth; Alex for Alexander; Jim for James; Jon for John. If you are looking for an immigrant ancestor, look for his or her name as spelled in the native language.

5. **SOUNDEX SEARCHES** Many electronic indexes allow for Soundex searches. This may help you to get positive results, despite possible misspellings. For other databases, you may want to say the name aloud. For example, when searching the surname Dwyer data entries are listed as Ware, Toire, Wire, and Weir. Note the phonetic spellings of names and try using different accents.

6. **RESEARCH LOG** When you are searching for multiple names, and multiple spellings for multiple years, it can be difficult to keep track of where you have searched, when, and for what. Keeping a log of the places you have searched and combination of search terms used, along with results, can save much duplicated effort. With Web sites that are constantly being updated, bugs worked out, and/or search features enhanced, you may want to go back occasionally to recheck for missing ancestors. Your log can tell you when you last checked a site. The free research calendar at Ancestry.com can be used to record your searches. <http://www.ancestry.com/save/charts/researchcal.htm>

7. **BEYOND THE INDEX** While indexes are becoming more and more detailed, there is still more to be found on the original documents. For example, the FamilySearch™ 1880 U.S. Census and National Index contains the following:

name	age
relationship	occupation
sex	birthplace
marital status	father's birthplace
race	mother's birthplace

But, you will not find the any of following information that can be found by looking at a copy of the original enumeration:

the family's address

how many families reside in the dwelling

month of birth for children born within the year

whether individuals were married that year

how many months an individual was unemployed

school attendance during the year

whether unable to read if age 10 or older

whether sick or temporarily disabled on the day of enumeration and the reason therefore

whether the individual was blind, deaf-mute, "idiotic," insane, or permanently disabled

In addition, as previously discussed, indexes may contain errors, causing you to miss family members that could be found in browsing the enumerations.

8. **USING ONLINE SOURCES TO SAVE TIME DURING LIBRARY AND ARCHIVE VISITS** With more and more census information becoming available online and on CD-ROM, by performing as many of these searches from the comfort of your home, you can free up valuable research time to search other records and resources when the opportunity arises to visit a facility with a large genealogical collection.

9. **PRINT IT OUT** Each CD-ROM or Web site is slightly different, but it is always worth the time and toner to print out a hard copy of pertinent census records for further review. This paper copy can be placed in a binder or folder and accessed when you are not at your computer. The paper copy also helps to ensure that you do not introduce any mistakes into your records while transcribing. A paper copy allows you to compare your new findings with offline information more easily and handwriting or reading errors can be corrected on further review or looking back at the printed form.

INTERPRETING CENSUS INFORMATION

Professional researchers recommend that photocopies or computer printouts be made of census pages whenever possible. The advantages of an actual copy over a transcription are several: the possibility of mistakes being made in the transcription process are eliminated; a copy will include neighbors and provide an overview of the population makeup of the area (except in cases where names are listed in alphabetical order instead of in order of visitation); and a copy makes it easy to go back and reevaluate information as new discoveries are made in the research process.

While information in the census may be quite accurate, at times the order in which data has been entered can be misleading. For example, a head of household recorded in 1820, 1830, or 1840 may not be the oldest person in the house. With only age ranges to distinguish, it is impossible to know who may be a grandparent, a younger brother, or a man with both parents still living at home. Individuals listed in early censuses in any age grouping could be servants, visitors, or boarders not related to the family. Even in 1880 and later, the relationships noted apply to heads of household only. Children listed as sons and daughters of the head of household may be unrelated to the wife.

CENSUS RECORDS AND THE ROLE OF THE NATIONAL ARCHIVES

The National Archives has custody of the federally created census records, including the published 1790 census schedules, negative photostatic copies of the 1800, 1810, 1820, and 1830 census schedules, originals of the 1840, 1850, 1860, and 1870 census schedules, the surviving fragments of the 1890 schedules, and microfilm copies of the 1900, 1910, and 1920 schedules. Due to their fragile condition, some of the original schedules have been retired and are not available to researchers. The original 1880 census schedules went back to the states and are no longer in the custody of the National Archives. A research book entitled *Guide to Genealogical Research in the National Archives*, 3rd ed. (Washington, D.C.: National Archives and Records Administration, 2001), provides detailed information on federally-created census records from 1790 to 1910. According to the Guide, "Because copies of the census records are now available at the archives field branches, NARA no longer searches schedules in response to mail requests. The National Archives will fur-

National Archives Building, Washington D.C.

nish photocopies of census pages only when the researcher can cite the state, county, enumeration district (for 1880, 1900 and 1910), volume number, and exact page on which a family is enumerated." Information about this and other NARA publications is available at the NARA Web site <http://www.nara.gov/publications/>.

MICROFILM COPIES

The National Archives has reproduced all of the available federal population census schedules on microfilm. Copies of available 1790 to 1930 censuses for all states and territories can be used in the Microfilm Research Room in the National Archives in Washington, D.C., regional branches of the National Archives, at the Family History Library of The Church of Jesus Christ of Latter-day Saints in Salt Lake City and in its family history centers, and at many other private and public libraries. The added options of borrowing census schedules from microfilm lending companies or purchasing microfilm copies from the National Archives make the census one of the most readily available record sources.

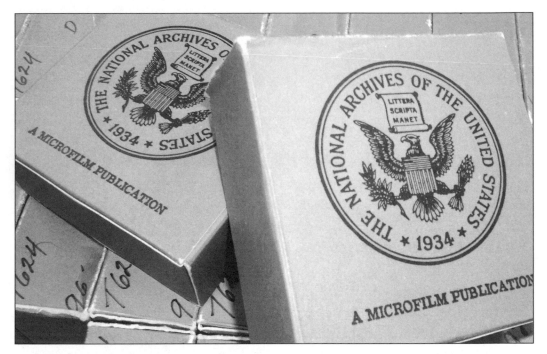

Rolls of National Archive Census Microfilm

LIMITATIONS OF MICROFILM COPIES

As noted earlier, microfilming of the census schedules, indexes, and other heavily-used records in the National Archives took place in the 1940s, when the technology was in its infancy. The microfilms of most of the censuses for most years are quite legible. However, there are thousands of census pages from various states and years that cannot be read because of poor focusing or because of too much or too little lighting. Pages of original census schedules were inadvertently skipped when microfilming took place—some pages may have stuck together when turned, and some may have been missing when the microfilming began. For example, nine pages were missed during the microfilming of the 1820 Virginia schedule. They were subsequently identified and indexed by Gerald M. Petty in "Virginia 1820 Federal Census: Names Not on the Microfilm Copy," *Virginia Genealogist* 18 (1974): 136–39. In another case, more than 1,000 Illinoisans with names beginning with the letter O were somehow missed when the rest of the 1880 Soundex index was microfilmed. The missing section for the letter O was later transcribed from the original cards by Nancy Gubb Frederick, *1880 Illinois Census Index, Soundex Codes O-200 to O-240* (Evanston, Ill.: the compiler, 1981).

Unfortunately, since the 1900, 1910, and 1920 census originals were destroyed, it will be impossible to re-microfilm any illegible pages or pages missed in the original microfilming of schedules for those census years. As mentioned previously, however, advances in scanning technology have provided a way to improve the legibility of some of these damaged pages.

RESTRICTIONS ON ACCESS TO POST-1930 CENSUS RECORDS

To protect the privacy of living individuals, access to population schedules is restricted for seventy-two years after the census is taken, so they are not available to researchers during that time. The Personal Service Branch, Bureau of the Census, P.O. Box 1545, Jeffersonville, IN 47131, will provide, for a fee, official transcripts of census records from 1940 to 2000. Access is restricted to whomever the information is about, their authorized representatives, or, in the case of deceased persons, their heirs or administrators. Use Form BC-600 (See Appendix III) to request information. Since the Census Day for 1940 was 1 April 1940, this census is scheduled to be released on 1 April 2012.

A U.S. Census Geographer works on coverage maps for the 1930 census. *(Source: U.S. Census Bureau, Public Information Office.)*

FEDERAL POPULATION CENSUS RESEARCH PROCEDURES

1. HOW TO FIND CENSUS RECORDS

All available federal census schedules, from 1790 to 1930, have been microfilmed and are available at the National Archives in Washington, D.C., at the National Archives' regional archives in twelve states, at the LDS Family History Library and LDS family history centers throughout North America, at many large libraries, and through microfilm lending companies. Some state and local agencies may have census schedules only for the state or area served.

In addition to the microfilmed copies of the federal census schedules, digital copies are also increasingly available online and on CD-ROM. These resources can be accessed from personal computers at home or at a library, are generally searchable, and can save researchers a good deal of time and money. Ask your local librarian if your library has access to a U.S. Federal Census collection online or on CD-ROM. See Appendix I for contact information of groups and organizations that produce this type of resource.

2. STARTING INFORMATION

It is usually best to begin a census search in the most recently available census records and to work from what is already known about a family. With any luck, birthplaces and other clues found in these more recent records will point to locations of earlier residency.

3. ARRANGEMENT OF CENSUS RECORDS

The microfilm census schedules are arranged by census year and thereunder alphabetically by name of state; then, with a few exceptions, alphabetically by name of county. To begin researching microfilmed census records, a researcher must know in which state the subject of interest lived during the census year, and may need to know the county and an exact address if the name is common.

In early census years or in sparsely populated areas, one roll of microfilm may contain all the schedules for one county or several small counties. However, in heavily populated areas, there may be many rolls for a single county. The arrangement of surnames on a page of the schedule is usually in the order in which the enumerator visited the households. To search for a particular name in the microfilm schedules may necessitate scanning every page of a district; however, the increasingly numerous indexes to federal censuses and finding aids have dramatically reduced such tedious work. Finding a particular name in most electronic and digital copies of the schedules is much easier with their built-in global search function.

4. INDEXES

Federal census indexes have been compiled and published for every state up to and including 1850; many states have been indexed up to and including 1870; and The Church of Jesus Christ of Latter-day Saints has now completed a nationwide index for 1880 which is available on CD-ROM from FamilySearch™. Indexes may be in book, microfilm, computer diskette, or CD-ROM form. They are also available in database format online. There are indexes or partial indexes for the 1880, 1900, 1910, and 1920 censuses. Within a short time it is probable that there will be online indexes available for all extant censuses that have been microfilmed. Archives and libraries that have copies of census microfilm generally have indexes to complement their collections.

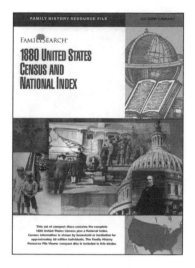

5. CATALOGS

Four catalogs produced by the National Archives Trust Fund Board are especially helpful in conducting research in federal census records (See sidebar on the following page for ordering information). They are:

National Archives Trust Fund Board. *The 1790–1890 Federal Population Censuses: Catalog of National Archives Microfilm*. Washington, D.C.: National Archives Trust Fund Board, 1993. This catalog is arranged chronologically, thereunder by state or territory, and then by county. Given for each microfilm publication is the series number and the total number of microfilm rolls in the enumeration. The catalog further identifies each microfilm roll by number and contents.

_____. *1900 Federal Population Census: A Catalog of Microfilm Copies of the Schedules*. Washington, D.C.: 1978. This catalog lists the 1,854 rolls of microfilm on which the 1900 population census schedules appear. The census schedules are arranged by state or territory and then by county. Numbers for the 7,846 rolls of 1900 Soundex indexes appear in the second half of the book.

_____. *The 1910 Federal Population Census: A Catalog of Microfilm Copies of the Schedules*. Washington, D.C.: 1982. This catalog lists the 1,784 rolls of microfilm on which the 1910 population census schedules appear. The census schedules are arranged by state or territory and then by county. Numbers for the 4,642 rolls of 1910 Soundex/Miracode indexes appear in the second half of the catalog.

_____. *The 1920 Federal Population Census: Catalog of National Archives Microfilm*. Washington, D.C..: 1991. This catalog lists the 8,585 rolls of 1920 Soundex indexes in the front portion of the book. The catalog lists 2,076 rolls of 1920 census schedules arranged by state or territory and then by county.

The 1790-1890 Federal Population Censuses, Revised
8.5" x 11", 96 pages
National Archives and Records Administration,
1979, 1993, 1997
#200032 Softcover $3.50
ISBN 0-911333-63-0

1900 Federal Population Census, Revised
8.5" x 11", 84 pages
National Archives and Records Administration,
1978, 1996
#200031 Softcover $3.50
ISBN 0-911333-14-2

The 1910 Federal Population Census
8.5" x 11", 44 pages
National Archives and Records Administration, 1982
#200009 Softcover $3.50
ISBN 0-911333-15-0

1920 Federal Population Census, Revised
8.5" x 11", 96 pages
National Archives and Records Administration,
1991, 1992
#200042 Softcover $3.50
ISBN 0-911333-86-X

1930 Federal Population Census
8.5" x 11", 112 pages
National Archives and Records Administration, 2002
#200043 Softcover $3.50
ISBN 1-880875-25-X

ORDERING INFORMATION

Payment. A check (payable to the National Archives Trust Fund) must accompany each order unless payment is made by credit card. VISA, MasterCard, American Express, and Discover (Novus) are accepted; simply provide the account number, expiration date, and cardholder signature. Persons placing credit card orders may also call toll free 1–800–234–8861. (301–713–6800 in the Washington, DC area) Orders may also be faxed to 301–713–6169.

Purchase orders. Government agencies, educational institutions, and businesses may order on an accounts–receivable basis by submitting either an official purchase or letterhead with authorized order signatures. Send your order to the address shown below, or fax to 301–713–6499. (If faxed, please do not send a confirming copy by mail.)

Trade (retail) orders. All NARA books in print may be purchased for resale at a 20% discount as long as 10 or more copies of the same title are purchased. Higher discounts may be available for single-title orders of 250 or more copies; please inquire.

Bookseller returns: full credit (no refunds) will be extended to all returns within 180 days of shipment as long as the copies are in clean, saleable condition and are accompanied by a packing slip with applicable National Archives Service Order numbers. Damaged or defective books or books shipped in error may be returned for replacement within 30 days of receipt. Booksellers must request authorization and shipping instructions from the Customer Service Center (NWCC2) before the materials are returned.

Shipping/handling.

* Please add $3 for orders up to $50
* Add $5 for orders between $50.01 and $100
* For orders over $100, add 5% of merchandise total
* Please specify exact title(s) and order number(s)
* Send payment, with your name, address, and day-time telephone number, to: National Archives Trust Fund, NWCC2, Dept. 2001, P.O. Box 100793, Atlanta, GA 30384–0793.

Please allow 3 to 4 weeks for delivery.
Prices and availability subject to change without notice.

Researching the Individual Censuses

T he information contained in the U.S. Federal Census schedules varies dramatically from the first census in 1790 to the latest available census of 1930. What started in colonial times as a basic head-count evolved into a somewhat lengthy interrogation that yielded tremendous amounts of information useful in genealogical research.

Following is a summary of what to expect in each census schedule, along with research tips. Also, see page 153 for a summary of questions asked in each census.

1790 CENSUS

The 1790 census was begun on 2 August 1790. The marshals were expected to finish the census within nine months of the Census Day—by 1 May 1791. Although most of the returns were in long before the deadline, Congress had to extend the count until 1 March 1792. By that time some people probably were counted who had not been born or present in 1790. The official census population count was 3,929,214.

QUESTIONS ASKED IN THE 1790 CENSUS

The 1790 Census called for: name of family head; number of free white males of sixteen years and older; number of free white males under sixteen; number of free white females; number of slaves; number of other persons; and sometimes town or district of residence.

The 1790 census instructed the marshals to identify, by age brackets, free white males sixteen years of age or older and those under sixteen. This was designed to determine the country's industrial and military capabilities. Additionally, the first census was to count the number of free white females; all other free persons regardless of race or gender; and slaves. A twenty-dollar fine, to be split between the marshals' assistants and the

154 Names of Heads of Families	Free White Males of 16 years & upwards including Heads of Families	Free White Males under Sixteen Years	Free White Females including Heads of Families	All other Free Persons	Slaves
Greenwich					
Cond Bower	1		1		
Jno Derr	1	3	3		
Andw Werner	1		1		
Dav Dresler	1	2	2		
Andw Dresler	1	2	5		
Michl Laub	2		1		
Peter Dommeyer	1	1	4		
Michl Eary	2		2		
Geo Herring	3		4		
Geo Herring Junr	2		3		
Saml Groß	1	2	1		
Adam Gensel	1	3	3		
Andw Kamp	1	3	2		
Jno Herring	1		2		
Simon Gruber	2	1	5		
Geo Kemp	1		1		
Fredk Kamp	1		2		
Adam Didrich	1	4	3		
Widow Minigh	2	1	3		
Jno Witt	1		5		
Andw Boligh	1	1	5		
Nichs Lieb	1	3	4		
Jacob Arnold	1		2		
Jacob Greenwalt	1	4	5		
Michl Boligh	1		3		
Michl Croll	2	1	2		
Benedict Neidlinger	1	1	4		
Jno Folk	1		2		
Franw Arnold	2	2	4		
Carried Over	38	34	84		

1790 Census
Schedule

government, would be levied against anyone who refused to answer the enumerator's questions.

OTHER SIGNIFICANT FACTS ABOUT THE 1790 CENSUS

The Constitution called for a census of all "Persons . . . excluding Indians not taxed" for the purpose of apportioning seats in the House of Representatives and assessing direct federal taxes. The "Indians not taxed" were those not living in the settled areas. In later years, Native Americans everywhere were considered part of the total population, but not all were included in the apportionment figures until 1940.

The government did not provide printed forms or even paper until 1830. It was up to each assistant to copy his census return on whatever paper he could find and post it in two public places in his assigned area. Those who saw and could read them were supposed to check for discrepancies or omissions. The highest pay rate, two cents per person, barely covered expenses, especially where settlers were scattered and living in places that were difficult to find or access.

The jurisdictions of the thirteen original states stretched over an area of seventeen present-day states. Census schedules survive for only two-thirds of those states. The surviving schedules were indexed by state and published by the Bureau of the Census in the early 1900s. The index, *Bureau of the Census, Heads of Families at the First Census of the United States Taken in the Year 1790,* 12 vols. (Washington, D.C.: Government Printing Office, 1908), can be found in most research libraries; it has been reprinted by various publishers over the years.

Both the original and printed 1790 census schedules are available on microfilm for Connecticut, Maine (then part of Massachusetts), Maryland, Massachusetts, New Hampshire, New York, North Carolina, Pennsylvania, Rhode Island, South Carolina, and Vermont (figure 2). The schedules for Delaware, Georgia, Kentucky, New Jersey, Tennessee, and Virginia were burned during the War of 1812. (There are substitutes

HEADS OF FAMILIES—NEW YORK. 13

ALBANY COUNTY—Continued.

NAME OF HEAD OF FAMILY.	Free white males of 16 years and upward, including heads of families.	Free white males under 16 years.	Free white females, including heads of families.	All other free persons.	Slaves.	NAME OF HEAD OF FAMILY.	Free white males of 16 years and upward, including heads of families.	Free white males under 16 years.	Free white females, including heads of families.	All other free persons.	Slaves.	NAME OF HEAD OF FAMILY.	Free white males of 16 years and upward, including heads of families.	Free white males under 16 years.	Free white females, including heads of families.	All other free persons.	Slaves.
ALBANY CITY, FIRST WARD—continued.						**ALBANY CITY, SECOND WARD—continued.**						**ALBANY CITY, THIRD WARD—continued.**					
Yates, Peter W	2		8		2	McFarson, Hugh	1	1	1			Stringer, Samuel	2	1	2		2
Staats, Henry	3	1	5		2	Barber, John	3		3			Lush, Stephen	1	3	3		2
Radlie, Philip	1		2		2	Watson, Matthew	2	2	2	1		Wendell, — H	1		3		4
Hilton, William	1	1	1			Easterly, Thomas	2	3	4			Douw, Volkert A	1		1		4
ALBANY CITY, SECOND WARD.						Norwood, Mary			4			Lansing, John Jacob	1	1	1		
						Fonda, Jacobus	1		3			Evertson, Bernardus	2	5	4		1
Cuyler, Jacob	2	3	1		4	Bogert, Barent	1	1				lansing, Garrit	1		1		
Groesbeck, John	2	5	4		1	Mersales, Gysbert	1		4		2	lush, Richard	1		2		
De Garmo, Bastian	4	1	4			Cuyler, Philip	1		3			Graham, John	1	2	2		
Rogardus, Jacob	1					Hooker, Samuel	3	3	3			Defrust, Isaac	2	3	3		4
Cavenaugh, William	2	1	3			Hanson, John J	1	3	4			Veeder, Abraham	1	2	1		
Groesbeck, David	2		1		2	Swits, Cornelius	1		3			Va Vechten, Teunis T	2	3	3		2
Woodruff, Hanlock	2	1	4			Van Schaaick, Cornelius	1		1			Dexter, Samuel	1		2		
Hanson, John	2					Mersailes, John	1		3			Douw, Peter W	1		2		3
Blucker, Catherine		2	5		3	Pruyn, Casparus	3	1	2	1	3	Beekman, Elizabeth			2		3
Beekman, John J	1	1	4		6	Tiffany, Silvester	3	2	2		1	Glen, Cornelius	1		2		1
Fellows, William	2		1			Whipple, Benjamin	4		5			Caldwell, James	5	3	6		5
Batist, —	2			1		Cuyler, Abraham	2		5		5	Makey, John	2		5		5
Hagerdy, William	1	2	1		1	Ten Eyck, Harmanus	1	2	4		2	Willett, Elbert	2		3		1
Lansing, Jacob	1		1		2	Va Rensselaer, Jeremiah	2		5		5	Sim, Peter	2	2	2		(*)
Bradt, Aaron	2	3	3			Va Schuriyne, Cornelius	1		3		12	Orr, Isabel	1		2		(*)
Nehemiah, John	1	3	3			Bogert, Abraham	1		1		1	Waters, David	1				(*)
Bradt, John A	1	3	1			Douglass, Thomas		3	4			Hale, Daniel	4	1	3		2
Dunkavy, James	1		3			Ryan, Patrick	2		2			Bloodgood, James	6		1		5
Barrington, Nicholas	1		2			McGurgy, Edward	1		2			Brower, Barent	1		1		(*)
Pruyne, Margaret			2			Dale, William	1	2	2			Roseboom, Eve			3		2
Muclaroy, Richard	1	1	3			Cammeron, John	1	1	2			Fonda, David	1	3	5		2
Devenbagh, Frederick	1		3			Campbell, John	1		2			Groesbeck, Garrit	1		2		(*)
Brower, John	1	4				Haynes, Thomas	1		1		(*)	Cuyler, John	1				(*)
McKenney, John	1		5			McDonald, Donald	1		1		(*)	Kirk, John	1	1	2		(*)
Groesbeck, Cornelius	1	1	3			Bruce, Robert	1		1		(*)	Boyd, John	3	2	2		2
Van Vrankin, Moses R	1	1	3		1	Archer, George	1	1	2		(*)	Hunn, Thomas	2		2		
Willitt, Edward, Jun	2		1		(*)	Andrews, Joseph	1	1	2		(*)	Gansevoort, Harman	1	1	1		7
Kennear, James	1	1	2			Hannah, Samuel	1		2		(*)	Gansevoort, Leonard, Jun					(*)
Ruby, Conradt	2	1	1			Smith, James	2	1	1		(*)	Bleeker, Barent	1	1	6		(*)
Park, Henry	1		2			McGourk, James	1		2		(*)	McMillen, John	1		2		(*)
Davis, Peter	1	1	3			McGourk, Robert	1	1	2		(*)	Evertson, Henry	2	1	2		(*)
Sturges, Isaac	1				(*)	Welch, Joseph	1		3			Yates, Abraham, Jun	2	5	3		(*)
Milligan, James	1		1		(*)	Ackerson, James	1		3		(*)	Westerlo, Ellardus	1	1	3		(*)
Giles, William	1		1			Morslelus, John G	2		5		1	Gansevoort, Peter	3	2	2		(*)
Winne, Jacob	1	4	2			Watson, Alexander	1		1		(*)	Ten Broek, John	3	2	4		(*)
Finch, Isaac	1		2			Crom, John	1		2	3		Truax, Henry	1	1	2		7
Van Ness, John	2	1				Burgess, John	1		3		(*)	Glen, Henry	3	1	3		7
Fadon, John	1	4	2			Mulhance, Peter	1		4		(*)	Schuyler, Abraham	2		3		9
Hawk, Christopher	1	2	5			Ellison, Abraham	1	1	4		(*)	Cuyler, Jacob, Jun	2	1	1		2
Billson, John	1		5			Lawson, Henry	1	1	2		(*)	Wallace, Benjamin	3		2		
Shaw, Ezra	1		1		(*)	Stevenson, Mary			2		(*)	Vesscher, Nanning H	1		4		
Roberts, John	1	1	1		(*)	Legrange, Jacobus	1		3		(*)	Bisbrown, Thomas	1		1		2
Amos, Thomas				2	(*)	Chesham, George	1		3		(*)	Lansing, Jeremiah	1	2	1		
Stoop, Catherine		1	4		(*)	McCloud, Donald	1	1	4			Beauman, Charles	1		2		
Visscher, Sarah	1	1	2		(*)	Forsight, Alexander	1	3	2		(*)	Visscher, Teunis	1		2		6
Van Dusen, Aaron	1		4		(*)	Barkley, James	1		3		(*)	Vandelbergh, William	2		3		3
Fonda, Isaac D	1		2		(*)	McMurray, Thomas	1	1	3		(*)	Van Husen, Cathelina			3		
Visscher, Tuenis G	1		3		(*)	Hendrick, Jacob	1		2	(*)	(*)	Chesney, James	1		4		5
Johnston, John	1		2		(*)	Ostrander, John	3	1	2		(*)	Wendell, Barbara			4		
Driskie, Jeremiah	1	3	1		(*)	Myer, Carol	1		2		(*)	Bradford, Thomas	1	1	6		
Bleeker, Nicholas	1	2	1		(*)	Waggoner, Andrew	1		2			McGibbon, Peter	1	1			
Edgar, Gregg	1		1		(*)	Wilmot, John	1	1	5		(*)	Tolbert, William	1		7		
Patrick, James	1		2		(*)	McManac, William	1	1	2		(*)	Richards, Ezra	1		3		
Vanloan, Jacob	1	3	3		(*)	Keating, Garret	2		2		(*)	Vander Zee, Walter	1	1	5		
Bleeker, John J	4	2	3	(*)	(*)	Snyder, Daniel	1	1	2			Killburn, York			4	3	
Bleeker, Jacob	1		1		4	Heath, John	1	3	1			Ram, John	1		4		
Bleeker, Jacob, Jun	1	2	2			Staals, Henry	2		2			McHargh, John	1		4		5
Cameron, William	2	2	1			Carson, Alexander	1		2			Van Iveren, Rynier	2		2		5
Andrew, John	2	1	1			Bromley, Samuel	1		2			Ten Broek, Abraham	1		3		12
Bleeker, John R	3		2		3	Horse, George	1		2			Vander Heyden, Jacob	1	2	4		3
Lansing, Gerandus	1		1		5	Hay, Alexander	1		3			Hunn, William	2	2	2		1
Bleeker, John N	3		6		1	McMickle, John	3	2	4			Williamson, Timothy	1		2		
Bleeker, Catelintia	1		4		2	Christie, John	1		2			Dunbar, William	1	3	3		1
Brower, Cornelius	2		2			Whitney, William	1	2	4			Visscher, Garrit T	4		1		
Lyn, Aaron	1	2	3			McKown, William	1	2	3			Icebrass, Hannah			1		
Barrington, Lewis	2	2	4			Bradt, Daniel	1	2	3			McReady, William	1	3	7		
Magee, John	1		2			Truax, John J	1		5			Miller, Philip, Jun	1	1	4		1
Boyd, John	4		2			Kagle, Cornelius	1	1	3			Van Vronkin, Garrit	1		2		
Hanson, Albert	2		2			James, John				3		Gates, John	1	2	4		1
Staats, Barent O	1		1		2	Winne, Killian D	2	1	2			Vanderhurg, Garrit	1		2		1
Van Zant, John W	1		3			**ALBANY CITY, THIRD WARD.**						Graverato, Henry	2		2		1
McDurmot, Michael	1		1									Slingerland, Jacob	1		3		
Rider, Barent	1		3			Lansing, Abraham A	1	1	4		6	Graham, Theodorus					
Carson, John	1	4	2			Blair, James	1		5			Van Wyck	2	1	3		4
Fuller, James	4	5	2			Sharp, Conradt	1	3	3			Roff, John	1		2		
Meggs, Seth	1		2			Van Iveren, Rynier			2			Bradt, Henry	1		3		
Pruyn, John F	1		2		6	Van Duser, Peter		2	2			Douw, Catherine			2		2
Merchant, George	3	2	5	1		Young, Peter	1		3			Leonard, Enock	1	1	2		
Visscher, Matthew	3		2			Truax, Isaac	1		2		2	Wynkoop, Jacobus	2		3		2
Ten Eyck, Hendrick	1	1	6			Van Arnam, Isaac		2	3		3	Sharp, Peter	2	2	2		
Jackroum, Jack	1	1		7		Lansing, John, Jun		1	4		4	de frust, Philip	1		2		
Lansing, Simon	2	2	4		4	Lansing, Sanders	1		2		2	de frust, Philip, Jun	1				2
Fonda, Nicholas	1		2			Walsh, Dudley	1	1	3			Verplank, William	1	1	2		2
Brown, William	1	2	4			Ten Broeck, Dirick	1		3		5	Winne, Jellis	1	2	3		1
												Lansing, Philip	1	2	3		

Illegible.

Figure 2. From *1790 Federal Census, Albany County, New York* (Baltimore: Genealogical Publishing Co.,1971, 13). All extant 1790 census schedules have been reprinted more than once. Copies are readily available in most public and research libraries.

for most of these.) Published and microfilmed 1790 schedules for Virginia were reconstructed from state enumerations and tax lists. (See list of these schedules on page 93.)

RESEARCH TIPS FOR THE 1790 CENSUS

Because of the availability of the printed 1790 census schedules, researchers tend to overlook the importance of consulting the original schedules, which are readily available on microfilm. As in most cases, the researcher who relies on printed transcripts may miss important information and clues found only in the original version.

The 1790 census records are useful for identifying the locality to be searched for other types of records for a named individual. The 1790 census will, in most cases, help distinguish the target family from others of the same name; identify immediate neighbors who may be related; identify slaveholders; and spot spelling variations of surnames. Free men "of color" are listed as heads of household by name. Slaves appear in age groupings by name of owner. By combining those age groupings with probate inventories and tax list data, it is sometimes possible to determine names of other family members and the birth order of those individuals.

For a state-by-state listing of census schedules, see *The 1790–1890 Federal Population Censuses: Catalog of National Archives Microfilm* (Washington, D.C.: National Archives Trust Fund Board, 1993). For boundary changes and identification of missing census schedules, see William Thorndale and William Dollarhide, *Map Guide to the U.S. Federal Censuses, 1790–1920* (Baltimore: Genealogical Publishing Co., 1987).

1800 CENSUS

The 1800 census was begun on 4 August 1800. The count was to be completed within nine months. The official census population count was 5,308,483.

QUESTIONS ASKED IN THE 1800 CENSUS

Name of family head; number of free white males and females in age categories: 0 to 10, 10 to 16, 16 to 26, 26 to 45, 45 and older; number of other free persons except Indians not taxed; number of slaves; and town or district and county of residence.

OTHER SIGNIFICANT FACTS ABOUT THE 1800 CENSUS

Most 1800 census entries are arranged in the order of visitation, but some have been rearranged to appear in alphabetical order by initial letter of the surname.

RESEARCH TIPS FOR THE 1800 CENSUS

The 1800 census records are useful in identifying the locality to be searched for other types of records for a named individual. The 1800 census will, in most cases, help distinguish the target family from others of the same name; help to determine family size; locate possible relatives with the same name; identify immediate neighbors who may be related; identify slaveholders; and spot spelling variations of surnames. Free men "of color" are listed as heads of household by name. Slaves appear in age groupings by name of owner. By combining those age groupings with probate inventories and tax list data, it is sometimes possible to determine names and birth order of other family members.

For a state-by-state listing of census schedules, see *The 1790–1890 Federal Population Censuses: Catalog of National Archives Microfilm* (Washington, D.C.: National Archives Trust Fund Board, 1993) (cited earlier). For boundary changes and identification of missing census schedules, see William Thorndale and William Dollarhide, *Map Guide to the U.S. Federal Censuses, 1790–1920* (Baltimore: Genealogical Publishing Co., 1987).

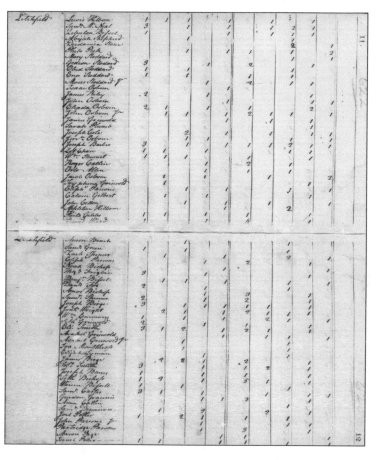

1800 Census Schedule

1810 CENSUS

The 1810 census was begun on 6 August 1810. The count was due within nine months, but the due date was extended by law to ten months. The official census population count was 7,239,881.

QUESTIONS ASKED IN THE 1810 CENSUS

The 1810 Census called for: name of family head; number of free white males and females in age categories: 0 to 10, 10 to 16, 16 to 26, 26 to 45, 45 and older; number of other free persons except Indians not taxed; number of slaves; and town or district and county of residence.

RESEARCH TIPS FOR THE 1810 CENSUS

The 1810 census records are useful in identifying the locality to be searched for other types of records for a named individual. The 1810 census will, in most cases, help

1810 Census
Schedule

distinguish the target family from others of the same name; help to determine family size; locate possible relatives with the same name; identify immediate neighbors who may be related; identify slave-holders; and spot spelling variations of surnames. Free men "of color" are named as heads of household. Slaves appear in age groupings by name of owner. By combining those age groupings with probate inventories and tax list data, it is sometimes possible to determine names of other family members and the birth order of those individuals. Manufacturing schedules are scattered among the 1810 population schedules.

For a state-by-state listing of census schedules, see *The 1790–1890 Federal Population Censuses: Catalog of National Archives Microfilm* (Washington, D.C.: National Archives Trust Fund Board, 1993). For boundary changes and identification of missing census schedules, see William Thorndale and William Dollarhide, *Map Guide to the U.S. Federal Censuses, 1790–1920* (Baltimore: Genealogical Publishing Co., 1987).

1820 CENSUS

The 1820 census was begun on 7 August 1820. The count was due within six months but was extended by law to allow completion within thirteen months. The official census population count was 9,638,453.

QUESTIONS ASKED IN THE 1820 CENSUS

• The 1820 Census called for: name of family head; number of free white males and females in age categories 0 to 10, 10 to 16, 16 to 18 (males only), 16 to 26, 26 to 45, 45 and older; number of other free persons except Indians not taxed; number of slaves; and town or district and county of residence. Additionally, the 1820 census for the first time asked the number of free white males 16 to 18; number of persons not naturalized; number engaged in agriculture, commercial, or manufacture; number of "colored" persons (sometimes in age categories); and number of other persons except Indians.

RESEARCH TIPS FOR THE 1820 CENSUS

The 1820 census records are useful in identifying the locality to be searched for other types of records for a named individual. The 1820 census will, in most cases, help distinguish the target family from others of the same name; help to determine family size; locate possible relatives with the same name; identify immediate neighbors who may be related; identify slaveholders; and spot spelling variations of surnames. Free men "of color" are listed as heads of household by name. Slaves appear in age groupings by name of owner. By combining those age groupings with probate inventories and tax list date, it is sometimes possible to determine names of other family members and the birth order of those individuals.

The added questions in the 1820 census break down ages so that it is possible to gauge the age of young men more accurately. However, the redundancy of asking the number of free white males "Between 16 and 18," and "Of 16 and under 26," "Of 26 and under 45," "Of 45 and upwards," is frequently cause for confusion in attempts to calculate the total number of persons in a given household. The column regarding naturalization status may be some indication of length of residency in the United States and the possibility of finding naturalization papers in a local court.

The questions asked regarding number and nature of those involved in agriculture, commercial, or manufacturing enterprises allow researchers to make some distinctions about the occupation of the head and any others in the household who were employed. Some, though admittedly not much, identifying information is available where schedules go beyond stating the number of "colored" persons and provide an age breakdown as well. The 1820 manufacturing schedules are on twenty-nine separate rolls of microfilm.

For a state-by-state listing of census schedules, see *The 1790–1890 Federal Population Censuses: Catalog of National Archives Microfilm* (Washington, D.C.: National Archives Trust Fund Board, 1993). For boundary changes

1820 Census
Schedule

and identification of missing census schedules, see William Thorndale and William Dollarhide, *Map Guide to the U.S. Federal Censuses, 1790–1920* (Baltimore: Genealogical Publishing Co., 1987).

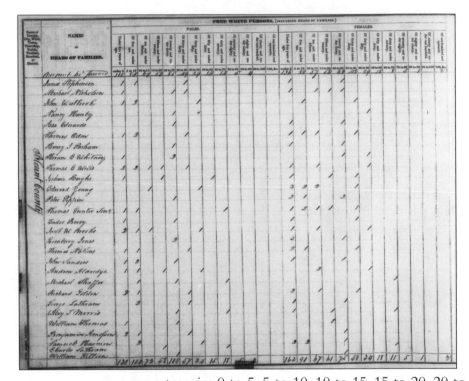

1830 Census
Schedule

1830 CENSUS

The 1830 census was begun on 1 June 1830. The enumeration was to be completed within six months but was extended to allow completion within twelve months. The official census population count was 12,860,702.

QUESTIONS ASKED IN THE 1830 CENSUS

The 1830 Census form called for: name of head of household; number of free white males and females in age categories 0 to 5, 5 to 10, 10 to 15, 15 to 20, 20 to 30, 30 to 40, 40 to 50, 50 to 60, 60 to 70, 70 to 80, 80 to 90, 90 to 100, over 100; number of slaves and free "colored" persons in age categories; categories for deaf, dumb, and blind persons and aliens; town or district; and county of residence.

OTHER SIGNIFICANT FACTS ABOUT THE 1830 CENSUS

The 1830 census was the first for which the government provided uniform, printed forms to enumerators for the purpose of recording answers to census questions.

RESEARCH TIPS FOR THE 1830 CENSUS

The 1830 census records are useful in identifying the locality to be searched for other types of records for a named individual. The 1830 census will, in most cases, help distinguish the target family from others of the same name; help to determine family size; locate possible relatives with the same name; identify immediate neighbors who may be related; identify slaveholders; and spot spelling variations of surnames. Free men "of color" are listed as heads of household by name. Slaves appear in age groupings by name of owner. By combining those age groupings with probate inventories and tax list data, it is sometimes possible to determine names of other family members and the birth order of those individuals.

The 1830 census went a step further in breaking down ages, thus allowing more precise knowledge of the household configuration. With the age categories expanded to include those one hundred years and older, it is possible to have a better idea of life spans during that time period. The addition of information regarding those who were deaf, dumb, and blind is an indication that there may be related guardianship or institutional records. The presence of aliens in a household suggests the possibility that those individuals may eventually have been naturalized in a nearby court.

For a state-by-state listing of census schedules, see *The 1790–1890 Federal Population Censuses: Catalog of National Archives Microfilm* (Washington, D.C.: National Archives Trust Fund Board, 1993). For boundary changes and identification of missing census schedules, see William Thorndale and William Dollarhide, *Map Guide to the U.S. Federal Censuses, 1790–1920* (Baltimore: Genealogical Publishing Co., 1987).

1840 CENSUS

The 1840 census was begun on 1 June 1840. The enumeration was to be completed within nine months but was extended to eighteen months. The official census population count was 17,063,353.

1840 Census
Schedule

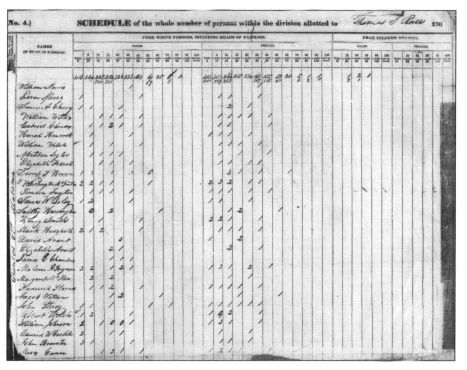

QUESTIONS ASKED IN THE 1840 CENSUS

The 1840 Census form called for: name of head of household; number of free white males and females in age categories 0 to 5, 5 to 10, 10 to 15, 15 to 20, 20 to 30, 30 to 40, 40 to 50, 50 to 60, 60 to 70, 70 to 80, 80 to 90, 90 to 100, over 100; number of slaves and free "colored" persons in age categories; categories for deaf, dumb, and blind persons and aliens; town or district; and county of residence.

Additionally, the 1840 census, asked for the first time, the ages of revolutionary war pensioners and the number of individuals engaged in mining, agriculture, commerce, manufacturing and trade, navigation of the ocean, navigation of canals, lakes and rivers, learned professions and engineers; number in school, number in family over age twenty-one who could not read and write, and the number of insane.

RESEARCH TIPS FOR THE 1840 CENSUS

The same research strategies used in the previous census apply to the 1840. A significant bonus comes from the question regarding revolutionary war pensioners. A search of revolutionary war sources may provide a wealth of genealogical information. A refinement of the occupation categories makes it possible to pursue other occupational sources and easier to distinguish individuals of the same name in the ever-growing population. Reading and writing skills and some indication of the educational level attained add an interesting and more personal dimension to a family history. An indication of the "insane" within a household might point to guardianship or institutional records. For a state-by-state listing of census schedules, see *The 1790–1890 Federal Population Censuses: Catalog of National Archives Microfilm* (Washington, D.C.: National Archives Trust Fund Board, 1993). For boundary changes and identification of missing census schedules, see William Thorndale and William Dollarhide, *Map Guide to the U.S. Federal Censuses, 1790–1920* (Baltimore: Genealogical Publishing Co., 1987).

1850 CENSUS

The 1850 census was begun on 1 June 1850. The enumeration was to be completed within five months. The official census population count was 23,191,876.

QUESTIONS ASKED IN THE 1850 CENSUS

The 1850 Census form called for: number of dwelling house and family, in order of visitation; name; age; sex; color; territory or country of birth; whether the person attended school or was married within the year; whether the person could read or write if over age twenty; whether the person was deaf-mute, blind, insane, or "idiotic"; whether or not a fugitive from the state; and real estate value. The census also asked the occupation of males over age fifteen.

Separate slave schedules for 1850 asked the name of each slaveowner, the number of slaves owned, and the number of slaves manumitted (released from slavery). While the schedules, unfortunately, do not name individual slaves, they asked the age, color, sex, and whether or not slaves were deaf-mute, blind, insane, or idiotic; and whether or not the slave was a fugitive from the state.

OTHER SIGNIFICANT FACTS ABOUT THE 1850 CENSUS

The 1850 census is frequently referred to as the first modern census because of dramatically improved techniques employed for it and repeated in later years. Printed

instructions to the enumerators account for a greater degree of accuracy compared with earlier censuses. The instructions explained the responsibilities of enumerators, census procedures, the manner of completing the schedules, and the intent behind census questions. "In the 1850 census and thereafter, enumerators were required by law to make their count by personal inquiry at every dwelling and with every family, and not otherwise."[8] As enumerations of districts were completed, the enumerator was instructed to make two additional copies: one to be filed with the clerk of the county court, one to be sent to the secretary of the state or territory, and one of the three to be sent to the Census Office for tabulation.

1850 Census Schedule

The census was to show the names of persons who died after 1 June of the census year and to omit children born after that date. It should be noted that many of the census takers did not get around to their assigned districts until late in 1850; some were as late as October and November.

The enumeration was to list every person in the United States except Indians living on government reservations or living on unsettled tracts of land. Indians not in tribal relations, whether of mixed blood or not, who were not living among the white population or on the outskirts of towns, were counted as part of the taxable population. The count was designed to determine the apportioning of representatives among the states.

RESEARCH TIPS FOR THE 1850 CENSUS

The 1850 schedules included the free and slave population and mortality, agriculture, and industry data. The inclusion of so much personal data for the first time in the 1850 census is an obvious boon to genealogists and social historians. For the first time it is possible to identify families and other groups by name. The inclusion of birthplaces for every individual allow for the plotting of migrational routes.

Ages provided in the 1850 census allow researchers to establish dates for searching vital records. While few states officially recorded vital records that early, religious and other records may be pursued with estimated dates of birth gleaned from the census.

The identification of previous residences points to still other record sources to be searched in named localities. The indication of real estate ownership would suggest that land and tax records should be searched. The 1850 census may provide starting information for searching marriage records, probates, and a number of other genealogically important records. Probable family relationships may also be determined through 1850 census records, though it is easy to come to the wrong conclusions. The 1850 census provides valuable insights into occupations and property value. It may also make it possible to spot remarriages and step-relationships and to determine approximate life spans.

For a state-by-state listing of census schedules, see *The 1790–1890 Federal Population Censuses: Catalog of National Archives Microfilm* (Washington, D.C..: National Archives Trust Fund Board, 1993). For boundary changes and identification of missing census schedules, see William Thorndale and William Dollarhide, *Map Guide to the U.S. Federal Censuses, 1790–1920.* (Baltimore: Genealogical Publishing Co., 1987).

1860 CENSUS

The 1860 census was begun on 1 June 1860. The enumeration was to be completed within five months. The official census population count was 31,443,321.

QUESTIONS ASKED IN THE 1860 CENSUS

For all free persons, the census asked: number of dwelling house and family, in order of visitation; name; age; sex; color; occupation of persons over age fifteen; value of real estate; value of personal estate; name of state, territory, or country of birth; whether the person was married during the year; whether the person attended school during the year; persons over 20 years of age who cannot read and write; and whether the person was deaf-mute, blind, insane, an "idiot," a pauper, or a convict.

The information in the slave schedules is the same as those for 1850.

OTHER SIGNIFICANT FACTS ABOUT THE 1860 CENSUS

The 1860 census was the first to ask those being queried to reveal the value of their personal estates. As enumerations of districts were completed, enumerators were instructed to make two copies: one to be filed with the clerk of the county court, one to be sent to the secretary of the state or territory, and the third to be sent to the Census Office for tabulation.

The birthplaces of individuals were to be specific as to the state or territory in the United States and the country of birth if foreign born. For example, designations of England, Scotland, Ireland, and Wales and the German states of Prussia, Baden, Bavaria, Württemberg, and Hesse-Darmstadt were preferred to Great Britain and Germany.

RESEARCH TIPS FOR THE 1860 CENSUS

Research strategies remain the same as those suggested for the 1850 census because information included in the 1850 and 1860 schedules is essentially the same, except for the addition of the question concerning personal estates. While the added column may be a general indicator of a person's assets, it is doubtful that individuals were likely to disclose true figures for fear of being taxed accordingly.

For a state-by-state listing of census schedules, see *The 1790–1890 Federal Population Censuses: Catalog of National Archives Microfilm* (Washington, D.C.: National Archives Trust Fund Board, 1993). For boundary changes and identification of missing census schedules, see William Thorndale and William Dollarhide, *Map Guide to the U.S. Federal Censuses, 1790–1920* (Baltimore: Genealogical Publishing Co., 1987).

1860 Census Schedule

1870 CENSUS

The 1870 census was begun on 1 June 1870. The enumeration was to be completed within five months. The official census population count was 38,558,371.

QUESTIONS ASKED IN THE 1870 CENSUS

The 1870 census form called for dwelling houses to be numbered in the order of visitation; families numbered in order of visitation; and the name of every person whose place of abode on the first day of June 1870 was with the family. The census further

1870 Census
Schedule

asked the age of each individual at the last birthday. If a child was under one year of age, months of age were to be stated in fractions, such as 1/12. Additionally, the census asked the sex, color, profession, and occupation or trade of every inhabitant. There were also columns for disclosure of value of real estate and personal property. The 1870 census asked for the place of birth, specifically in which state or territory of the United States, or in which country if foreign born (including the province if born in Germany). The schedule provided space to indicate whether or not the father and the mother of the individual was foreign born, and if an individual was born or married within the year, the month in which the event occurred was to be entered. The census also asked for those who had attended school within the year; those who could not read; those who could not write; and the deaf and dumb, blind, insane and the "idiotic" to be identified. Finally, the schedules had space to identify any male citizen of the United States of age twenty-one and older, and any male citizen of the United States age twenty-one and older whose right to vote was denied or abridged on grounds other than rebellion or other crime. (Also see "Non-Population Schedules and Special Federal Censuses," on page 69.)

OTHER SIGNIFICANT FACTS ABOUT THE 1870 CENSUS

The 1870 census may identify survivors of the Civil War, thus suggesting that military records may be found. Conversely, if an individual does not appear in the 1870 census as expected, it may be a clue that the person was a casualty of the war. In the absence of so many other records from the South for this era, information from the 1870 census can be especially important. A caveat, however, is found in *Map Guide to the U.S. Federal Censuses 1790–1920*, in which it is stated that "The 1870 census in the Southern States omits a great many persons."

RESEARCH TIPS FOR THE 1870 CENSUS

The 1870 census is the first census in which parents of foreign birth are indicated—a real boon in identifying immigrant ancestors. Immigrants who were naturalized and eligible to vote are identified, suggesting follow-up in court and naturalization sources. Indications of a person's color that were intended to be more precise—white (W), black (B), Chinese (C), Indian (I), mulatto (M)—may be helpful in determining individuals' origins. (Also see "Non-Population Schedules and Special Federal Censuses," on page 69.)

For a state-by-state listing of census schedules, see *The 1790–1890 Federal Population Censuses: Catalog of National Archives Microfilm* (Washington, D.C.: National Archives Trust Fund Board, 1993). For boundary changes and identification of missing census schedules, see William Thorndale and William Dollarhide, *Map Guide to the U.S. Federal Censuses, 1790–1920* (Baltimore: Genealogical Publishing Co., 1987).

1880 CENSUS

The 1880 census was begun on 1 June 1880. The enumeration was to be completed within thirty days, or within two weeks for communities with populations of 10,000 or more. The official census population count was 50,189,209.

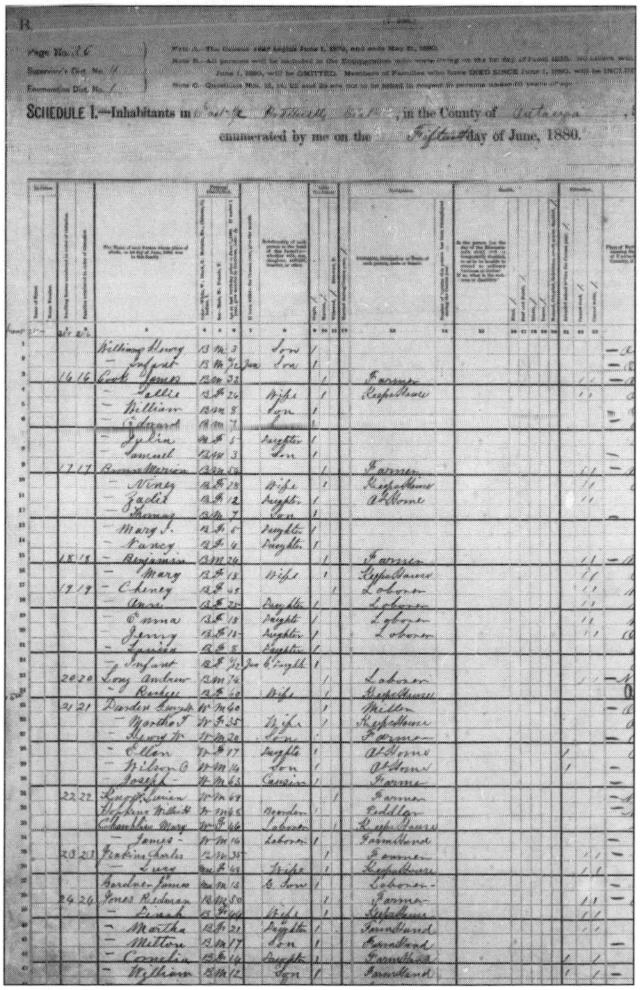

QUESTIONS ASKED IN THE 1880 CENSUS

For each person in every household, the census asked number of dwelling house and family, in order of visitation; name; whether white, black, mulatto, Indian, or Chinese; sex, age; month of birth if born within the year; relationship to the head of the household; whether single, married, widowed, or divorced; whether married within the year; occupation and months unemployed; name of state, territory, or country of birth; parents' birthplaces; school attendance within the year; whether unable to read if age ten or older; and whether sick or temporarily disabled on the day of enumeration and the reason therefore. Those who were blind, deaf-mute, "idiotic," insane, or permanently disabled were also indicated as such.

1880 Census Schedule

37

OTHER SIGNIFICANT FACTS ABOUT THE 1880 CENSUS

In addition to identifying the state, county, and other subdivisions, the 1880 census was the first to provide the name of the street and house number for urban households. The 1880 census was also the first to identify relationship to the head of household; illness or disability at the time the census was taken; marital status; number of months unemployed during the year; and the state or country of birth of every individual's father and mother. Individuals who were born or died after 1 June 1880 were not to be included in the 1880 census, even though the enumerator may not have questioned them until well after that date. Indians not taxed are not in regular population schedules. Some may appear in special Indian schedules. (Also see "Non-Population Schedules and Special Federal Censuses," on page 69.)

RESEARCH TIPS FOR THE 1880 CENSUS

The 1880 census makes it possible to identify the state or country of birth for parents, which is especially important for tracing movements of immigrant ancestors. The census may be used to supplement birth or marriage records for the census year or even to partially replace them where vital records are not recorded elsewhere. The census may also be useful in discovering previously unknown surnames of married daughters, mothers-in-law, cousins, and other relatives living with the family. This is the first census to state relationship to the head of household, but the wife may not be the mother of the children. The 1880 census may also provide clues to genetic symptoms and diseases in earlier generations of a family.

For a state-by-state listing of census schedules, see *The 1790–1890 Federal Population Censuses: Catalog of National Archives Microfilm* (Washington, D.C.: National Archives Trust Fund Board, 1993). For boundary changes and identification of missing census schedules, see William Thorndale and William Dollarhide, *Map Guide to the U.S. Federal Censuses, 1790–1920* (Baltimore: Genealogical Publishing Co., 1987). Also available are 1885 territorial censuses for Colorado, Florida, Nebraska, Dakota Territory, and New Mexico.

1890 CENSUS

The 1890 census was begun on 1 June 1890. The enumeration was to be completed within thirty days, or within two weeks for communities with populations of more than 10,000. The official census population count was 62,979,766.

QUESTIONS ASKED IN THE 1890 CENSUS

The surviving 1890 schedules provide the address, number of families in the house, number of persons in the house, and number of persons in the family. Individuals are listed by name; whether a soldier, sailor, or marine during the Civil War; and whether Union or Confederate or whether the widow of a veteran; relationship to head of family; whether white, black, mulatto, quadroon, octoroon, Chinese, Japanese, or Indian; sex; age; marital status; whether married during the year; if a mother, number of children and number living; place of birth of the individual and his or her father and mother; if foreign born, how many years in the United States; whether naturalized or in the process of naturalization; profession, trade, or occupation; months unemployed during census year; ability to read and write; ability to speak English (if not, language or dialect spoken); whether suffering from acute or chronic disease (if so, name of disease and length of time afflicted); whether defective in mind, sight, hearing, or speech; or whether crippled, maimed, or deformed (with name of defect); whether a prisoner, convict, homeless child, or pauper; whether the home is rented or owned by the head or a member of the family (if so, whether mortgaged); if the head of family was a farmer, if he or a family member rented or owned the farm; and, if mortgaged, the post office address of the owner.

1890 Census Schedule

OTHER SIGNIFICANT FACTS ABOUT THE 1890 CENSUS

Most of the original 1890 population schedules were destroyed or badly damaged by a fire in the Commerce Department in 1921. Records enumerating only 6,160 individuals—less than one percent of the schedules—survived. Unfortunately, no complete schedules for a state, county, or community survived, but only the following fragments:

1. Alabama: Perry County (Perryville Beat No. 11 and Severe Beat No. 8).
2. District of Columbia: Q. Thirteenth, Fourteenth, R.Q. Corcoran, fifteenth, S.R. and Riggs streets, Johnson Avenue, and S Street.
3. Georgia: Muscogee County (Columbus).
4. Illinois: McDonough County, Mound Township.
5. Minnesota: Wright County, Rockford.

6. New Jersey: Hudson County, Jersey City.
7. New York: Westchester County, Eastchester, Suffolk County, Brookhaven Township.
8. North Carolina: Gaston County, South Point Township and River Bend Township; Cleveland County, Township No. 2.
9. Ohio: Hamilton County (Cincinnati) and Clinton County, Wayne Township.
10. South Dakota: Union County, Jefferson Township.
11. Texas: Ellis County, J.P. no. 6, Mountain Peak, and Ovila Precinct; Hood County, Precinct no. 5; Rusk County, Precinct no. 6 and J.P. no. 7; Trinity County, Trinity Town, and Precinct no. 2; Kaufman County, Kaufman.

See the following indexes to these schedules:
• *Index to the Eleventh Census of the United States*. National Archives microfilm M496.
• Nelson, Ken. *1890 Census Index Register*. Salt Lake City: Genealogical Society of Utah, 1984.
• Swenson, Helen Smothers. *Index to 1890 Census of the United States*. Round Rock, Tex.: the author, 1981.

RESEARCH TIPS FOR THE 1890 CENSUS

Because it is well-known that the 1890 census records were destroyed by fire, few researchers think to check the index to the remaining schedules. (See "Federal Population Census Indexes and Finding Aids" on page 51.)

Special 1890 schedules enumerating Union veterans and widows of Union veterans of the Civil War are sometimes useful as a substitute for the missing 1890 population schedules. (Also see "Non-Population Schedules and Special Federal Censuses," on page 69.)

For a state-by-state listing of census schedules, see *The 1790–1890 Federal Population Censuses: Catalog of National Archives Microfilm* (Washington, D.C.: National Archives Trust Fund Board, 1993). For boundary changes and identification of missing census schedules, see William Thorndale and William Dollarhide, *Map Guide to the U.S. Federal Censuses, 1790–1920* (Baltimore: Genealogical Publishing Co., 1987).

THE 1890 CENSUS SUBSTITUTE

Ancestry.com, the National Archives and Records Administration, and the Allen County Public Library have teamed up to provide the first definitive online substitute for the missing census. More than 20 million records have been identified for inclusion in the collection, and additions will be made regularly as they become available for posting. It will include fragments of the original 1890 census that survived the fire, special veterans schedules, several Native American tribe censuses for years surrounding 1890, state censuses (1885 or 1895), city and county directories, alumni directories, and voter registration documents. You can access the census substitute at <http://www.ancestry.com/search/rectype/census/1890sub/main.htm>.

1900 CENSUS

The 1900 census was begun on 1 June 1900. The enumeration was to be completed within thirty days, or within two weeks for communities with populations of more than 10,000. The official census population count was 76,212,168.

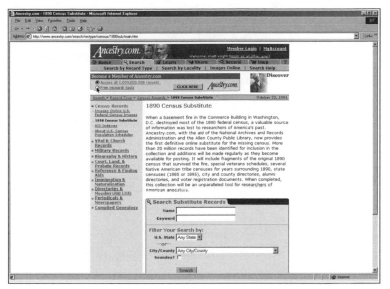

The Ancestry.com 1890 Federal Census Substitute Project Web page.

QUESTIONS ASKED IN THE 1900 CENSUS

The 1900 population schedules provide the number of dwelling house and family, in order of visitation; name of each person in the household; address; relationship to the head of the household; color or race; sex; month and year of birth; age at last birthday; marital status; the number of years married; the total number of children born of the mother; the number of those children living; places of birth of each individual and the parents of each individual; if the individual was foreign born, the year of immigration and the number of years in the United States; the citizenship status of foreign-born individuals over age twenty-one; occupation; number of months unemployed; whether the person attended school within the year; number of months in school, whether the person could read, write, and speak English; whether the home was owned or rented; whether the home was on a farm; and whether the home was mortgaged.

OTHER SIGNIFICANT FACTS ABOUT THE 1900 CENSUS

The 1900 census is the only available census that provides columns for including the exact month and year of birth of every person enumerated. Previous censuses, and even the 1910, 1920, and 1930 censuses, include only the ages. The 1900 census is also the only census to include space to record the number of years couples were married, the number of children born to the mother, and how many were still living. This census was also the first to indicate how long an immigrant had been in the country and whether naturalized; whether a home or farm was owned or rented, and whether the owned property was free of mortgage.

RESEARCH TIPS FOR THE 1900 CENSUS

Because the Soundex index to the 1900 census is regarded as one of the most inclusive and accurate of the federally created indexes, it is recommended as a good starting point for beginning researchers. Most beginning researchers have or are able to find some knowledge of family names and residences that will serve as a starting point for searching the 1900 Soundex index. (See "Federal Population Census Indexes and Finding Aids" on page 51.) The 1900 census is an excellent tool for determining dates and places to search for marriage records, birth records of children, deaths of children, and the marriages of children not listed. It is also a means of verifying family traditions, identifying unknown family members, and linking what is known to other sources, such as earlier censuses, naturalization records (especially declarations of intent to become citizens), school attendance rolls, property holdings, and employment and occupational records. These records can help to trace and document ethnic origins, and identify overseas and shipboard military service.

1900 Census Schedule

NATIVITY			CITIZENSHIP			OCCUPATION, TRADE, OR PROFESSION		EDUCATION				OWNERSHIP OF HOME			
Place of birth of each person and parents of each person enumerated. If born in the United States, give the *State* or *Territory*; if of foreign birth, give the *Country* only			Year of immigration to the United States	Number of years in the United States	Naturalization	of each person TEN YEARS of age and over		Attended school (in months)	Can read	Can write	Can speak English	Owned or rented	Owned free or mortgaged	Farm or house	Number of farm schedule
Place of birth of this PERSON	Place of birth of FATHER of this person	Place of birth of MOTHER of this person				OCCUPATION	Months not employed								
13	14	15	16	17	18	19	20	21	22	23	24	25	26	27	28

Note that some Indian schedules are kept at the end of the schedules for the state instead of the county.

For additional information on the 1900 census, see National Archives, *1900 Federal Population Census: A Catalog of Microfilm Copies of the Schedules* (Washington, D.C.: 1978). For boundary changes and identification of missing census schedules, see William Thorndale and William Dollarhide, *Map Guide to the U.S. Federal Censuses, 1790–1920* (Baltimore: Genealogical Publishing Co., 1987).

1910 CENSUS

The 1910 census was begun on 15 April 1910. The enumeration was to be completed within thirty days, or within two weeks for communities with populations of more than 5,000. The official census population count was 92,228,496.

Standard sections ranging from Nativity to Trade and Education were included in the 1900 census form. Ownership of home was no longer supplemental. Note column 19; a person only had to be 10 years of age to be employed. *(Source: U.S. Census Bureau)*

QUESTIONS ASKED IN THE 1910 CENSUS

The 1910 census schedules record number of dwelling house and family, in order of visitation: street address; each person's name and relationship to the head of household; sex; color or race; age at last birthday; marital status; length of present marriage; if a mother, number of children and number of living children; birthplace and parents' birthplaces; if foreign born, year of immigration and citizenship status; language spoken; occupation; type of industry employed in; whether employer, employee, or self-employed; number of weeks unemployed in 1909 if applicable; whether out of work on 15 April 1910; ability to read and write; if attended daytime school since 1 September 1909; if home was rented or owned; if owned, whether free or mortgaged; if home was a house or a farm; if a veteran of the Union or Confederate army or navy; if blind in both eyes, and if deaf and dumb. The Indian schedule also recorded the tribe and/or band.

RESEARCH TIPS FOR THE 1910 CENSUS

The quality of the microfilming of the 1910 census seems especially poor when compared to other census schedules. Overexposure in microfilming schedules for Mississippi, for example, rendered hundreds of pages illegible. Additionally, the omission rate in the 1910 Miracode/Soundex appears to be greater than in most other indexes. In many cases, individuals not indexed are present in the census schedules, so

1910 Census
Schedule

it is especially advisable for researchers to continue a search in the actual schedules even though a name fails to show up in an index.

The 1910 census, while not providing as much precise information as the 1900 census (such as exact birth month, years married, and number of children born to the mother), is still a good tool for determining approximate dates and places to search for marriage records, birth and death records of children, and the marriages of children not listed. The 1910 census sometimes makes it possible to verify family traditions, identify unknown family members, and link what is known to other sources, such as earlier censuses, naturalization records (especially declarations of intent to become citizens), school attendance rolls, property holdings, and employment and occupational records. These records will also verify Civil War service, trace and document ethnic origins, and locate military and naval personnel in hospitals, ships, and stations and those stationed in the Philippines, Alaska, Hawaii, and Puerto Rico.

For additional information on the 1910 census, see National Archives, *The 1910 Federal Population Census: A Catalog of Microfilm Copies of the Schedules* (Washington,

D.C.: 1982). For boundary changes and identification of missing census schedules, see William Thorndale and William Dollarhide, *Map Guide to the U.S. Federal Censuses, 1790–1920* (Baltimore: Genealogical Publishing Co., 1987).

1920 CENSUS

The 1920 census was begun on 1 January 1920. The enumeration was to be completed within thirty days, or within two weeks for communities with populations of more than 2,500. The official census population count was 106,021,537.

QUESTIONS ASKED IN THE 1920 CENSUS

The 1920 Census form called for: Name of street, avenue road, etc.; house number or farm; number of dwelling in order of visitation; number of family in order of visitation; name of each person whose place of abode was with the family; relationship of person enumerated to the head of the family; whether home owned or rented; if owned, whether free or mortgaged; sex; color or race; age at last birthday; whether single, married, widowed, or divorced; year of immigration to United States; whether naturalized or alien; if naturalized, year of naturalization; whether attended school any time since 1 September 1919; whether able to read; whether able to write; person's place of birth; mother tongue; father's place of birth; father's mother tongue; mother's place of birth; mother's mother tongue; whether able to speak English; trade, profession, or particular kind of work done; industry, business, or establishment in which at work; whether employer, salary or wage worker, or working on own account; number of farm schedule.

The 1920 census asked the year of naturalization and included a separate column for "Mother Tongue." (*Source: U.S. Census Bureau*)

OTHER SIGNIFICANT FACTS ABOUT THE 1920 CENSUS

The date of the enumeration appears on the heading of each page of the census schedule. All responses were to reflect the individual's status as of 1 January 1920, even if the status had changed between 1 January and the day of enumeration. Children born between 1 January and the day of enumeration were not to be listed, while individuals alive on 1 January but deceased when the enumerator arrived were to be counted.

Unlike the 1910 census, the 1920 census did not have questions regarding unemployment, Union or Confederate military service, number of children, or duration of marriage. It did, however, include four new question columns: one asked the year of naturalization and three inquired about mother tongue. The 1920 census also asked the year of arrival and status of every foreign-born person, and inquired about the year of naturalization for those individuals who had become U.S. citizens. In 1920 the census included, for the first time, Guam, American Samoa, and the Panama Canal Zone.

Also unlike the 1910 census, the 1920 census has a microfilmed index for each state and territory.

Due to boundary modifications in Europe resulting from World War I, some individuals were uncertain about how to identify their national origin. Enumerators were instructed to spell out the name of the city, state, province, or region of respondents who declared that they or their parents had been born in Germany, Austria-Hungary, Russia, or Turkey. Interpretation of the birthplace varied from one enumerator to another. Some failed to identify specific birthplaces within those named countries, and others provided an exact birthplace in countries not designated in the instructions. See Department of Commerce, Bureau of the Census, *Fourteenth Census of the United States, January 1, 1920: Instructions to Enumerators* (Washington, D.C.: Government Printing Office, 1919).

There are no separate Indian population schedules in the 1920 census. Inhabitants of reservations were enumerated in the general population schedules.

Enumerators were instructed not to report servicemen in the family enumerations but to treat them as residents of their duty posts. The 1920 census includes schedules and a Soundex index for overseas military and naval forces.

Soundex cards for institutions are found at the end of each state's Soundex index. It is important to note that many institutions, even if enumerated at their street addresses, are found at the end of the enumeration section.

The original 1920 census schedules were destroyed by authorization of the Eighty-third Congress, so it is not possible to consult originals when microfilm copies prove unreadable.

RESEARCH TIPS FOR THE 1920 CENSUS

Since nearly everyone has some knowledge or access to knowledge of family names, relationships, and the family's state of residence in 1920, most genealogical instructors recommend the 1920 census as the best starting point for research in federal records. Working from known information about the most recent generations, an efficient researcher works backwards in time to discover family relationships and to determine where additional records may be found.

The 1920 census is a good tool for determining approximate dates and places to search for marriage records, birth and death records of children, and the marriages of children not listed. The 1920 census sometimes makes it possible to verify family traditions, identify unknown family members, and link what is known to other sources, such as earlier censuses, school attendance rolls, property holdings, and employment and occupational records. In several instances, women, rather than men, have been listed as head of household in the 1920 Soundex index (figure 3); therefore, a search focused on a male name may be unsuccessful.

1920 Census Schedule

The 1920 census asked the foreign-born for the year of their arrival in the United States, making it easier to pinpoint the date of passenger arrival records. It also asked the naturalization status of every foreign-born person and inquired about the year of naturalization for those individuals who had become U.S. citizens, thus facilitating searches in naturalization records.

Due to the more specific questions asked of immigrants from Germany, Austria-Hungary, Russia, and Turkey regarding their birthplaces and those of their parents, many researchers will be able to discover the exact towns or regions from which their families emigrated. The fact that the 1920 census asked for the mother tongue of each respondent and that of each parent will further help to define the origins of many families.

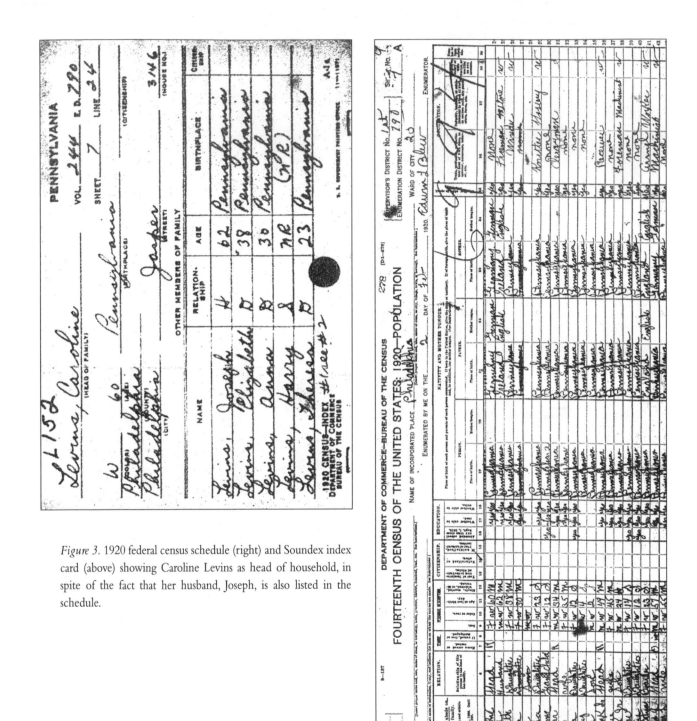

Figure 3. 1920 federal census schedule (right) and Soundex index card (above) showing Caroline Levins as head of household, in spite of the fact that her husband, Joseph, is also listed in the schedule.

For additional information regarding the 1920 census, see the following sources:

Green, Kellee. "The Fourteenth Numbering of the People: The 1920 Census." *Prologue* (Summer 1991): 131–45.

National Archives. *The 1920 Federal Population Census: Catalog of National Archives Microfilm.* Washington, D.C.: National Archives Trust Fund Board, 1991.

Shepard, JoAnne (Bureau of the Census). *Age Search Information.* Washington, D.C.: Government Printing Office, 1990.

For boundary changes and identification of missing census schedules, see William Thorndale and William Dollarhide, *Map Guide to the U.S. Federal Census, 1790–1920* (Baltimore: Genealogical Publishing Co., 1987).

1930 CENSUS

The 1930 census was taken on April 1, 1930. The official census population count was 123,202,624.

QUESTIONS ASKED IN THE 1930 CENSUS

The 1930 Census form called for: street, avenue, road, house number, number of dwelling house in order of visitation, number of family in order of visitation; name of each person whose place of abode on April 1, 1930, was in this family; relationship of this person to the head of the family; home owned or rented, value of home, if owned, or monthly rental, if rented; radio set; does this family live on a farm?; sex; color or race; age at last birthday; marital condition; age at first marriage, attended school or college any time since Sept. 1, 1929; whether able to read or write; place of birth—person, place of birth—father, place of birth—mother; language spoken in home before coming to the United States; year of immigration into the United States; naturalization; whether able to speak English; trade, profession, or particular kind of work done, Industry of business, class of worker; whether actually at work yesterday, If not, line number on unemployment schedule; where a veterans of U.S. military or naval force—yes or no, what war or expedition; number of farm schedule (Note: The farm schedules have not survived).

OTHER SIGNIFICANT FACTS ABOUT THE 1930 CENSUS

A WPA Soundex exists for the 1930 census for the following states only: Alabama, Arkansas, Florida, Georgia, Louisiana, Mississippi, North Carolina, South Carolina,

Tennessee, and Virginia. The following counties were Soundexed for Kentucky: Bell, Floyd, Harlan, Kenton, Mehlenberg, Perry, and Pike. The following West Virginia counties were indexed: Fayette, Harrison, Kanawha, Logan, McDowell, Mercer, and Raleigh.

All of the Soundex indexes are in the traditional format, with the exception of Georgia, which is in Miracode. All of the Soundexed states, except for Georgia, list the institutions at the end of the publication. There appear to be no mixed codes for the 1930 census.

RESEARCH TIPS FOR THE 1930 CENSUS

To effectively search the 1930 census, know as much about where the person lived as is possible.

The following finding aids will be available at the National Archives in Washington, D.C. and at NARA's regional records services facilities.

• *Enumeration District Maps for the Fifteenth Census of the United States, 1930.* (National Archives Microfilm Publication M1930), 35 rolls.

• *Index to Selected City Streets and Enumeration Districts, 1930.* (National Archives Microfilm Publication M1931), 11 rolls.

• *Descriptions of Census Enumeration Districts, 1830-1950.* (National Archives Microfilm Publication T1224), rolls 61-90.

For additional information on the 1930 census, see the 1930 census Web site at <http://www.nara.gov/genealogy/1930cen.html>.

Note: To complement its collection of 1930 resources, The National Archives has also purchased copies of city directories for 1928-1932. For a complete list of which directories NARA has, see the 1930 Web site. These are not National Archives publications, but can be purchase from Primary Source Microfilm (an imprint of the Gale Group). For ordering information call 1-800-444-0799.

Census Indexes
and Finding Aids

The census is a clear reflection of population growth in the United States. The millions of names and figures added to the census totals over the years have made indexing, particularly of the most populous states, a formidable and expensive task. Recent developments in technology have facilitated indexing and publication, and now a significant and ever-growing number of later statewide and even nationwide census schedules have been indexed.

INDEXES ON CD-ROM AND ONLINE

Unlike the 1880 Soundex, which is only a partial index, the LDS Church's FamilySearch™ 1880 United States Census and National Index is an every-name index with entries including name, relation to head of household, sex, marital status, race, age, birth place, occupation, and father and mother's birth place. The 1880 Census CD-ROMs are available for sale at the FamilySearch™ site <http://www.family-search.org>. Ancestry.com offers Accelerated Information Systems (AIS) Federal Census Indexes on CD-ROM that cover the years 1790–1880, as well as the 1910 Miracode. These indexes, plus a number of other state and local census indexes are also available at: <http://www.ancestry.com/census>. HeritageQuest's Family Quest Archives CD-ROM collection, available at <www.heritagequest.com>, contains complete head of household indexes to U.S. Federal Censuses for the 1790, 1800, 1810, and 1870 censuses. Partial indexes are available for 1850, 1900, and 1910.

Over the past several years, online census indexes have increased in both number and scope. Ancestry.com is nearing completion of its project to add a searchable database of indexed images of every U.S. Federal Census schedule to its Web site. And Genealogy.com currently offers the 1900 U.S. Federal census with an every-name index on its subscriber site. Another site, Census4All.com, has begun an every-name index to the 1910 U.S. Federal Census with Rhode Island and New Hampshire presently available. The Census4All indexes can be searched for free, and a list of other members of the household or copies of the actual census schedules desired can be ordered for a fee. (See Appendix I for a listing of digital and electronic census data providers.)

Fortunately for researchers, libraries with good genealogy collections usually make it a priority to acquire these popular and important indexes, on CD or by subscription on the Internet, as soon as they become available.

In addition to the commercial online census index projects, volunteers from around the country have responded to the need for finding aids by producing, in various formats, indexes to many of the federal censuses. One such volunteer effort, The USGenWeb Census Project can be accessed online at <http://www.rootsweb.com/~census/states.htm>. Other sites provide links to census data online. These include:

Census Links.com <http://www.censuslinks.com>
Census-Online.com <http://www.census-online.com/>
Cyndi's List – Census <http://www.cyndislist.com/census.htm>

CENSUS INDEX LIMITATIONS

A common mistake made by beginners is to consult an index, find a name, extract the index information—and go no further. Many seem unaware that census indexes are simply finding aids. While there is a certain element of excitement in discovering an ancestor's name in an index, there is greater satisfaction in store for those who view the fuller picture provided in the actual census schedules.

A well-prepared index includes a preface explaining the index parameters (for example, whether it is an every-name index or if only heads of household are included) and identifying specific problems encountered in the process of compiling the index. The wise researcher will read every preface carefully.

In most published census indexes, only the heads of households are listed. If an individual was a child when the census was taken, and if the name of his or her father, mother, or other head of the household in which he or she lived is not known, a long and tedious search may be in store. It may be necessary to look at different census schedules for every entry for a given surname in an index before her household is found.

Regardless of the care taken by the creator of an index to make it accurate, no index is perfect. Omissions, misinterpreted names, and misspellings creep into virtually all census indexes. Some indexes are not useful for tracing individuals because information was culled from microfilm that was nearly impossible to read, and sometimes the microfilmed version itself lacks certain information. Examples of the latter are the published federal census indexes from 1790 to 1840. Like the censuses themselves, the indexes are of limited use in finding individuals because only heads of household are listed. Likewise, most post-1840 census indexes include only heads of household and "strays."

Frequently, names are actually included in an index but cannot be found because they are misspelled to the extent that they are unrecognizable. Some surnames have been incorrectly alphabetized when indexers could not decipher even the first letter of a surname. In some handwriting styles, the letter L resembles an S; thus, the handwritten surname Lee might become See in an index. Handwriting styles have caused indexing problems when certain similar-appearing letters have been confused, including T and F; J, G, and Y; I and J; K and R; O and Q; P and R; and U and W.

PAGE NUMBERING PROBLEMS

Pages of census schedules were originally numbered by the census taker; when the schedules were later arranged and bound, they were often renumbered with a hand stamp. It is common for some volumes to have two or more series of page numbers. A stamped number, when it is present, is usually the page reference used in printed census indexes. It is very important to determine which page number the census indexer was using. Sometimes in the AIS index, for example, the indexer was inconsistent with the page number that he or she used, making it difficult to find names.

HISTORY AND QUALITY OF CENSUS INDEXES

Computer technology has revolutionized the process of indexing census schedules. Computer-produced census indexes are becoming increasingly available in book, microfiche, CD-ROM, and online forms. Despite the advanced technology, however, no index is error-free. Misinterpretations of handwritten census manuscripts and transcription mistakes continue to thwart research, particularly when the first letter of a name is entered into an index incorrectly.

While a number of individuals and genealogical societies have used computers to create census indexes, most such indexes have been created by commercial firms. The oldest of these firms is Accelerated Indexing Systems. Accelerated Indexing produced indexes for every extant state and territory census through 1860 and some for later years, as well as a number of special censuses and census substitutes. These indexes are available online and in CD-ROM format (see page 51).

The schedules for some states and areas have been indexed more than once by different organizations and commercial publishers. But though the year and the locality indexed may be the same, formats and contents can differ dramatically. Names may have

Table 1: Phonetic Substitutes

a	e,i,o,u,y,ey,eh	lm (as in *calm*)	m,mm,mb,mn
au	ow,ou	m	mm,lm,mb,mn,n
b	p,v,bb,pp	mb (as in *comb*)	mm,lm,mn
bb	b,p,pp	n	nn,ng,gn (as in *gnat*),kn,m
c (as in *catch*)	k,g,gh,q,cc,ck	ng	n,nk,ch,k,q
c (as in *chin*)	ch,cz,s,sh,tch,tsh,z,dg	nk	ng,ch,k,q
ch	c,k,g,gh,sh,h (as in *Chanukah*), ju (as in San *Juan*)	nn	n
		o	a,e,i,u,aw,ow,eau (as in *beau*)
chr	kr,gr,cr	oey	oy,oe,oi
ck	k,c,g,q	oe	oy,oe,oey
cr	kr,chr,gr	oo	u,ow,ew
cz	c,ch,ts,tz,s,sh,tcr,tsh	ou	u,au,ow,ew.oo
d	dd,t,dt	ow	au,ou.eau (as in *beau*)
dd	d,t,tt	oy	oi,oe,oey
dg (as in *dodge*)	g,j,ch,gg,tj	p	b,pp,ph,bb
ds (as in *bends*)	z,ts	pf	f,pfph,gh,v,lf
dt	d,t,tt	ph	f,gh (as in *laugh*),pf,lf,p
e	a,ee,i,o,u,y,ie,ea	ps (as in *psalm*)	s
ea	e,i,y,ie,ei	q	c,ch,g,k,gh,cc,ck,ng,nk
eau (as in *beau*)	o,aw,ow,au,ou	r	rr,wr,rh
ee	ie,e,i,y,ea,ei	rh	r,rr,wr
ew	u,oo,ou	rr	r,rh,wr
f	v,ph,pf,gh,il (as in *calf*),ff	s	c,sh,tch,z,cz,ss,x
ff	f,ph,gh,v,lf (as in *calf*)	sch (as in *school*)	sh,s,sc,sk,sq
g	c,ch,gg,gh,j,k,q,dg,h (as in *Gila* Monster)	sch (as in *Schwarz*)	s,sh
		sch (as in *Tisch*)	sh,tsh,tch,ch,cz,ti (as in *nation*),ss
gg	g,ch,k,q,j	sh	s,c,ch,cz,sch,ti (as in *nation*),ss
gh (as in *ghost*)	c,ch,g,gg,ch,k,q	sk	sch,sh,s,sc,sq
gh (as in *laugh*)	f,ph,pf,v,lf	sq	sc,sk,sch,sh
gn (as in *gnat*)	n,kn	ss	s,c,ch,ci,sh,sc,z
gr	chr,ke	t	d,dd,tt,th
h	(h is sometimes omitted) ch,wh,w,g (as in *Gila* Monster),ju (as in San *Juan*)	tch	s,sh,c,ch,cz,s,tsh
		th	t,tt,d
i	a,e,o,u,y,ei,uy,aye	ti (as in *nation*)	sh,si,tsh,tch,ch
ie	e,i,y,ee,ea,ei	tj	j,g,ch,dh,dg,tch,tsch,s
ih	y,i,ei,ii	tt	d,dd,t,th,dt
j	ch,g,dg,gg	ts	tz,cz,z,tzts,cz,z
ju (as in San *Juan*)	h,wh,ch	u	a,e,i,omou,ew,oo
k	c,ch,g,gh,q,nk,cc,ck	v	b,f,lf,w
kn (as in *knot*)	n,gn	w	wh,v,au,ow,h,ju (as in San *Juan*)
kr	chr,cr,gr	wh	w,h,ju (as in San *Juan*), oa
ks	x	wr	r,rh,rr
l	ll	x	s,z,ks,chs
lf (as in *calf*)	f,v,ph,pf,gh	y	i,e,ij
ll	l,th	z	s,c,sh,sch,x,ds

been interpreted differently; some publications may include names missed by others; and some may include much more than county, township, and page and microfilm numbers after the names of heads of households. It is wise to check every index when more than one is available for a given time and place.

Misspellings can be found on several levels. The census enumerator may have misunderstood the name and written it incorrectly. (See Table 1). Even if the enumerator got it right, the indexer may have misread the enumerator's handwriting or had other difficulties reading the old and fading microfilm. (See Table 2).

Many indexes, up to and including the 1920 census, cover individual counties only. They can prove especially useful when a name or names cannot be found in a statewide compilation. Because local indexes are frequently compiled by genealogical societies and indexers who tend to be familiar with local name spellings and geographical distinctions, their reliability is sometimes greater than the larger indexes.

Statewide censuses are sometimes interfiled with other sources in single personal name indexes available in state archives. The addresses of state archives and state historical societies are given in Appendix II.

Indexes From 1790 to 1840

The federal government led the way in publishing census indexes when, in the early 1900s, it published indexed volumes of the extant 1790 census schedules for each state. The individual state volumes have since been privately reprinted and are widely available in libraries with genealogy collections. Some indexes for

Table 2: Frequently Misread Letters

Letter	Misread as	Letter	Misread as
A	H,C,O	Q	Z,D,I,J,G,C
a	o,u,ei,ie,n,w	q	g,y,z,f,ej,ij,j
B	R,P,S	R	Pi,B,S,Pe,Pr,Re
b	li,le,t,h,l	r	e,s,i,ei,a
C	G,E,O,Ce	S	L,I,J,St,Se,F,G,R,T
c	e,i,o,u	s	r,i,e,c
D	G,S,I,J,T,lr	sc	x
d	u,a,n,ie,ei,ee,ct,o	ss	fs,p,rr,w,m,n
E	C,G,Ee	T	F,S,L,D,Q
e	i,c	t	l,f,lr,i
ee	u,n,ll,a,o,ie,ei,w	te	k
F	T,S,G,Ti,L	tt	ll
f	s,i,g,q,t	U	V,A,O,N,H
G	S,Q,Z,Ci,L,Se,ls	u	ee,a,o,n,ie,ci,ll,w
g	y,z,q,f	V	N,W,lr,Jr,B
H	N,W,He,Sl,St,A,F	v	u,n,b,rr,s,r,o,ee,ei,
h	K,li,lc,le	W	M,N,U,H,St
I	J,L,S,Q,F,T	w	m,rr,ur,nr,ui,ni,eu,en
i	e,c,l	X	H,Z,N,J
ie	ei,u,ee,n,a,o,w,il	x	sc,c,r
J	I,L,S,Q,F,T,P	Y	T,F,Z,Q
j	y,g,f,q,z	y	g,q,j,z,p,ej,ij,if
Jno	Mr,Mo	Z	G,Q,Y
K	H,R,B,tr,te	z	g,q,y,j,p
k	h,le,lr,te,R,B,H		
L	S,T,F		
l	e,i,t		
ll	tt,ee,u,a,o,ie,ei		
M	W,H,N,A,Al,Me		
m	w,rr,ni,in,iv, ev,ai,ui,iu		
N	H,W,V,St,Ne		
n	u,a,o,ee,ie,ei,w,m		
O	C,U,V,D		
o	a,u,n,ee,ll,ie,ei,tt		
P	R,B,I,J,S,L		
p	ss,g,js,k,f,fs,fa,fi,fr		

the years 1790 to 1820 also include the tallies listed for each family. These tallies would be listed as such:

Where census data is given, it appears in columns. For example:

The columns have the following meanings:

1790
a. free white males age sixteen and older
b. free white males under age sixteen
c. free white females
d. all other free persons
e. slaves

1800-10
a. free white males to age ten (under age ten)
b. free white males to age sixteen (of ten and under sixteen)
c. free white males to age twenty-six (of sixteen and under twenty-six)
d. free white males to age forty-five (of twenty-six and under forty-five)
e. free white males over age forty-five
f. free white females to age ten (under age ten)
g. free white females to age sixteen (of ten and under sixteen)
h. free white females to age twenty-six (of sixteen and under twenty-six)
i. free white females to age forty-five (of twenty-six and under forty-five)

j. free white females over age forty-five
k. other free persons (except Indians not taxed)
l. slaves

1820
a. free white males to age ten (under age ten)
b. free white males to age sixteen (of ten and under sixteen)
c. free white males between ages sixteen and eighteen
d. free white males to age twenty-six (of sixteen and under twenty-six)
e. free white males to age forty-five (of twenty-six and under forty-five)
f. free white males over age forty-five
g. free white females to age ten (under age ten)
h. free white females to age sixteen (of ten and under sixteen)
i. free white females to age twenty-six (of sixteen and under twenty-six)
j. free white females to age forty-five (of twenty-six and under forty-five)
k. free white females over age forty-five
l. slaves
m. free colored persons

Indexes from 1850 to 1870

Many statewide indexes for censuses after 1850 include only heads of household and the names of persons in households whose names were different than that of the household head. Obviously, then, a large percentage of the actual population of a state is excluded from such an index. This is especially a problem with common names, and when a child's or woman's name is known but that of the head of household is not.

1880 Soundex

Until recent years, the fastest method for finding names in the 1880 census for most states was to use the Soundex, a partial index that includes only households with children ten years old and under in residence. Compiled by the Work Projects Administration (WPA), the Soundex index was designed to identify those who would be eligible for

Social Security. (An explanation of the Soundex coding system follows this section.)

Important to remember when using the 1880 Soundex is that, while a large portion of the population is not indexed because many families had no children ten years old or under, all individuals and families were supposed to have been included in the original census schedules. Some of the original Soundex index cards survive and have been distributed among various state and local agencies; others have apparently been destroyed. Some of the 1880 cards were lost or misfiled before or when they were microfilmed.

Use the Soundex to determine surname distribution throughout the state. This can be an important clue if you don't know which county to search for a family. You can identify family naming patterns (because each person in the family is listed on the Soundex card with relationships stated), find orphaned children living with persons of other surnames, and identify grandparents living under the same roof. They are listed in the census schedule, even though they may not be indexed separately (figure 4). As mentioned, the LDS Church offers an every-name index to the 1880 Census in electronic format (See page 51).

1890 Index

A card file to the names on the surviving 1890 schedules is available on two rolls of microfilm titled *Index to the Eleventh Census of the United States, 1890* (National Archives microfilm M496). The index is also available in printed form.

Ken Nelson, comp., *1890 Census Index Register* (Salt Lake City: Genealogical Society of Utah, 1984), is an index to the 6,160 names in the surviving fragments of this census. Available on microfilm (1,421,673, item 11), it is also to be found in the reference area of the Family History Library (Family History Library book Ref 973 X2n 1890). Also see Helen Smothers Swenson, *Index to 1890 Census of the United States* (cited earlier), and "Veterans Schedules, 1840–1890," (page 40).

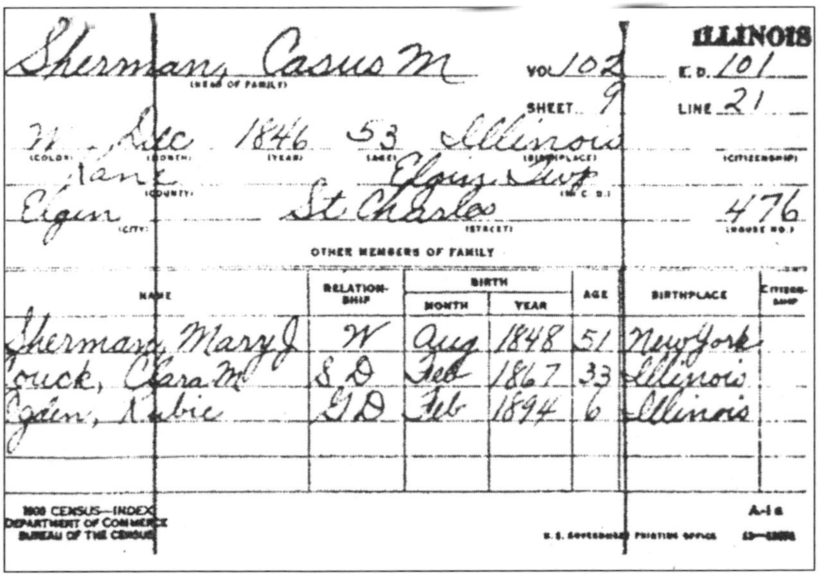
Sherman, Casus M (HEAD OF FAMILY) VOL. 102 ILLINOIS E.D. 101
SHEET 9 LINE 21
W (COLOR) Dec (MONTH) 1846 (YEAR) 53 (AGE) Illinois (BIRTHPLACE) (CITIZENSHIP)
Kane (COUNTY) Elgin Twp (M.C.D.)
Elgin (CITY) St. Charles (STREET) 476 (HOUSE NO.)

OTHER MEMBERS OF FAMILY

NAME	RELATION-SHIP	BIRTH MONTH	BIRTH YEAR	AGE	BIRTHPLACE	CITIZEN-SHIP
Sherman, Mary J	W	Aug	1848	51	New York	
[illegible], Clara M	S D	Feb	1867	33	Illinois	
[illegible], [illegible]	G D	Feb	1894	6	Illinois	

1900 CENSUS—INDEX DEPARTMENT OF COMMERCE BUREAU OF THE CENSUS
A-1a
U. S. GOVERNMENT PRINTING OFFICE

Figure 4. Illinois Soundex household card for Casus M. Sherman in 1900 Federal Population Census. A Catalog of Microfilm Copies of the Schedules (Washington, D.C.: Government Printing Office, 1978), appendix.

1900 Index

The Soundex index to the 1900 census is regarded as one of the most inclusive and accurate of the federally-created indexes. It serves as an efficient key to locating households and individuals in the most genealogically informative census ever taken. Unlike the 1880 census, the 1900 census identifies all heads of household and every adult whose name is different from that of the head of household (figure 5).

1910 Indexes

The most notable problem with the 1910 census has traditionally been the lack of indexes for most states. Miracode/Soundex indexes exist for only twenty-one states: Alabama, Arkansas, California, Florida, Georgia, Illinois, Kansas, Kentucky, Louisiana, Michigan, Mississippi, Missouri, North Carolina, Ohio, Oklahoma, Pennsylvania, South Carolina, Tennessee, Texas, Virginia, and West Virginia. Since Soundex/Miracode indexes are not available for the remaining states, researchers must rely on city directories, county landowners' atlases, enumeration districts, or specially created finding tools (such as the special index to streets and enumeration districts for certain cities), or conduct tedious, page-by-page searches of the census schedules. (For a detailed description, see "Federal Population Census Indexes and Finding Aids" on page 51.)

Soundex and Miracode (a slightly modified version of Soundex) indexes were created by the Bureau of the Census for the twenty-one states that lacked a centralized vital statistics bureau at the time the indexes were created. The Miracode system uses the same phonetic code and abbreviations as the Soundex system, but Miracode cards list the visitation numbers assigned by the enumerators, while Soundex cards show the page and line numbers on the appropriate census schedules. With the exception of Louisiana, which uses both, the following states have been indexed using either the Soundex or Miracode systems: Alabama, Arkansas, California, Florida, Georgia, Illinois, Kansas, Kentucky, Louisiana, Michigan, Mississippi, Missouri, North Carolina, Ohio, Oklahoma, Pennsylvania, South Carolina, Tennessee, Texas, Virginia, and West Virginia. Both indexing systems give the surname, first name, state and county of residence, city (if applicable), race, age, and place of birth as well as the volume number and enumeration district number of the census schedule from which the information was obtained. Some large cities are indexed separately in the 1910 census. Be sure to see separate Soundex listings in the National Archives microfilm catalog for some metropolitan areas in Alabama, Georgia, Louisiana, Pennsylvania, and Tennessee.

The 1910 Census City Street Finding Aid

The Federation of Genealogical Societies (FGS) promoted and coordinated the funding to microfilm an important finding aid for the 1910 census. A city street finding aid, it was created by the Bureau of the Census to facilitate its work of searching the original schedules for age and other personal data in response to inquiries from individuals and government agencies. This index to city streets and census enumeration districts for

Figure 5. 1880 federal census schedule for St. Patrick's Orphan Asylum, Rochester, New York, p. 39.

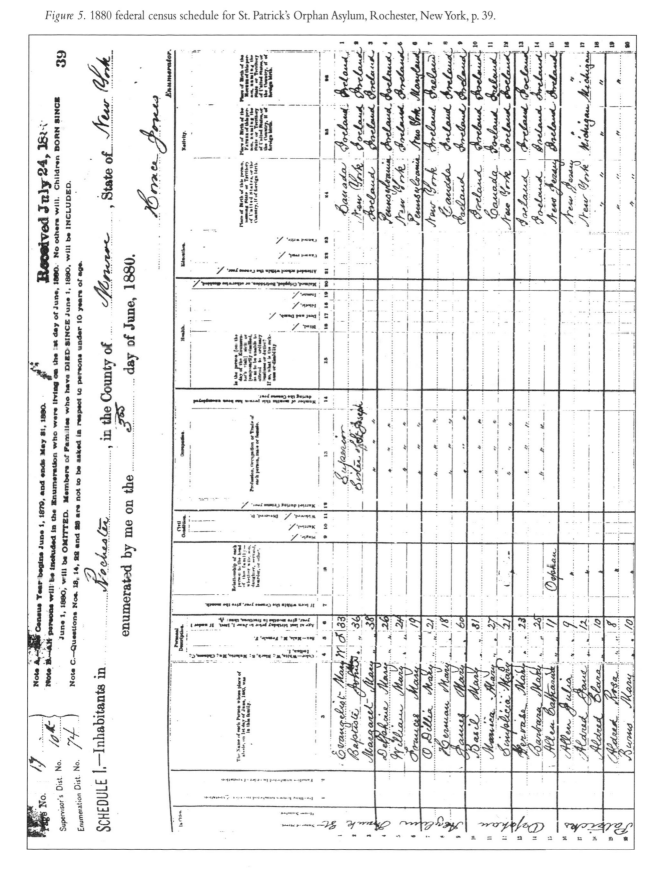

thirty-nine cities in the 1910 federal population census is widely available on fifty sheets of microfiche. The index enables users of the population schedules to translate specific street addresses into the appropriate enumeration district number and corresponding volume number of the microfilmed schedules. The city schedules were selected for indexing by the Bureau of the Census based on the frequency of requests for information. The indexes were originally in bound volumes, but they were disbound for microfilming. With the exception of several of the larger cities, the index for each city occupied a single volume. The original arrangement of the indexes has been preserved, with the exception that the boroughs of Manhattan and the Bronx, Richmond (Staten Island), and Brooklyn have been placed under the heading "New York City." There is no index for the borough of Queens.

Entries in the index give for each city a list of city streets and house numbers and show the appropriate enumeration district. The records are arranged alphabetically by name of city and thereunder by street. Named streets, arranged alphabetically, are listed first, followed by numerical streets. Immediately preceding the index portion of each volume is a table listing the enumeration districts covered in the volume, with a cross-reference to the corresponding volume of the original population schedules.

The thirty-nine cities included in the 1910 index are:

Akron, Ohio	Newark, New Jersey
Atlanta, Georgia	New York City (excluding Queens)
Baltimore, Maryland	Oklahoma City, Oklahoma
Canton, Ohio	Omaha, Nebraska
Charlotte, North Carolina	Patterson, New Jersey
Chicago, Illinois	Peoria, Illinois
Cleveland, Ohio	Philadelphia, Pennsylvania
Dayton, Ohio	Phoenix, Arizona
Denver, Colorado	Reading, Pennsylvania
Detroit, Michigan	Richmond, Virginia
District of Columbia	San Antonio, Texas
Elizabeth, New Jersey	San Diego, California
Erie, Pennsylvania	San Francisco, California
Fort Wayne, Indiana	Seattle, Washington
Gary, Indiana	South Bend, Indiana
Grand Rapids, Michigan	Tampa, Florida
Indianapolis, Indiana	Tulsa, Oklahoma
Kansas City, Kansas	Wichita, Kansas
Long Beach, California	Youngstown, Ohio
Los Angeles and Los Angeles County	

The 1910 street index can dramatically reduce the problems and time expenditure involved in searching large cities for which there are thousands of pages of census entries.

1920 Census/Soundex

The 2,074 rolls of microfilm for the 1920 census are Soundex indexed on 8,590 rolls of microfilm. The Soundex includes all of the states as well as the then territories of Alaska and Hawaii. The Canal Zone, Puerto Rico, Guam, American Samoa, the Virgin Islands, and military, naval, and various institutions are also indexed.

While the percentage of mistakes and omissions in census indexes is disappointingly high, it is generally agreed that even an imperfect index can be an invaluable time-saver and is certainly better than no index at all. Improved technology and better editing are making most new compilations more inclusive and more accurate.

1930 Census/Soundex

The 1930 U.S. Federal Census was released by the National Archives and Records Administration 1 April 2002. Soundex indexes are available for the states of Alabama, Arkansas, Florida, Georgia, Kentucky (only Bell, Floyd, Harlan, Kenton, Muhlenberg, Perry, and Pike counties), Louisiana, Mississippi, North Carolina, South Carolina, Tennessee, Virginia, and West Virginia (only Fayette, Harrison, Kanawha, Logan, McDowell, Mercer, and Raleigh counties).

To aid in locating entries for other areas, geographic descriptions of census enumeration districts are reproduced in NARA microfilm publication T1224. In addition, NARA has purchased a large number of city directories from a commercial vendor for use in its facilities. More details can be found on NARA's Web site at: <http://www.nara.gov/genealogy/1930cen.html>.

BEYOND THE INDEX

Experienced researchers know that there is much more to a census search than merely checking an index—whether that index is a book, a microfilmed version of the Soundex, or a computerized database. Unfortunately, too many beginners give up the search if the name sought does not appear in the index; if it does appear, they often seem content with the minimal information found in the index. Those who do not take the time to get the full picture provided by careful study of the actual census schedules usually miss important information and clues to further research. The study should include not only the subject of the search but the general area in which that person lived. To focus on only one name or one family in a given census is to see only a partial picture—somewhat like reading one chapter of a fascinating book.

THE SOUNDEX INDEX SYSTEM

An index and filing system called the Soundex is the key to finding the names of individuals among the millions listed in the 1880, 1900, 1910, 1920, and, for some states, 1930 federal censuses. The Soundex indexes include heads of households and persons of different surnames in each household.

The Soundex indexes are coded surname (last name) indexes based on the progression of consonants rather than the spelling of the surname. This coding system was developed and implemented by the WPA in the 1930s for the Social Security Administration in response to that agency's need to identify individuals who would be eligible to apply for old-age benefits. Because early birth records are unavailable in a number of states, the 1880 census manuscripts became the most dependable means of verifying dates of birth for people who would qualify—those born in the 1870s. Widespread misspelling caused so many problems in matching names, however, that the Soundex system was adopted. Because locating eligible Social Security beneficiaries was the sole reason for creating the 1880 Soundex, only households with children ten years of age or under were included in that index. All households were included in the Soundex indexes for the 1900, 1910, and 1920 censuses.

HOW THE SOUNDEX WORKS

Soundex index entries are arranged on cards, first in Soundex code order and then alphabetically by first name of the head of household. For each person in the house, the Soundex card should show name, race, month and year of birth, age, citizenship status, place of residence by state and county, civil division, and, where appropriate for urban dwellers, the city name, house number, and street name. The cards also list the volume number, enumeration district number, and page and line numbers of the original schedules from which the information was taken.

Coding a Surname

To search for a name it is necessary to first determine its Soundex code. Every Soundex code consists of a letter and three numbers; for example, S655. The letter is always the first letter of the surname. The numbers are assigned according to the Soundex coding guide below.

Code key letters and equivalents:

1 B, P, F, V
2 C, S, K, G, J, Q, X, Z
3 D, T

4 L
5 M, N
6 R

The letters A, E, I, O, U, W, Y, and H are disregarded. Consonants in each surname which sound alike have the same code.

Use of Zero in Coding Surnames

A surname that yields no code numbers, such as Lee, is L000; one yielding only one code number, such as Kuhne, takes two zeros and is coded as K500; and one yielding two code numbers takes just one zero; thus, Ebell is coded as E140. No more than three digits are ever used, so Ebelson would be coded as E142, not E1425.

Names with Prefixes

Because the Soundex does not treat prefixes consistently, surnames beginning with, for example, Van, Vander, Von, De, Di, or Le may be listed with or without the prefix, making it necessary to search for both possibilities. Search for the surname van Devanter, for example, with and without the "van-" prefix. Mc- and Mac- are not considered prefixes.

Names with Adjacent Letters Having the Same Equivalent Number

When two key letters or equivalents appear together or one key letter immediately follows or precedes an equivalent, the two are coded as one letter with a single number. (Surnames may have different letters that are adjacent and have the same number equivalent.) Pfeiffer, for example, is coded P160. Because the P and the F are both coded as 1, only one (P) is used. The letters e and i separate the coded Pf from the second and third appearance of the letter f, so one of these is coded. The double f again requires that only one be considered in the code. The letter r is represented by 6, and in the absence of additional consonants, the code is rounded off with a zero. Other examples of double-letter names are Lennon (L550), Kelly (K400), Buerck (B620), Lloyd (L300), Schaefer (S160), Szucs (S200), and Orricks (O620). Occasionally the indexers themselves made mistakes in coding names, so it may be useful to look for a name in another code. Also be aware that some immigrants with difficult last names may have been soundexed under their first name; these names would then be listed alphabetically by last name.

Different Names within a Single Code

With this indexing formula, many different surnames may be included within the same Soundex code. For example, the similar-sounding surnames Scherman, Schurman, Sherman, Shireman, and Shurman are indexed together as S655 and will appear in the same group with other surnames, such as Sauerman or Sermon. Names that do not sound alike may also be included within a single code: Sinclair, Singler, Snegolski, Snuckel, Sanislo, San Miguel, Sungaila, and Szmegalski are all coded as S524.

Alphabetical Arrangement of First or Given Names within the Code

As described above, multiple surnames appear within most Soundex codes. Within each Soundex code, the individual and family cards are arranged alphabetically by given name. Marked divider cards separate most Soundex codes. Look also for known nicknames, middle names, or abbreviations of the first name.

Mixed Codes

Divider cards show most code numbers, but not all. For instance, one divider may be numbered 350 and the next one 400. Between the two divided cards there may be names coded 353, 350, 360, 365, and 355, but instead of being in numerical order they are interfiled alphabetically by given name.

Soundex Reference Guide

For those who are unsure of their Soundex skills, most genealogical software programs and many genealogy Web sites include a Soundex Calculator. Also, most genealogical libraries have a copy of Bradley W. Steuart, *The Soundex Reference Guide: Soundex Codes to Over 125,000 Surnames* (Bountiful, Utah: Precision Indexing, 1990).

Soundex Abbreviations

In addition to the letter/numerical codes, Soundex also uses a number of abbreviations, most of which relate to residents' relationships to the head of the household (see table 3). NR (not recorded) is a frequently found abbreviation.

Native Americans, Asians, and Nuns

Names of nuns, Native Americans, and Asians pose special problems. Phonetically spelled Asian and Native American names were either coded as one continuous name or by what seemed to be a surname. For example, the Native American name Shinka-Wa-Sa may have been coded as Shinka (S520) or Sa (S000). Nuns were coded as if "Sister" were the surname, and they appear in each state's Soundex under the code S236, but not necessarily in alphabetical order.

SOUNDEX RESEARCH TIPS

The Soundex indexes can be especially useful in identifying family units, because all members of the household are listed on the Soundex cards under the name of the

Table 3. Soundex Abbreviations: Relationships to Head of Household

A	Aunt	GM	Grandmother	SF	Stepfather
AdD	Adopted daughter	GNi	Grandniece	SFL	Stepfather-in-law
AdS	Adopted son	GS	Grandson	Si	Sister
At	Attendant	GU	Great-uncle	SiL	Sister-in-law
B	Brother	Hh	Hired hand	SL	Son-in-law
BL	Brother-in-law	I	Inmate	SM	Stepmother
Bo	Boarder	L	Lodger	SML	Stepmother-in-law
C	Cousin	M	Mother	SS	Stepson
D	Daughter	ML	Mother-in-law	SSi	Stepsister
DL	Daughter-in-law	N	Nephew	SSiL	Stepsister-in-law
F	Father	Ni	Niece	SSL	Stepson-in-law
FB	Foster brother	Nu	Nurse	Su	Superintendent
FF	Foster father	O	Officer	U	Uncle
FL	Father-in-law	P	Patient	W	Wife
FM	Foster mother	Pa	Partner (share common abode)	Wa	Warden
FSi	Foster sister	Pr	Prisoner		
GA	Great aunt	Pri	Principal		
GD	Granddaughter	Pu	Pupil	**Citizenship Status**	
GF	Grandfather	R	Roomer	A	Alien
GGF	Great-grandfather	S	Son	NA	Naturalized
GGM	Great-grandmother	SB	Stepbrother	PA	First papers filed
GGGF	Great-great-grandfather	SBL	Stepbrother-in-law	NR	Not recorded
GGGM	Great-great-grandmother	Se	Servant		

head of the household. Often, census searches begin with only a surname and the name of the state in which a person or family lived in a given census year. In such cases, the Soundex can be a means of determining surname distribution throughout the state. A search can often be narrowed to a smaller geographic area within a state. Once the county of origin is determined through census work, whole new paths of research open up. The Soundex can also be used to locate orphaned children living with persons of other surnames and to identify families with grandparents living under the same roof. They are sometimes listed on the Soundex cards, even though they may not be indexed separately.

1900, 1910, AND 1920 CENSUS ENUMERATION DISTRICT DESCRIPTIONS

Because of errors in transcribed names and because of variant spellings of names, a researcher may not be able to locate an entry in the Soundex system for a given head of family or individual living in a specific area. And though a name does not appear in the Soundex, the possibility exists that the individual being sought was indeed enumerated but was somehow missed or incorrectly coded in the indexing process. Those wishing to bypass the 1900, 1910, or 1920 Soundexes and to consult

Using the Soundex—A Case Study

Courtesy of
Suzanne Russo, AG

The first step in searching for an ancestor in the census is to identify the ancestor's name and then list everything you know about him or her, e.g. names, dates, locations. The initial target person should be the head of household for the census year you are searching, since heads of household and people with different last names were usually indexed. A general rule is to search the last census year that is available to you in which your ancestor could have lived, and then to work backward in time.

The following search in the 1920 U.S. Federal Census illustrates the basic steps to finding your ancestors in the census. While this example focuses on a search of the 1920 Census at an LDS Family History Center, the same steps will be helpful searches at other libraries.

1. Identify What You Know

For this example, I searched the census for Matteo Russo, my great-grandfather. I already knew that he was born around 1885 in Palermo, Sicily, and that his wife's name is Maria. I also knew that he immigrated to St. Louis, Missouri in the early 1900s and that his children are Phillie Russo, Natale Russo (born about 1915), Tony Russo, Zena Russo, and Dominic Russo.

2. Choose a Census Year

I decided to search the 1920 U.S. Federal Census. Usually, it is best to start with the most recent information available so you can more easily work backward from the known to the unknown.

3. Locate the Soundex Code

The census for the years 1880, 1900, 1920 and parts of 1910 and 1930 have indexes on microfilm known as either Soundex or Miracode. The Soundex system indexes individuals by the sound of their last name. This helps to increase the chance of finding an ancestor if his or her name was misspelled or changed in any way by a census enumerator. Each group of surnames has a code. Use the Soundex system to find the code for your surname of interest. (See page 62) Some libraries have computers or books that aid in finding your surname code. In this example, the surname code for Russo is R200.

4. Locate the Soundex Film

Many LDS Family History Centers and libraries with census film collections have books or binders with the film numbers of both the Soundex and the census. Some libraries have a different numbering system. These film numbers are usually arranged by state and then by Soundex code. Some libraries have labeled their film drawers sufficiently so that you can go to the film drawer and recognize the film that you need by looking for the state (usually arranged in alphabetical order) and then for your Soundex code.

Once I found the film number, I went to the drawer with the 1920 Soundex film and looked first for the state (they should be arranged alphabetically) and then the Soundex code. The box is labeled "U.S. 1920 Soundex, Missouri: R200 John thru R226." There is another film for Missouri that is labeled R200. It contains the index for R163 Williams thru R200 John.

The Soundex system indexes the surname by the sound of the last name and then lists in alphabetical order the first name. Because I was looking for Matteo Russo, I searched the film that began with "R200 John" first.

5. Search for Your Ancestor

After I placed the microfilm on the film reader, I scrolled through it until I found the Soundex code of R200. Once I had found the code, I looked for the first name of the ancestor, then I searched for the surname along with other identifying information such as age, sex, color, birthplace, or name of spouse and children.

I searched the microfilm for a Matteo Russo, white, about forty to forty-five years old, who had the birthplace of Italy or Sicily, and whose wife was Maria, Marie, Mary or any other variation of the name.

As I searched, I passed up the portion of the film that should have contained Matteo Russo. There was no Matteo listed between the Matt and Matthews so I looked for other variations of the name and I looked through all of the first names that began with "M" to see if the first name was misspelled or altered in some way. Could my ancestor have been indexed under a nickname?

As I scrolled through the microfilm, I came to a section that lists several people with the name Mike Russo. One came from Naples, Italy. (I already knew that my ancestor was from Sicily.) Another came from Italy but was too young and not enumerated with a wife named Mary or any of the names of the children that I knew belonged in my ancestral family. I finally came across a forty-year-old Mike Russo, living in St. Louis, Missouri, who was born in Sicily. His wife was listed as Mary and the children were Philipia, Tony, Natale, Dominick, and Vincentia.

I realized this could be my ancestor. According to the information that I already had on the family, it seemed like

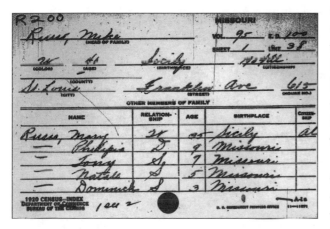

a good bet. But I continued to scroll through the rest of the "Ms" to see if there were other possibilities. A further look didn't yield any results, and based upon several known clues about the family, I was fairly certain that I had found the correct family.

Once I had located the correct Soundex card, I recorded all the information it contained for use in finding the actual census page. Remember, the Soundex card is not the census, it is merely an index to the census.

In the upper right-hand corner of the Soundex card, I found the information that would lead me to the census page. I recorded the name of my ancestor, the city, county, state, enumeration district, sheet number, and line number. Making a copy of the index card is always a nice addition to a family history. (If you are searching a Miracode index, look for the name of ancestor, state, county, city, volume, enumeration district, and visitation number.)

From the Soundex card, I recorded the following the information:

Mike Russo
St. Louis, St. Louis, Missouri
Enumeration District 100
Sheet 1
Line 38

6. Search the Census

Since I am at a Family History Center, I am ready to go get the film. I went to the census film drawers for the 1920 census and found the film that contains the state, county, city and enumeration district. If I had been searching at another library or archive, I would likely have had to go to a separate index to find the film number. I scrolled through the film until I found the correct county and city, then I looked for the enumeration district and sheet number. (These are generally in the upper right-hand corner of the census page.) When I had located these, I looked for the line number of my ancestor along the right-hand side of the page.

Following the line across the page, I found Mike Russo and his family. I made a copy and recorded the information onto a census extract sheet. Further investigation and interviews with relatives about my Russo relatives revealed that "Mike" was indeed Matteo's nickname. In that light, it makes a lot of sense that I found him listed that way on the census.

Of course, not every census search ends so successfully. Remember to keep looking and not to get discouraged. If you don't find your ancestor in the census he or she should be in, realize that the federal census-taking system has never been perfect. No matter how thoroughly you conduct your search, your family may not even be there.

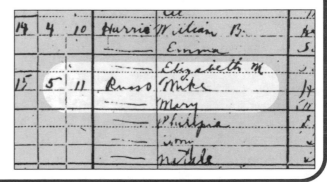

the actual schedules for a given town, a minor civil division or geographic area, or a ward of a large city need to know the enumeration district numbers assigned to the particular place.

Arranged alphabetically by state and thereunder by county, the Census Enumeration District Descriptions identify the specific enumeration district numbers assigned within states, counties, and cities. Note that the district boundaries are described in the microfilm series as they were when the censuses were taken and may have changed significantly since then.

Further information on Census Enumeration District Descriptions for the 1900, 1910, and 1920 censuses is provided in the introduction pages of the following National Archives catalogs:

• *1900 Federal Population Census*. National Archives Trust Fund Board, 1978.
• *The 1910 Federal Population Census*. National Archives Trust Fund Board, 1982.
• *The 1920 Federal Population Census*. National Archives Trust Fund Board, 1991.

CENSUS LOCATOR MAPS AND TOOLS FOR CITIES

Even though an ever-growing number of indexes are available to facilitate research in cities and towns, few, if any, indexes are complete. A significant number of city dwellers, though present in the actual census schedules, were missed or misplaced in the indexing process. To remedy the situation, historians, researchers, and librarians have compiled finding aids for a number of metropolitan areas. Historian Keith Schlesinger devised a system to locate individuals overlooked by Soundex and other indexing processes. Schlesinger gleaned addresses from city directories, which he found both accurate and accessible, then plotted them on maps of census enumeration districts, which normally followed the boundaries of voting precincts in most cities. By narrowing the search for a non-indexed individual to one or two enumeration districts, this scheme permits the researcher to escape the confinement of the Soundex. The technique is described in Keith Schlesinger and Peggy Tuck Sinko, "Urban Finding Aid for Manuscript Census Searches," *National Genealogical Society Quarterly* 69 (3) (September 1981): 171–80.

The staff of the Newberry Library in Chicago has created enumeration district maps for Chicago for the 1880, 1900, and 1910 censuses. Similar maps are available for other cities, and at least one, Mary Lou Craver Mariner and Patricia Roughan Bellows, *A Research Aid for the Massachusetts 1910 Federal Census* (Sudbury, Mass: Computerized Assistance, 1988), has been published.

The Family History Library has some unpublished finding aids for some cities that are filed in notebooks with other materials in the census area of the library. The library has also compiled or revised some census finding aids for cities. *Guide to the Use of the*

United States Census Office 10th Census 1880 New York City was originally compiled by Barbara Hillman in 1963 for use at the New York Public Library. This unpublished finding aid was revised in 1985 by Raymond G. Matthews. The newer, forty-one-page guide reproduces 1880 Manhattan street maps and assembly and election districts, and converts ward numbers to corresponding Family History Library census microfilm call numbers. The 1880 finding aid has been published on microfiche (Family History Library microfiche no. 6047913).

The *U.S. 1910 Federal Census: Unindexed States, A Guide to Finding Census Enumeration Districts for Unindexed Cities, Towns, and Villages* is a Family History Library finding aid compiled by G. Eileen Buckway, Marva Blalock, Elizabeth Caruso, Raymond G. Matthews, and Ken Nelson. It is an alphabetical directory, arranged by state, that lists the names of cities and towns not indexed by Soundex or Miracode. It provides the name of the county, enumeration district number, and Family History Library microfilm number for the corresponding 1910 census. For large cities, it gives additional aids, such as call numbers for city directories, street address indexes, enumeration district maps, and others. It is in the reference area at the Family History Library (Family History Library book Ref 973 X2bu 1910; microfiche no. 6101340).

Street Indexes to the 1910 Census: Boston, Massachusetts; Des Moines, Iowa; Minneapolis, Minnesota; Queens, New York; Salt Lake City, Utah (Malmberg, Malmberg, Blalock, Atwood, and Payne, 1990) is yet another Family History Library finding aid. It is a time-saving directory that lists street addresses for the named densely populated areas that were not indexed in 1910. This uncataloged finding aid may be located in reference binder 49b on the second floor of the library or on microfiche (no. 6104151).

For researchers having problems locating addresses for the New York Metropolitan area in the state's 1915 census, the Family History Library has made available two important finding aids: *New York City 1915 State Census Street Address Index* vol. 1, *Manhattan*, is an alphabetical listing of all Manhattan addresses, giving the assembly district, election district, block, and Family History Library microfilm numbers. It was compiled by Elaine Justesen and Ann Hughes and edited by Raymond G. Matthews in 1992 (Family History Library book 974.71 X22m v.1.; microfiche no. 6101203). Vol. 2, *Brooklyn*, an equally valuable finding aid, was compiled by Lois Owen and Theodore R. Nelson and edited by Raymond G. Matthews in 1993 (Family History Library book 974.71 X22m, v.2; microfiche no. 6101620).

A page from the 1850 Agricultural Census Schedule for Meisenburg Township, Lehigh County, Pennsylvania.

SCHEDULE 4.—Productions of Agriculture in *Meisenburg Township* **enumerated by me, on the** *Twentieth* **day of** *August*

Name of Owner, Agent, or Manager of the Farm.	Acres of Land.		Cash value of Farm.	Value of farming Implements and Machinery.	Live Stock, June 1st, 1850.								Wheat, bushels of.	Rye, bushels of.	Indian Corn, bushels of.	Oats, bushels of.
	Improved.	Unimproved.			Horses.	Asses and Mules.	Milch Cows.	Working Oxen.	Other Cattle.	Sheep.	Swine.	Value of Live Stock.				
1	2	3	4	5	6	7	8	9	10	11	12	13	14	15	16	17
Salomon Hollien	80	26	3500	200	3		3		1	4	8	325	12	150	100	20
Daniel Hollien	70	10	3000	150	2		4		3	3	5	300	18	200	40	
Abraham Neely	80	20	3500	200	4		5		10	3	13	400	40	275	50	25
Michael Neely	80	20	3500	200	4		5		4	3	12	350	40	275	40	25
Nathan Buchman	87	7	3500	200	3		5		2	6	9	370	110	200	50	40
Bastien Scherling	70	10	3500	200	3		3		1		8	355	50	250	100	160
Henry Kramlich	66	14	3500	250	3		4			6	7	390		150	50	40
Nathan Walbert	80	10	2200	150	1		4		3	1	3	250	20	200	75	20
George Faith	20	4	1000				2				1	55	5	50	30	10
Paul Bleiler	130	40	6000	200	2		4		1		4	190	150	350	200	30
Nicol Weis	15	5	1200	50	1		2		1	2	3	80		40	20	
Michael Weis	60	20	3000	200	2		4		4	3	7	300	30	200	100	80
Peter Rabinold	78	12	3000	250	1		4		1	2	3	290	100	250	40	75
Henry Weis	74	18	3000	250	2		4		1	3	4	165	10	200	100	60
Nathan Xander	60	9	1500	100	2		3		2	3	6	150	10	100	50	40
Daniel Sechler	55	25	2200	100	2		5		1		6	200	100	100	100	80
Dennis Bachman	90	18	3500	150	3		2		2	5	1	250	50	150	100	50
Nicholas Neely	50	60	3000	100	2		5		1		4	205		150	50	20
Abraham Frey	40	6	1300		3		3			4	3	70	10	40	30	15
Daniel Greenawalt	70	40	3000	150	2		5		5	3	6	270	70	70	100	60
Charles Greenawalt	75	35	5000	200	2		6		3	6	6	300	65	160	150	70
John Gern	105	15	3500	200	2		2		3	3	3	205	100	200	150	100
Elijah Old	57	11	2500	100	3		3			3	1	155	20	50	30	12
Thomas Gern	85	25	3500	150	3		4		4	6	10	300	30	150	150	30
William Sheafer	53	7	1000	100	2		2		1	2	2	140	30	80	40	15
Henry Neely	50	20	2000	100	2		2				7	150		100	40	
Henry Faith	14	1	900	50	1		2				4	115	8	25	15	20
John Faith	22	3	1200				2				2	40		45	15	16
Charles Faith	19	3	1000	50	1		2			1	4	80	10	40	20	25
David Steire	133	46	10000	350	6		7		4	6	5	645	300	350	200	50
Jonas Ebert	25		1100	50	1		3			3	1	105	14	70	50	
Abraham Neely	87	8	3000	200	2		5		4	5	9	275	15	200	80	65
Jacob Neely	85	15	3000	200	3		5		2	4	7	320	40	200	100	70
Charles Danner	70	15	3000	150	4		5		2	3	4	325	125	150	75	50
George Danner	58	2	2000	150	2	1	3		1	4	4	220	25	60	50	100
George Leiherspiece	100	44	2500	100	3	5	3		1		2	170	15	70	75	50
Jacob Faatz	19	2	1200	30	1		2		1		4	135	8	65	35	
Wm. L. Eisenhart	36	7	1500	45	1		2		3		6	180		100	100	20
Jacob Gern	140	90	14000	250	6		9		10		9	933	600	200	150	300
Page	2507	603	141648	5540	95		152		88	86	224	7696	2449	5798	3930	2326

Non-Population Schedules and Special Censuses

I n addition to the population schedules, federal, state and local governments have requested special information for administrative decisions. These special schedules can be quite useful for family historians.

1885 CENSUS

An act of 3 March 1879 provided that any state could take an interdecennial census with partial reimbursement by the federal government. Colorado, Florida, Nebraska, and the territories of Dakota and New Mexico returned schedules to the secretary of the interior. The schedules are numbered 1, 2, 3, and 5.

- **Schedule No. 1: Inhabitants** Lists the number of dwellings and families. It also identifies each inhabitant by name, color, sex, age, relationship to head of family, marital status, occupation, place of birth, place of birth of parents, literacy, and kind of sickness or disability, if any.

- **Schedule No. 2: Agriculture** Gives the name of the farm owner and his tenure, acreage, farm value, expenses, estimated value of farm products, number and kind of livestock, and amount and kind of produce.

- **Schedule No. 3: Products of industry** Lists the name of the owning corporation or individual, name of business or products, amount of capital invested, number of employees, wages and hours, number of months in operation during the year, value of materials used, value of products, and amount and type of power used.

- **Schedule No. 5: Mortality** Lists the name, age, sex, color, marital status, place of birth, place of birth of parents, and occupation, and gives the cause of death for every person who died within the year ending 31 May 1885.

The schedules are interfiled and arranged alphabetically by state and then by county. Schedules for a number of counties are missing. The National Archives has microfilmed the Colorado (M158, eight rolls) and Nebraska (M352, fifty-six rolls) schedules. The originals are in the National Archives.

RESEARCH TIPS FOR THE 1885 CENSUS

The 1885 census is useful for locating data about individuals who were living on rapidly growing frontiers: Arizona, Colorado, New Mexico, Nebraska, Florida, and North and South Dakota; for locating and documenting newly arrived immigrants from Europe; and for documenting small businessmen and farmers—many of them immigrants—who were just getting started in their businesses. The manufacturers schedule for 1885 is the latest one available for research.

MORTALITY SCHEDULES, 1850–1885

The 1850, 1860, 1870, 1880, and 1885 censuses included inquiries about persons who had died in the twelve months immediately preceding the enumeration. Mortality schedules list deaths from 1 June through 31 May of 1849–50, 1859–60, 1869–70, 1879–80, and 1884–85. They provide nationwide, state-by-state death registers that predate the recording of vital statistics in most states. While deaths are under-reported, the mortality schedules remain an invaluable source of information (figure 6).

Mortality schedules asked for the deceased's name, sex, age, color (white, black, mulatto), whether widowed, place of birth (state, territory, or country), month in which the death occurred, profession/occupation/trade, disease or cause of death, and number of days ill. In 1870, parents' birthplaces was added. In 1880, the place where a disease was contracted and how long the deceased person was a citizen or resident of the area were included (fractions mean months when less than one year).

Before the National Archives was established in 1934, the federal government offered the manuscripts of the mortality schedules to the respective states. Those schedules not accepted by the states were given to the National Library of the Daughters of the American Revolution. Copies, indexes, and printed schedules are also available in many libraries (summarized in table 4).

The United States Census Mortality Schedule Register is an inventory listing microfilm and book numbers for the mortality schedules and indexes at the Family History Library. An appendix lists where the records are found for twelve states whose

Name	Age	Sex	Birthplace	Month of Death	Trade	Disease	Days Ill
Benton County, Sauk Rapids District							
AYR [AYER], Frederick	13	M	Minnesota	August		Affect lungs	[not given]
CRAWFORD, Leonard	1	M	Maine	February		Chronic	"
Ramsey County							
GERVAIS, Pierre	8	M	Minnesota	May		Unknown	42
DONNAR, Magdelin	60	F	Canada	April		Fever	15
BOUVAIS, Antoine	80	M	"	January	Farmer	Pulmonary	30
BIBOT, Zoe	25	F	"	April		Cholera	2
BAPTISTE, John	2	M	"	December		Pulmonary	30
PONCIN, Sophie	7	F	Minnesota	July		Cholera	3
RAMSEY, Alex, Jr.	4	M	Pennsylvania	"		Fever	14
FORBES, W. A.	6/12	M	Minnesota	March		Brain inflammation	21
GLASS, Phoebe	8	F	Wisconsin	February		Burned	2
BARBER, Mary Jane	3	F	Iowa	August		Conjestion	3
Albert	2	M	"	"		"	3
LUMLEY, John	23	M	Ohio	July	Stonemason	Cholera	1
GREEN, James	40	M	Pennsylvania	"	Trader	"	1
GLADDEN, Elijah	35	M	Ohio	"	None	"	5
ROBERT, Francis	25	M	Missouri	December	Trader	Consumption	90
GOODHUE, James, Jr.	2	M	Wisconsin	"		Teething	20

Figure 6. From Patricia C. Harpole and Mary Nagle, eds., *1850 Mortality Schedule, Minnesota Territorial Census* (St. Paul: Minnesota Historical Society, 1972), 100.

schedules are not at the library. Originally compiled by Stephen M. Charter and Floyd E. Hebdon in 1990, the thirty-seven-page guide was revised by Raymond G. Matthews in 1992. The second edition includes twelve pages of introduction to this important material. While the reference is not available in book form outside the second-floor reference area of the Family History Library, the library has reproduced it on microfiche that can be borrowed through LDS family history centers and a few other libraries (microfiche no. 6101876).

Frequently overlooked by family historians, mortality schedules comprise a particularly interesting group of records. Until recently, few were indexed. Lowell M. Volkel indexed the Illinois mortality schedules for 1850 in *Illinois Mortality Schedule 1850*, 3 vols. (Indianapolis: Heritage House, 1972); for 1860 in *Illinois Mortality Schedule 1860*, 5 vols. (Indianapolis: Heritage House, 1979); and those that survive for 1870 (the 1870 mortality schedules for more than half of the counties in Illinois are missing) in *Illinois Mortality Schedule 1870*, 2 vols. (Indianapolis: Heritage House, 1985). A more recent compilation is James W. Warren, *Minnesota 1900 Census Mortality Schedules* (St. Paul, Minn.: Warren Research & Marketing, 1991–92). As computers make indexing projects more manageable, we can expect more of these obscure yet genealogically valuable materials to be indexed. All statewide mortality schedules are indexed from 1850 to 1880 and for 1885 (South Dakota only) on microfiche by Accelerated Indexing Systems, and there is a CD-ROM index by Automated Archives, Inc.

RESEARCH TIPS FOR MORTALITY SCHEDULES

Mortality schedules are useful for tracing and documenting genetic symptoms and diseases and verifying and documenting African American, Chinese, and Native

Table 4: Mortality Schedule Depositories

An asterisk (*) indicates publication. An underline (_) indicates that it has been indexed. For addresses of national and state archives, and the Family History Library, see Appendix II.

State	1850	1860	1870	1880	1885	FHL	DAR	NARA Micropublications	State Archives	State Historical Society	Comments
Alabama	•	•	•	•					•		
Arizona	•*̲	•*̲	•*̲	•*̲		•			•		Printed and indexed; State Department of Archives
Arkansas			•*	•*		•	•	T655			
California	•	•	•̲	•			•				DAR has 1870 only
Colorado			•*	•*	•	•	•	T655			
Connecticut	•	•	•	•		•			•		
Delaware	•	•	•	•					•		
Dist. of Col.	•̲	•̲	•̲	•*̲			•	T655			
Florida	•	•	•	•	•		•		•		NARA has 1885 only
Georgia	•*	•	•	•		•	•	T655			
Idaho			•*	•*		•				•	
Illinois	•*	•*	•	•				T1156	•		
Indiana	•*̲	•̲	•̲	•̲			•		•		DAR has Jefferson County only
Iowa	•	•	•	•				T1156		•	
Kansas		•*	•*	•*		•	•	T1130			
Kentucky	•*̲	•̲	•̲	•̲		•	•	T1130			
Louisiana	•*̲	•̲	•̲	•̲		•	•	T655			
Maine	•	•	•	•	•						Originals in Office of Vital Statistics
Maryland	•̲	•	•	•					•		
Massachusetts	•̲	•	•	•			•	T1204			DAR has 1850 only
Michigan	•*̲	•*	•*	•*			•	T1163			
Minnesota	•	•	•			•	•	•		•	NARA has 1870 only
Mississippi	•*	•	•	•					•		
Missouri	•̲	•̲	•	•			•			•	DAR has 1850-60 only
Montana		•	•				•	GR6		•	
Nebraska		•*	•*	•*	•		•	T1128		•	NARA has 1885 only
Nevada		•	•				•			•	DAR has 1870 only
New Hampshire	•	•	•	•		•			•		
New Jersey	•	•	•	•			•	GR21	•		
New Mexico	•	•	•	•	•					•	NARA has 1885 only
New York	•	•	•	•			•			•	DAR has 1850 and city of Buffalo only
North Carolina	•	•	•	•	•		•	GR1	•		
North Dakota		•	•	•*	•	•			•	•	FHL has 1880 only
Ohio	•*	•		•	•	•		T1159	•		
Oregon	•*	•*	•*	•*					•		
Pennsylvania	•	•	•*	•		•	•	T956	•		DAR has Mifflin County only
Rhode Island	•	•̲	•̲	•̲		•					
South Dakota		•	•	•	•*	•					FHL has 1880 only; NARA has 1885

State	1850	1860	1870	1880	1885	FHL	DAR	NARA Micropublications	State Archives	State Historical Society	Comments
Tennessee	•	•		•		•	•	T655			FHL has 1850-60 only
Texas	•*	•*	•	•		•		T1134	•		FHL has 1850-60 only
Utah	•	•	•	•		•		T1134			State copy, LDS Historical Department, Salt Lake City; FHL has 1870 only; originals at Texas State University
Vermont	•*	•*	•	•				GR7	•		NARA has 1870 only
Virginia	•	•	•	•		•		T1132			State library has 1850, 1870-80; Duke University has 1860; FJL has 1870
Washington		•	•	•		•		T1154			
West Virginia	•*	•*	•*	•*		•			•		
Wisconsin	•	•	•	•		•				•	Milwaukee Public Library has 1860-80; DAR has 1850-70
Wyoming			•	•		•					Originals in State Law Library, Cheyenne

1. FHL: LDS Family History Library, Salt Lake City, Utah.
2. DAR: Daughters of the American Revolution, Washington, D.C.
3. NARA: National Archives and Records Administration, Washington, D.C.

American ancestry. By using these schedules to document death dates and family members, it is possible to follow up with focused searches in obituaries, mortuary records, cemeteries, and probate records. They can also provide clues to migration points and supplement information in population schedules.

VETERANS SCHEDULES, 1840–1890

Revolutionary War pensioners were recorded on the reverse (verso) of each page of the 1840 population schedules. Since slaves were also recorded on the verso of the schedules, it is easy to miss pensioner names, especially in parts of the United States where few or no slaves were recorded. Also, many elderly veterans or their widows were living in the households of married daughters or grandchildren who had different surnames or who lived in places not yet associated with the family. By government order, the names of these pensioners were also published in a volume called *A Census of Pensioners for Revolutionary or Military Services* (1841, various years. Reprint. Baltimore: Genealogical Publishing Co., 1996). The names of some men who had received state or Congressional pensions were inadvertently included with the revolutionary war veterans. The Genealogical Society of Utah indexed the volume in *A General Index to a Census of Pensioners . . . 1840* (Baltimore: Genealogical Publishing Co., 1965). These volumes are available in most research libraries. Figure 7 is the pensioner's list for Maine.

The National Archives has the surviving schedules of a special 1890 census of Union veterans and widows of veterans. They are on microfilm M123 (118 rolls). The

Figure 7. Revolutionary War veterans and military pensioners of Maine, 1840, in *A Census for Revolutionary or Military Services* (1841. Reprint. Baltimore: Genealogical Publishing Co., 1954), 1.

CENSUS

OF

PENSIONERS FOR REVOLUTIONARY AND MILITARY SERVICES,

AS

RETURNED UNDER THE ACT FOR TAKING THE SIXTH CENSUS,

IN 1840.

STATE OF MAINE.

Names of pensioners for revolutionary or military services.	Ages.	Names of heads of families with whom pensioners resided June 1, 1840.	Names of pensioners for revolutionary or military services.	Ages.	Names of heads of families with whom pensioners resided June 1, 1840.
YORK COUNTY. **WATERBOROUGH.**			**YORK COUNTY—Continued.** **SHAPLEIGH.**		
Noah Ricker	78	Noah Ricker.	Keziah Warren	81	John Pitts.
Jonathan Knight	77	Simeon C. Knight.	Jonathan Horn	85	Simon Ross.
Moses Deshon	76	Moses Deshon.	Jonathan Ross	91	Gideon Ross.
Abigail Hutchens	87	Abigail Hutchens.	**SACO.**		
Elizabeth Smith	85	Abner Thing.	Stephen Googins	86	Alexander Googins.
Thomas Carpenter	76	Thomas Carpenter.	John Grace	79	Moses Grace.
Sarah McKenney	74	Rufus McKenney.	Abraham Tyler	77	Abraham Tyler.
John Hamilton	75	John Hamilton.	**PARSONSFIELD.**		
Caleb Lassell	79	Ivory Parcher.	Noah Wedgwood	81	Allen Henry.
Moses Rhodes	74	Moses Rhodes.	Levi Chadbourn	82	Levi Chadbourn.
SOUTH BERWICK.			James Brown	83	Edmund Chase.
Mary Chambertin	90	Josiah W. Seaver.	Jacob Eastman	77	Jacob Eastman.
Lydia Jay	92	Ivory Jay.	Josiah Davis	90	Enoch Hale.
Henry Beedle	80	Henry Beedle.	Wentworth Lord	84	Wentworth Lord.
Timothy Berdens	76	John Brooks.	William Campnell	80	Nathan Moulton, jr.
Peliliah Stevens	83	John Welch.	George Newbegin	76	George Newbegin.
Barsham Allen	76	Barsham Allen.	Thomas Pendexter	88	Thomas Pendexter.
Charles Sargent	86	Charles Sargent.	John Stone	82	John Stone.
Lydia Marr	72	Reuben Bennett.	Thomas Towle	98	Thomas Towle.
John Hearl	85	John Hearl.	Nathan Wiggin	80	Nathan Wiggin.
Peace Peirce	69	Samuel Peirce.	Jonathan Wingate	82	Lot Wedgwood.
Hannah Peirce	81	Hannah Peirce.	**NORTH BERWICK.**		
Betsey Nasan	81	Betsey Nasan.	Ichabod Wentworth	52	Ichabod Wentworth.
Seammon Chadbourn	85	Seammon Chadbourn.	Absalom Stacpole	88	Absalom Stacpole.
Benjamin Nealey	58	Benjamin Nealey.	Jacob Allen	82	Jacob Allen.
WELLS.			Simeon Applebee	88	Benjamin Applebee.
Aaron Warren	83	Walter Warren.	Jonathan Hamilton	85	Abraham Henderson.
Samuel M. Jefferd	77	Samuel Jefferd.	**NEWFIELD.**		
Mary Gawen	73	James Goodwin.	Simeon Tibbets	88	Silvester Tibbets.
Joseph Hilton	85	Joseph Hilton.	Ebenezer Colby	81	Ebenezer Colby.
Miriam Littlefield	85	Joseph Littlefield, 3d.	Paul Roberts	78	Nathaniel Roberts.
Daniel Stuart	87	Joseph Stuart.	**LYMAN.**		
William Eaton	85	William Eaton.	Nathan Raymond	86	Francis Eldreg.
Abigail Hobbs	72	James Hobbs.	Thomas Murphey	85	Joseph Murphey.
David Hatch	79	David Hatch.	Joshua Gilpatrick	83	Benjamin Goodwin.
Joseph Williams	90	Moses Williams.	Silas Grant	86	Peter Grant.
Benjamin Penny	79	Benjamin Penny.	Jeremiah Roberts	86	Jeremiah Roberts.
Joseph Wheelwright	88	Joseph Wheelwright.	Rebecca Ricker	83	George W. Ricker.
SANFORD.			Simeon Chadbourn	91	Simeon Chadbourn.
John Hurton	77	John Hurton.	Elizabeth Lord	78	Elizabeth Lord.
Hepribeth Jacobs	85	Theodore Jacobs.	John Burbank	88	Reuben Goodwin.
Betsey Leavitt	72	Daniel L. Littlefield.	Uriah Hanscomb	59	Felard Davis.
Eunice Goodwin	72	John Lard.	William Clark	88	William Clark.
John Quint	79	John Quint.	Amaziah Goodwin	77	James Goodwin.
Samuel Shaw	83	Samuel M. Shaw.	Isaac Coffin	84	Issaac Coffin.
Samuel Shackford	79	Christopher Shackford.			
Robert Tripp	76	Robert Tripp.			
William Worster	86	Samuel Worster.			

schedules are those for Washington, D.C., approximately half of Kentucky, and Louisiana, Maine, Maryland, Massachusetts, Michigan, Minnesota, Mississippi, Missouri, Montana, Nebraska, Nevada, New Hampshire, New Jersey, New Mexico, New York, North Carolina, North Dakota, Ohio, Oklahoma, Oregon, Pennsylvania, Rhode Island, South Carolina, South Dakota, Tennessee, Texas, Utah, Vermont, Virginia, Washington, West Virginia, Wisconsin, Wyoming, Indian territories, and U.S.

ships and navy yards. Schedules for other states were destroyed in the 1921 fire that destroyed the 1890 population schedules. The schedules are arranged by state or territory, thereunder by county, and thereunder by minor subdivisions.

Each entry shows the name of a Union veteran of the Civil War; name of his widow, if appropriate; veteran's rank, company, regiment, or vessel; dates of enlistment and discharge and length or service in years, months, and days; post office address; nature of any disability; and remarks. In some areas, Confederate veterans were mistakenly listed as well.

Unlike the other census records described in this book, these schedules are part of the Records of the Veterans Administration (Record Group 15). They are discussed in Evangeline Thurber, "The 1890 Census Records of the Veterans of the Union Army," *National Genealogical Society Quarterly* 34 (March 1946): 7–9. Printed indexes are available for some of the 1890 census, and Ancestry.com has been indexing all of them as part of its 1890 Census Substitute (See page 40).

RESEARCH TIPS FOR SPECIAL VETERANS SCHEDULES

Veterans schedules can be used to verify military service and to identify the specific military unit in which a person served. A search of the state where an individual lived in 1890 may yield enough identifying information to follow up in service and pension records at the National Archives; it can often trace Civil War veterans to their places of origin. The 1890 veterans schedules have been indexed for every state for which schedules are extant (except Pennsylvania).

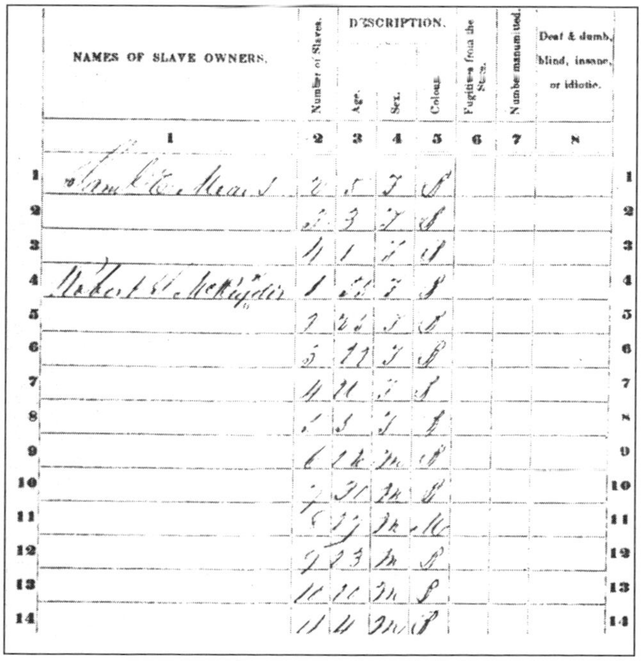

Figure 8. 1850 federal census (slave schedule), Fayette County, Kentucky.

SLAVE SCHEDULES, 1850–1860

Slaves were enumerated separately during the 1850 and 1860 censuses, though, unfortunately, most schedules do not provide personal names. In most cases, individuals were not named but were simply numbered and can be distinguished only by age, sex, and color; the names of owners are recorded. Figure 8 is a slave schedule for Kentucky. Few of the slave schedules have been indexed.

AGRICULTURE SCHEDULES, 1840–1910

Agriculture schedules are little known and rarely used by genealogists. They are scattered among a variety of archives in which they were deposited by the National Archives and Records Service. Most are not indexed, and only a few had been microfilmed until recently, when the National Archives asked that copies be returned for historical research. The schedules for 1890 were destroyed by fire, and those for 1900 and 1910 were destroyed by Congressional order. See table 5 for the locations of existing schedules.

RESEARCH TIPS FOR AGRICULTURE SCHEDULES

Agriculture censuses can be used to fill gaps when land and tax records are missing or incomplete; to distinguish between people with the same names; to document land holdings of ancestors with suitable follow-up in deeds, mortgages, tax rolls, and probate inventories; to verify and document black sharecroppers and white overseers who may not appear in other records; to identify free black men and their property holdings; and to trace migration and economic growth.

MANUFACTURERS SCHEDULES

The first census of manufacturers was taken in 1810. The returns were incomplete, and most of the schedules have been lost except for the few bound with the population schedules. Surviving 1810 manufacturers schedules are listed in appendix IX of Katherine H. Davidson and Charlotte M. Ashby, comps., *Preliminary Inventory of the Records of the Bureau of the Census, Preliminary Inventory 161* (Washington, D.C.: National Archives and Records Service, 1964).

The second census of manufacturers, taken in 1820, tabulated the owner's name, the location of the establishment, the number of employees, kind and quantity of machinery, capital invested, articles manufactured, annual production, and general remarks on the business and demand for its products. The schedules have been arranged alphabetically by county within each state to make research easier. The originals, deposited in the National Archives (Record Group 29), have been microfilmed with an index on each roll (M279, twenty-seven rolls). The Southeast, New England, Central Plains, and Mid-Atlantic regional archives of the National Archives have copies of the series. These indexes have been compiled and printed as *Indexes to Manufacturers' Census of 1820: An Edited Printing of the Original Indexes and Information* (Reprint. Knightstown, Ind.: Bookmark, n.d.).

No manufacturers schedule was compiled for the 1830 census. The 1840 schedules included only statistical information. Except for a few aggregate tables, nothing remains of these tallies.

From 1850 to 1870, the manufacturers schedule was called the "industry schedule." The purpose was to collect information about manufacturing, mining, fisheries, and mercantile, commercial, and trading businesses with an annual gross product of $500 or more. For each census year ending on 1 June, the enumerators recorded the name

Table 5: Summary of Special Census Schedules, 1850-80

For addresses of national, state, and library archives, and the Family History Library, see Appendix II.

State	Schedule	1850	1860	1870	1880	Location/Comments
District of Columbia	Agriculture	•	•	•	•	Duke University, Durham, N.C.
	Social statistics	•	•	•	•	
	Industry		•	•	•	
	Manufacturers				•	
Georgia	Agriculture	•	•	•	•	Duke University
	Social statistics	•	•	•	•	
	Manufacturers	•	•	•	•	
Illinois	Agriculture	•	•	•	•	State Historical Library
	Industry	•	•	•		
	Social statistics	•	•	•	•	
	Manufacturers				•	
Kentucky	Agriculture	•	•	•	•	Duke University
	Industry	•	•	•		
	Social statistics	•	•	•		
	Manufacturers				•	
Louisiana	Agriculture	•	•	•	•	Duke University; copy in state Department of Legislature Reference, Baton Rouge, La.
	Social statistics	•	•	•		
	Manufacturers				•	
Maryland	Agriculture	•	•			Hall of Records; social statistics schedule for Baltimore City/ County only survives
	Industry	•	•			
	Social statistics	•				
Massachusetts	Agriculture		•	•		State archives
	Industry		•	•		
	Social statistics		•			
Minnesota	Agriculture		•	•	•	Minnesota Historical Society
	Industry				•	
	Social statistics		•	•		
	Manufacturers		•	•	•	
Mississippi	Agriculture	•	•	•	•	Department of Archives
	Industry	•	•	•		
	Social statistics	•	•	•		
	Manufacturers				•	

State	Schedule	1850	1860	1870	1880	Location
Montana	Agriculture			•	•	1870, State Historical Society;1880 agricultural schedule at Duke University; other schedules at State Historical Society
	Industry			•		
	Social statistics			•		
	Manufacturers				•	
Nebraska	Agriculture		•	•	•	National Archives and Records Administration
	Industry		•	•	•	
	Social statistics		•	•		
	Manufacturers				•	
Nevada	Agriculture				•	Duke University
North Carolina	Agriculture	•	•	•	•	Department of Archives
	Industry	•	•	•	•	
	Social statistics	•	•	•		
	Manufacturers				•	
Pennsylvania	Agriculture	•	•	•	•	National Archives and Records Administration
	Industry	•	•	•	•	
	Social statistics	•	•	•	•	
	Manufacturers	•	•	•		
Tennessee	Agriculture	•	•	•	•	Duke University
	Industry	•	•	•		
	Social statistics	•	•	•		
	Manufacturers				•	
Texas	Agriculture	•	•	•	•	State library
	Industry	•	•	•	•	
	Social statistics	•	•	•		
	Manufacturers				•	
Utah	Agriculture	•	•	•	•	Genealogical Society of Utah has a microfilm of the three schedules; originals in LDS Historical Department
	Industry	•	•	•		
	Manufacturers				•	
	Mining			•		
Vermont	Agriculture	•	•	•		Public Records Commission
	Industry	•	•	•		
Virginia	Slave		•			Duke University, Durham, N.C.
	Agriculture		•			
	Industry		•			
	Social statistics		•			

Wisconsin	Agriculture	•	•	•	•	State Historical Society of Wisconsin
	Industry	•	•	•	•	
	Social statistics	•	•	•		
	Manufacturers				•	
Wyoming	Agriculture				•	Duke University

For those states not included in this table, check with the state archive or library first. (When these schedules were disposed of by the National Archives, state archives were given first rights to them.) Then check with the state historical society or state university with historical collections.

of the company or the owner; kind of business; amount of capital invested; and quantity and value of materials, labor, machinery, and products. Some of the regional archives of the National Archives have microfilm copies of the schedules for the specific states served by the region.

In 1880, the census reverted to the title "manufacturer's schedule." Special agents recorded industrial information for certain large industries and in cities of more than 8,000 inhabitants. These schedules are not now extant. However, the regular enumerators did continue to collect information on general industry schedules for twelve industries, and these schedules survive for some states. The manufacturer's schedules for later years were destroyed by Congressional order. See table 5 for the locations of extant schedules.

SOCIAL STATISTICS, 1850–1880

Social statistics schedules compiled from 1850 to 1880 contain three items of specific interest for the genealogist: (1) The schedules list cemetery facilities within city boundaries, including maps with cemeteries marked; names, addresses, and general description of all cemeteries; procedures for internment; cemeteries no longer functioning; and the reasons for their closing. (2) The schedules also list trade societies, lodges, clubs, and other groups with addresses, major branches, names of executive officers, and statistics showing members, meetings, and financial worth. The 1880 schedules were printed by the Government Printing Office, and most government document sections of public and university libraries have them. (3) The schedules list churches with a brief history, a statement of doctrine and policy, and a statistical summary of membership by county. The schedules for 1850 through 1900 are not listed in Davidson and Ashby, *Preliminary Inventory of the Records of the Bureau of the Census*. Those for 1906, 1916, and 1926 are printed; the originals were destroyed by order of Congress. Church records are especially helpful for researching immigrants, and the census of social statistics is a finding tool to locate the records of a specific group. See table 5 for the locations of extant schedules.

Special schedules are valuable because they document the lives of small businessmen and merchants who may not appear in land records. If population schedules give manufacturing occupations connected with industry, search the manufacturing schedules for more clues. It is also possible to trace the involvement of an individual in a fraternal club, trade society, or other social group.

STATE AND LOCAL CENSUSES

Population counts taken by state and local governments, though generally more difficult to find than the federal decennial censuses, can be very useful in family history research. In some cases, state and local census details will supplement information found in the federal counts; in others they may provide the only census information to be found for a given family or individual.

State Censuses

State censuses were often taken in years between the federal censuses. In some places, local censuses were designed to collect specific data, such as the financial strengths and needs of communities; tallies of school-age children and potential school populations to predict needs for teachers and facilities; censuses of military strength, cavalry horse resources, and grain storage; enumeration for revenue assessment and urban planning; and lists to monitor African Americans moving into northern cities.

As noted by Ann S. Lainhart in her comprehensive study *State Census Records* (Baltimore: Genealogical Publishing Co., 1992), tallies taken at the state level take on special importance for researchers attempting to fill in gaps left by missing censuses. For example, state and territorial censuses taken in Colorado, Florida, Iowa, Kansas, Nebraska, New Jersey, New Mexico, New York, North Dakota, and Wisconsin in years between 1885 and 1895 can partially compensate for the missing 1890 federal census schedules.

Additionally, some remarkably detailed state censuses are available for recent years. The Florida State Archives, for example, has 1935 and 1945 state enumerations. Like most other state schedules, the Florida state manuscripts are not indexed; they are arranged alphabetically by county and then geographically by election precincts. As with research in most state censuses, users must obtain election precinct numbers to expedite a search.

Probably no other state enumeration surpasses the 1925 Iowa state census in terms of genealogical value. In that year, Iowa asked for the names of all its residents and their relationship to the head of that household; place of abode (including house number and street in cities and towns); sex; color or race; age at last birthday; place of birth; marital status; if foreign born, year naturalized; number of years in the United States; number of years in Iowa; level of education; names of parents (including mother's maiden name); places of birth, age if living, and place of marriage of parents; nine specific questions relating to military service; nine questions regarding occupation; church affiliation; and six questions related to real estate, including the amount for which each listed property owner's house was insured.

A useful indication of what the Family History Library has on state and other censuses is "U.S. State and Special Census Register: A Listing of Family History Library Microfilm Numbers." It is an inventory, arranged by state and census year, describing the contents of each census and providing microfilm numbers for most known existing state censuses. The unpublished listing, compiled by G. Eileen Buckway and Fred Adams, was revised in 1992 and is available in the reference area of the Family History Library (Family History Library book Ref 973 X2be 1992; CCF 594855).

On the following page is a summary of state census schedules for the years 1623 to 1950 that includes the date, comments on them, and their current locations. (The notation "Ltd." following the census year indicates that only a partial census of the state was completed or is available. A census date is only included if at least the name of the head of the household is listed. Territory censuses are also included where applicable. Special thanks to Ann S. Lainhart for her assistance in preparing this summary.) The vast wealth of data available in these local enumerations can take several forms as the discussion will show.

LOCAL CENSUSES

Local population schedules usually resemble those of corresponding federal enumerations, but those taken in New York and Boston during the colonial period included details later incorporated in federal censuses. Beginning as early as 1703, some cities required that a census be taken of their population. Although these city/town censuses are not as numerous as the federal population schedules, some may be worth the time it takes to find them.

CENSUS SUBSTITUTES

In the absence of official census records, genealogists and historians have shown ingenuity in filling the resulting gaps. An interesting 1776 census was compiled from oaths of allegiance ordered by the colonial government of Maryland. Several of the lists are arranged in family units, with ages given for each person (figure 9). The pattern was

State Census Schedules, 1623 to 1950

Alabama
1818 Ltd., 1820 Ltd., 1821 Ltd., 1823, 1850, 1855, 1866, 1907 Ltd.

Alaska
1878 Ltd., 1879 Ltd., 1881 Ltd., 1885 Ltd., 1890–95 Ltd., 1904 Ltd., 1905 Ltd., 1906–07 Ltd., 1914 Ltd., 1917 Ltd.

Arizona
1866 Ltd., 1867 Ltd., 1869 Ltd., 1872 Ltd., 1874 Ltd., 1876 Ltd., 1880 Ltd., 1882 Ltd.

Arkansas
1823 Ltd., 1829 Ltd., 1865 Ltd., 1911 Ltd.

California
1788 Ltd., 1790 Ltd., 1796 Ltd., 1797–98 Ltd., 1816 Ltd., 1836 Ltd., 1844 Ltd., 1852

Colorado
1861, 1866 Ltd., 1885

Connecticut
No record of an applicable state census has been found.

Delaware
1782 Ltd.

District of Columbia
1803, 1867, 1878

Florida
1825, 1855 Ltd., 1866 Ltd., 1867 Ltd., 1868 Ltd., 1875 Ltd., 1885, 1895, 1935 Ltd., 1945 Ltd.

Georgia
1798 Ltd., 1800 Ltd., 1810 Ltd., 1827 Ltd., 1834 Ltd., 1838 Ltd., 1845 Ltd., 1852 Ltd., 1853 Ltd., 1859, 1865 Ltd., 1879 Ltd.

Hawaii
1878 Ltd., 1890, 1896 Ltd.

Idaho
No record of an applicable state census has been found.

Illinois
1810 Ltd., 1818 Ltd., 1820 Ltd., 1825 Ltd., 1830 Ltd., 1835 Ltd., 1840 Ltd., 1845 Ltd., 1855 Ltd., 1865 Ltd.

Indiana
1807 Ltd., 1853 Ltd., 1857 Ltd., 1871 Ltd., 1877 Ltd., 1883 Ltd., 1889 Ltd., 1901 Ltd., 1913 Ltd., 1919 Ltd., 1931 Ltd.

Iowa
1836 Ltd., 1838 Ltd., 1844 Ltd., 1846 Ltd., 1847 Ltd., 1849 Ltd., 1851 Ltd., 1852 Ltd., 1854 Ltd., 1856, 1885, 1895,1905, 1915, 1925

Kansas
1855 Ltd., 1865, 1875, 1885, 1895, 1905. 1915, 1925

Kentucky
No record of an applicable state census is available.

Louisiana
1853 Ltd., 1858 Ltd.

Maine
1837 Ltd.

Maryland
1776 Ltd., 1778 Ltd.

Massachusetts
1855, 1865

Michigan
1837 Ltd., 1845 Ltd., 1854, 1864, 1874, 1884, 1888 Ltd., 1894, 1904

Minnesota
1849 Ltd., 1853 Ltd., 1855 Ltd., 1857 Ltd., 1865 Ltd., 1875, 1885, 1895, 1905

Mississippi
1801 Ltd., 1805 Ltd., 1808 Ltd., 1810 Ltd., 1816 Ltd., 1818 Ltd., 1820 Ltd., 1822 Ltd., 1823 Ltd., 1824 Ltd., 1825 Ltd., 1830 Ltd., 1833 Ltd., 1837 Ltd., 1840 Ltd., 1841 Ltd., 1845 Ltd., 1850 Ltd., 1853 Ltd., 1860 Ltd., 1866 Ltd.

Missouri
1797 Ltd., 1803 Ltd., 1817 Ltd., 1819 Ltd., 1840 Ltd., 1844 Ltd., 1852 Ltd., 1856 Ltd., 1860 Ltd., 1864 Ltd., 1876 Ltd., 1880 Ltd.

Montana
No record of an applicable state census is available.

Nebraska
1854 Ltd., 1855 Ltd., 1856 Ltd., 1865 Ltd., 1869 Ltd., 1885

Nevada
1862–3 Ltd., 1875

New Hampshire
No record of an applicable state census has been found.

New Jersey
1855 Ltd., 1865 Ltd., 1875 Ltd., 1885, 1895, 1905, 1915

New Mexico
1790 Ltd., 1823 Ltd., 1845 Ltd., 1885 Ltd.

New York
1790 Ltd., 1825 Ltd., 1835, 1845, 1855, 1865, 1875, 1892, 1905, 1915, 1925

North Carolina
1786 Ltd.

North Dakota
1885 Ltd., 1915, 1925

Ohio
No actual state censuses were taken, but there are lists of eligible voters called quadrennial enumerations.

Oklahoma
1890 Ltd., 1907 Ltd.

Oregon
1842 Ltd., 1843 Ltd., 1845 Ltd., 1849 Ltd., 1850 Ltd., 1853 Ltd., 1854 Ltd., 1855 Ltd., 1856 Ltd., 1857 Ltd., 1858 Ltd., 1859 Ltd., 1865 Ltd., 1870 Ltd., 1875, 1885 Ltd., 1895, 1905

Pennsylvania
No record of an applicable state census has been found.

Rhode Island
1774 Ltd., 1777 Ltd., 1782 Ltd., 1865, 1875, 1885, 1905, 1915, 1925, 1935

South Carolina
1825 Ltd., 1839 Ltd., 1869 Ltd., 1875 Ltd.

South Dakota
1885 Ltd., 1895 Ltd., 1905, 1915, 1925, 1935, 1945

Tennessee
1891 Ltd.

Texas
1829–1836

Utah
1852 Index to Bishops Report, 1856 Territorial Census

Vermont
No record of an applicable state census has been found.

Virginia
1782 Ltd., 1783 Ltd., 1784 Ltd., 1785 Ltd., 1786 Ltd.

Washington
1856 Ltd., 1857 Ltd., 1858 Ltd., 1860 Ltd., 1871 Ltd., 1874 Ltd., 1877 Ltd., 1878 Ltd., 1879 Ltd., 1880 Ltd., 1881 Ltd., 1883 Ltd., 1885 Ltd., 1887 Ltd., 1889 Ltd., 1891 Ltd., 1892 Ltd., 1898 Ltd.

West Virginia
No record of an applicable state census has been found.

Wisconsin
1836, 1838 Ltd., 1842, 1846 Ltd., 1847 Ltd., 1855 Ltd., 1865 Ltd., 1875, 1885, 1895, 1905

Wyoming
1875 Ltd., 1878 Ltd.

later used for U.S. federal schedules. In 1778, a second census tallied those who opposed the American Revolution. Included on this second list are Quakers, Mennonites, and others who refused to take oaths, as well as some remaining Tories. Tax lists and city directories also make useful substitutes for missing censuses.

Figure 9. 1776 census of Susquehannah Hundred, Barford County, Maryland, from 1776 Census of Maryland (published by B. Sterling Carothers, 14423 Eddington Dr., Chesterfield, MO 63017).

```
1776 CENSUS OF SUSQUEHANNAH HUNDRED, HARFORD COUNTY, MD.
                    Taken by Charles Gilbert

Small, Robert        30    Horton, William     33    Macantraus, Hugh    24
   Elizabeth         21       Elisabeth        32       Feeby            31
   John            9mos.       William          14       Mary           3mos.
Beacor, George       15       Mary             12
Hare, Patience       11       James            10    Hall, Josias        24
                              Sarah             8    Mecarty, Owing      22
Small, John          27       Elisabeth         5    3 negroes
                              Ruth              1
Wilson, Andrew       46    2 negroes               Choislin, Thomas      41
   Lidiea            36                             Young, Thomas         40
   James             10    Cummins, Paul        35  Chisholm, Thomas      11
   Cathron            8       Hannah            27  Chisholm, John         7
   Benjamin           4       Samuel            9
   Andrew             2       James             3   Hampton, John         85
Hallett, John        25                                Ann                84
Prigg, Mary          25    Barns, Joseph        45
Brown, George        14                             Mitchel, John         31
                           Horner, James        29       Mary             34
Eare, Sarah (Widow)  39       Mary              28       Gaberil          19
   Mary              17       Elisabeth          7       Elisabeth         6
   Sarah              6       Thomas             6       Rachel            4
   Daniel             3       Casandrew          4       Fredrick          1
                              Mary Gilbert       1    Purkins, Ritchard   16
Rigdon, Charles      27    Baker, Jenny Mary    11    Taylor, Ritchard    12
Molton, Mathew       15    2 negroes
Sulliven, Nathaniel  13                             Cortny, Thomas        32
                           Clarke, Elizabeth    18       Sarah            27
Donovan William      23                                  Jonas            10
   Rachel            19    Culver, Benjamin     24       John              8
   Anos            6mos.       1 negro                    Hollas            6
                           Culver, Ann          62       Semelia           5
Duroin, Avariller    25       1 negro                    Sarah             3
   Delila             2    Suillovon, John      27       Thomas         2mos.
                              Margret           18    Brown, James        13
Judd, Daniel         40    Coolley, John        21       1 negro
   Hanah             39    Rigdon, Sarah        62
   William           17       Sarah             23    Knight, Jonathan    56
   Daniel            11    Pritchart, Mary      12       Ellender         46
   Joshua             9                                  Holliday, Mary   12
   Rachel             8    Bedelhall, John      27
   Ann                6    5 negroes                  West, Thomas        45
   Elisabeth          3                                  Ann              39
   James           3mos.   Michael, Belsher     48       Elisabeth        17
                              Ann               28       James            14
Thomson, Edward      45       John              14       Thomas           12
   Jamine            30       James             13       Samuel            6
   Martha            10       Bennet             8       Sarah             6
   Mallon             6       Jacob              6       Mary              3
   Mary               3       Susannah           4       Isaac             1
   William            1       Daniel             2
Sullavin, James      17       William         8mos.   Wright, Charles     30
                           Horten, John         23    Blackford, Thomas   66
Johns, Richard       43    4 negroes
                                 108
```

School Censuses

Traditionally, school censuses have been taken to ensure that local facilities and teachers are adequate, and to plan for future appropriations. These schedules count the children of school age. Some lists are in family units with parents' names included. Some list children with ages only (figure 10). School districts or archives of the institutions that created the records are the most likely to have these types of records.

Constable's or Sheriff's Census

The constable or sheriff's census (also called a police census) actually had little to do with law enforcement; but the local constable, often under the eye of the sheriff, was the official most often used to assemble data required for administrative decisions. For example, in 1769–1770, the governor of Connecticut required an enumeration of "how many parsons partayn to ech family, and how many boshels of wheat, and of Indian corne, ech famyly hath."

Another sheriff's census was taken to the Committee of Safety and Relief, 16 April 1814, to account for settlers on the Niagara Frontier (western New York) who were "victimized during the War of 1812." Money was raised in Albany by voluntary donation to provide aid for these settlers.

Pennsylvania's tax assessors took septennial (every seven years) censuses from 1763 to 1807, listing taxable inhabitants by township. Occasionally, the list covered males age sixteen to forty-five only, thus making a militia census. Tax assessors were exempt along with teachers, physicians, provincial and state government leaders, militia captains, and others. Their names were not included on the same lists. Exempt status was set by law.

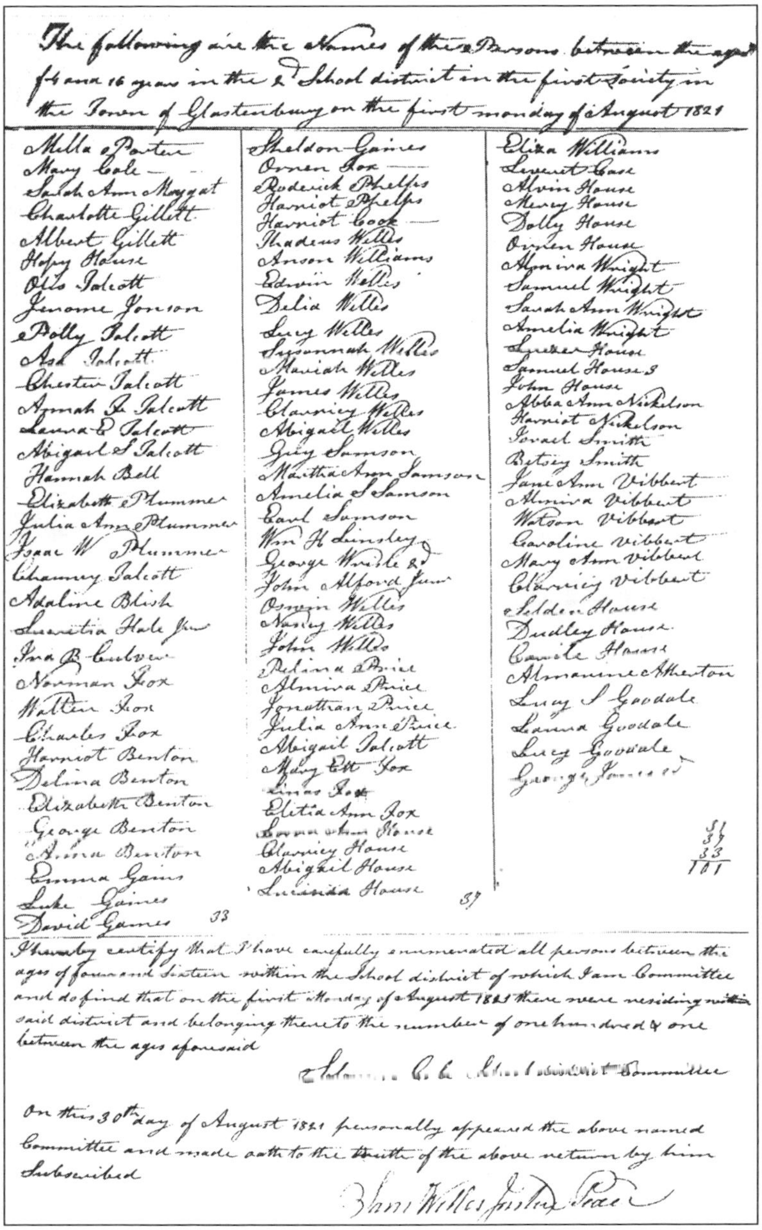

The following are the Names of the Persons between the ages of 4 and 16 years in the 2d School district in the first Society in the Town of Glastenbury on the first monday of August 1821

Milla Porter	Sheldon Gaines	Eliza Williams
Mary Cole	Orren Fox	Leverett Case
Sarah Ann Moggat	Roderick Phelps	Alvin House
Charlotte Gillett	Harriot Phelps	Mercy House
Albert Gillett	Harriot Cook	Dolly House
Hopy House	Thadeus Welles	Orren House
Otis Talcott	Anson Williams	Almira Wright
Jerome Jonson	Edwin Welles	Samuel Wright
Polly Talcott	Delia Welles	Sarah Ann Wright
Asa Talcott	Lucy Welles	Amelia Wright
Chester Talcott	Susannah Welles	[illegible] House
Azmah [illegible] Talcott	Mariah Welles	Samuel House 3
Laura E Talcott	James Welles	John House
Abigail S Talcott	Clarrisy Welles	Abba Ann Nickelson
Hannah Bell	Abigail Welles	Harriot Nickelson
Elizabeth Plummer	Guy Samson	Israel Smith
Julia Ann Plummer	Martha Ann Samson	Betsey Smith
Isaac W Plummer	Amelia S Samson	Jane Ann Vibbert
Chauncey Talcott	Earl Samson	Almira Vibbert
Adaline Blish	Wm H Linsley	Watson Vibbert
Lucretia Hale Jun	George [illegible] 2d	Caroline Vibbert
Ira B Culver	John Alford Jun	Mary Ann Vibbert
Norman Fox	Osmin Welles	Clarrisy Vibbert
Walter Fox	Nancy Welles	Selden House
Charles Fox	John Welles	Dudley House
Harriot Benton	Delina Price	Camile House
Delina Benton	Almira Price	[illegible] Atherton
Elizabeth Benton	Jonathan Price	Lucy S Goodale
George Benton	Julia Ann Price	Laura Goodale
Anna Benton	Abigail Talcott	Lucy Goodale
Emma Gains	Mary Ett Fox	George Jones 2d
Luke Gaines	Linus Fox	
David Gaines 33	Eletia Ann Fox	31
	[illegible] House	37
	Clarrisy House	33
	Abigail House	101
	Lucinda House 37	

I hereby certify that I have carefully enumerated all persons between the ages of four and sixteen within the School district of which I am Committee and do find that on the first Monday of August 1821 there were residing within said district and belonging thereto the number of one hundred & one between the ages aforesaid

[illegible] School district Committee

On this 30th day of August 1821 personally appeared the above named Committee and made oath to the truth of the above return by him subscribed

[illegible] Welles Justice Peace

Figure 10. First Monday of August, 1821, School Census, Glastonbury, Connecticut, P. 2. The Originals Are in the Connecticut State Library, Hartford.

Figure 11. Entry For the Joseph L. Pitts Family from the 1914 Census of LDS Church Members; Fhl 245155.

1914 CENSUS

Family Name Pitts

Ward Boise — Stake — Address Ida.

Date of Census Dec 10 1914

GIVEN NAMES	AGE	WARD RECORD NO.
PARENTS		
Joseph W	34	65
Francis	33	66
CHILDREN, OLDEST FIRST		
Mary Lucille	9	194
Evelyn	8	195
[illegible] H. S.	6	193
Phylis	1	
TOTAL		

Census taken by [illegible] Hellewell

Checked with Ward Record by Mary A. Hellewell Acting Ward Clerk

Figure 12. Entry for the John Frank Pincock family from the 1930 census of LDS church members; FHL 245155.

CENSUS OF CHURCH MEMBERS—1930

Sugar WARD — FAMILY NAME Pincock

Fremont STAKE — ADDRESS Sugar, Idaho R.F.D. #1

DATE TAKEN July 14, 1930

	SEX Male or Female	P. H'OOD MEMBER OR CHILD	WHEN BORN Day	Month	Year	WHERE BORN	SOCIAL RELATION	WARD RECORD NUMBER
Father's Name: John Frank	M	E.	15	January	1880	Utah	Married	545-[illegible]
Mother's Maiden Name: Susie S. Blackford	F	M	22	January	1881	England	Married	546-[illegible]
Children's Names—Oldest First: Joseph B.	M	T	8	May	1911	Idaho	Single	547-[illegible]
Alice	F	M	10	August	1913	Idaho	Single	548-[illegible]
Thelma	F	M	4	February	1915	Idaho	Single	549-[illegible]
Grace	F	M	10	April	1917	Idaho	Single	550-[illegible]
Ruth	F	M	4	January	1919	Idaho	Single	551-[illegible]
Grant	M	M	10	April	1922	Idaho	Single	552-[illegible]
Paul	M	C	27	May	1924	Idaho	Single	481-[illegible]

CENSUS TAKEN BY Eula Haldram

CHECKED WITH WARD RECORD BY [illegible] Davis WARD CLERK

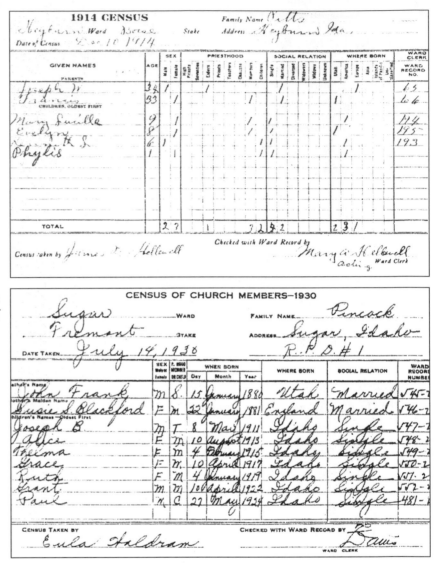

Church/Civil Censuses

In areas where a church was established and supported by the civil government, enumerating the population was often the responsibility of church officials. The most common examples come from New England, but others can be found among church wardens' records in Virginia and South Carolina.

As a more modern example, The Church of Jesus Christ of Latter-day Saints enumerated its members in Pottawatomie, Iowa, as part of the Iowa state census ordered in 1847 for all residents. These church schedules contain the standard information asked for in the Iowa tally but also include wagons, guns, number of family members ill, aged, or infirm, and oxen/cattle/horses. These data suggest a dual function for the census to comply with the Iowa law and to prepare for transporting a large body of people westward, a project even then under way (figure 11). Emigrating companies were enumerated in tens and hundreds before they embarked, the organization under which they traveled to Utah.

Other censuses were taken in Utah in 1852 and 1856. These tallies are valuable because many people did not survive the trek across the Great Plains and the Rockies; comparing the two censuses helps clarify mortality figures. Many of the companies that Brigham Young sent to colonize the Mormon Corridor before 1872 (Rocky Mountain valleys stretching from Mexico to Canada and from Las Vegas to San Bernardino, California) made summaries of individuals, professions, states of health, wagons, cattle, and weapons. Many of these schedules are among the collections of the LDS Church Historical Department, 50 North West Temple, Salt Lake City, UT 84150. More widely known are the twentieth-century census cards (1914 to 1960), which enumerate all LDS families in organized wards. They are available for research on microfilm at the Genealogical Society of Utah (figure 12).

SETTLERS CENSUS

Still another example is the Holland Land Company Census of 1806 (figure 13). The Holland Land Company had great difficulty getting payments from settlers on their lands in central and western New York. Its census assessed the resources of these settlers and, hence, their ability to pay. The 1806 data is especially valuable, as many of these people moved on before the 1810 federal census. For some, it is the only record of their stop in New York City.

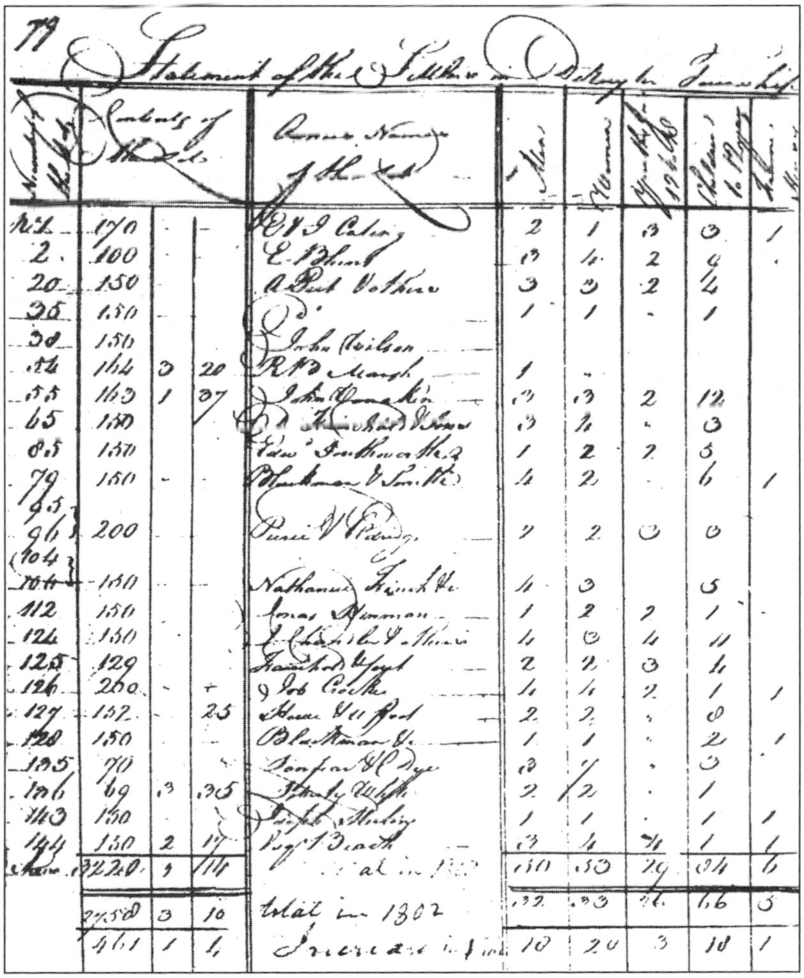

IMPORTANCE OF LOCAL CENSUSES

Local censuses can be useful in discovering the names of children who are listed in pre-1850 census schedules by age groupings only. Similarly, these censuses may be used to determine the number living in a household and compared with birth and death records. They may also verify specific residences of individuals who moved too rapidly to be recorded in other sources; and they may identify

Figure 13. Statement of settlers, Holland Land Company census, 1806. The original papers are in the possession of Central New York Park and Recreation Commission; microfilm copies are in Cornell University, Department of Manuscripts and Archives, Ithaca, NY 14853.

neighbors and other community members whose records can provide additional clues for tracing families and individuals back in time. Comparing local census schedules with tax records and other property sources is often one of the best ways to distinguish individuals of the same or similar names.

AFRICAN AMERICAN CENSUS SCHEDULES

From about 1830 on, northern cities increasingly felt the need to monitor African Americans who were moving from the South seeking freedom and work. In 1863, in the midst of the Civil War, Ohio called for the number and names of African

African Americans in The Federal Censuses

Courtesy of
David T. Thackery

It has been widely noted that African Americans were enumerated as all other U.S. residents from 1870 (the first census year following the Civil War and emancipation) onward. Prior to 1870, however, the situation was far different. Although free African Americans were enumerated by name in 1850 and 1860, slaves were consigned to special, far less informative, schedules in which they were listed anonymously under the names of their owners. The only personal information provided was usually that of age, gender, and racial identity (either black or mulatto). As in the free schedules, there was a column in which certain physical or mental infirmities could be noted. In some instances the census takers noted an occupation, usually carpenter or blacksmith, in this column. Slaves aged 100 years or more were given special treatment; their names were noted, and sometimes a short biographical sketch was included. In at least one instance, that of 1860 Hampshire County, Virginia, the names of all slaves were included on the schedules, but this happy exception may be the only instance when the instructions were not followed.

Sometimes the listings for large slaveholdings appear to take the form of family groupings, but in most cases slaves are listed from eldest to youngest with no apparent effort to portray family structure. In any event, the slave schedules themselves almost never provide conclusive evidence for the presence of a specific slave in the household or plantation of a particular slaveowner. At best, a census slave schedule can provide supporting evidence for a hypothesis derived from other sources.[8]

Prior to 1850 there were no special slave schedules for the manuscript census, as slave data was recorded as part of the general population schedules. In these, only the heads of household were enumerated by name.

In the absence of any contradictory information, it might be assumed that a family of freed people enumerated in the 1870 census was living not far from its last owner, whose surname they also bore. There would, of course, be reasons to dispute both assumptions. (Knowledge of the Civil War history of a locality could come into play here; for example, such relative stability would not have existed in a Georgia county that was in the path of Sherman's march to the sea.) Even so, this assumption represents one of the more obvious exploratory lines of research, especially in the absence of any other options. The first step in testing the hypothesis would be to search for slaveowners of the same surname in the 1860 slave schedules of the county in which the African American family resided in 1870.

Starting in 1850, another supplemental schedule, the mortality schedule, listed all deaths within a year before the regular census enumeration.[9] The deaths of blacks and mulattoes, both free and slave, are recorded in them, even though their names have not been included in many of the indexes to these schedules.[10] The deaths of slaves were generally enumerated in four fashions: unnamed (as in the slave schedules), but perhaps with the owner identified; by first name only; by first name and surname; and by first name with the owner noted.

Americans who had immigrated to Ohio from other states since 1 March 1861, their current township of residence, and their state of origin. Thirteen counties in southeastern Ohio submitted schedules. Hamilton County refused because the numbers were too great and its staff too limited.

Household censuses of Philadelphia's African American population were taken in 1838 and 1856 by the Pennsylvania Abolition Society and in 1847 by the Society of Friends. In addition to the variables listed in the federal census, the records of 11,600 households contain information describing membership in church, beneficial, and temperance societies; income, education level, and school attendance; house, ground, and water rent; how freedom was acquired; and the amount of property brought to Pennsylvania. These superb records constitute the most detailed information we have describing any population group in the mid-nineteenth century; they are being computer-processed as part of an urban-immigrant study of African Americans in Philadelphia conducted by Temple University.

The National Archives has issued a separate list of "Free Black Heads of Families in the First Census of the U.S. 1790" as Special List 34. This compilation by Debra L. Newman is available free of charge upon request from the National Archives. An expanded version for New York is Alice Eichholz and James M. Rose, comps., *Free Black Heads of Households in the New York State Federal Census 1790–1830*, Gale Genealogy and Local History Series, vol. 14 (Detroit: Gale Research Co., 1981).

RECONSTRUCTED 1790 CENSUS SCHEDULES

Census schedules are extant for only two-thirds of the thirteen states originally covered in the 1790 Census. Concerned genealogists have reconstructed substitute schedules for the missing states using tax lists and following the pattern set by the Bureau of the Census in *Bureau of the Census Records of State Enumerations, 1782–1785* (1908. Reprint. Baltimore: Genealogical Publishing Co., 1970). These substitutes for 1790 schedules include:

DELAWARE

Leon deValinger, Jr. *Reconstructed Census for Delaware*. Washington, D.C.: National
  Genealogical Society, 1954.

GEORGIA

Georgia Department of Archives and History. *Some Early Tax Digests of Georgia*. Atlanta:
  Department of Archives, 1926. Also available are several volumes of printed land lotteries, 1805 to 1820, available in most research libraries, and a pamphlet that describes
  the state's head-right (land bounty for attracting new settlers) and lottery system,

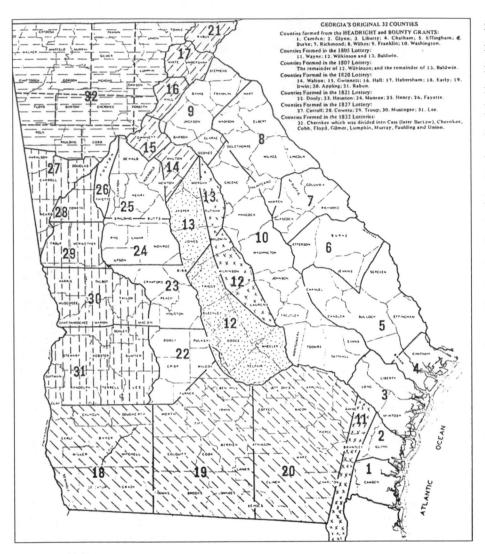

including eligibility qualifications. This pamphlet is available upon request from the Georgia Department of Archives and History, 330 Capitol Avenue S.W., Atlanta, GA 30334. Lotteries include precise description of qualifications for land ownership for each person drawing land in specific counties created as a result of the land awards. Figure 14 shows which years applied to which counties for lotteries.

KENTUCKY

Heinemann, Charles B. *"First Census" of Kentucky, 1790.* 1940. Reprint. Baltimore: Genealogical Publishing Co., 1971.

Figure 14. From the Rev. Silas Emmett Lucas, Jr., *The Creation of Georgia Counties, 1777-1932*; a separately published map, copyright 1982. Used with permission.

NEW JERSEY

Norton, James S. *New Jersey in 1793.* Distributed by The Everton Publishers, Box 368, Logan UT 84321. Based on military census lists and ratables.

Stryker-Rodda, Kenn. *Revolutionary Census of New Jersey: An Index, Based on Ratables of the Inhabitants During the Period of the American Revolution.* New Orleans: Polyanthos, 1972.

The Library of the Daughters of the American Revolution, Washington, D.C., has twenty-four microfilm rolls of New Jersey tax lists for 1783 which can also substitute for 1790 data.

TENNESSEE

Creekmore, Pollyanna. *Early East Tennessee Tax-Payers*. Easley, S.C.: Southern Historical Press, 1980. Originally printed in East Tennessee Historical Society Publications beginning in 1951.

Sistler, Byron, and Barbara Sistler. *Index to Early East Tennessee Tax Lists*. Nashville: Byron Sistler & Associates, 1977.

VIRGINIA

Bureau of the Census Records of State Enumerations, 1782–1785. 1908. Reprint. Baltimore: Genealogical Publishing Company, 1970.

Fothergill, Augusta B., and John M Naugle. Virginia Tax Payer 1782–1787. *Other Than Those Published in the United States Census Bureau*. 1940. Reprint. Baltimore: Genealogical Publishing Co., 1971.

Schreiner-Yantis, Nettie, and Virigina Love. *The 1787 Census of Virginia*. Baltimore: Genealogical Publishing Co., 1987.

Because substitutes for the 1790 census have been so useful, numerous reconstructions of other missing schedules are also under way. Tax lists, oaths of allegiance, land entities, militia lists, petitions, road records, and other sources, though never as complete as censuses, can go far toward filling the gaps left by lost or destroyed census schedules. Table 6 is a checklist of census substitutes.

In order to use substitutes effectively, it is important to know what specific categories of people are included in each source and which ones were left out. Many potential census substitutes are described in detail in *The Source: A Guidebook to American Genealogy* (1984. Reprint. Salt Lake City: Ancestry Incorporated, 1997), and some can be found printed with indexes. Still other sources have been stored, and sometimes forgotten, in various state archives, courthouses, and historical agencies.

CENSUSES OF NATIVE AMERICANS

In some years, separate censuses of Native Americans were taken by the federal government and the Bureau of Indian Affairs. While some early Native American populations were tabulated by missionary priests and colonial authorities, specific examples of such tallies have not been located.

The 1860 and 1870 federal censuses noted only Native Americans living in non-Native American households. Native Americans who were not taxed (living on

Table 6: A Checklist of Census Substitutes

Tax Rolls
___ Poll tax
___ Personal property
___ Real estate
___ 1863 income tax
___ 1798 property tax
___ Assessors' lists
___ Faculty lists
___ Rate lists

Land Records
___ Entries plats
___ Plat maps
___ Lotteries
___ Processioning lists
___ Perambulations
___ Ground rents
___ Quitrents
___ Debt books
___ Permits to settle
___ Land grant lists
___ Suspended land grants
___ Headright claims
___ Lists of indentured servants
___ Immigrant land allowances
___ Inquisitions
___ Devises' lists
___ Heir lists

Court Records
___ Oaths of allegiance
___ Registers of papists (Roman Catholics)
___ Lists of attorneys
___ Lists of constables
___ Lists of jurors
___ Jury pay lists
___ Jury attendance lists
___ Commissions of officials
___ Appointments of Justices of the peace
___ Lists of gamekeepers

Road Records
___ Petitions
___ Plats
___ Appointments of road officials

Voters' Records
___ Voters' register
___ Voters' lists
___ Poll books
___ Register of intended voters
___ Register of freemen
___ Lists of freeholders
___ Lists of rejected voters
___ Oaths of office
___ Loyalty oaths
___ Freemen admissions

Militia Records
___ Militia lists
___ Muster rolls
___ Muster-in rolls
___ Muster-out rolls
___ Payrolls
___ Lists of males over age 16
___ Troop returns
___ Enlistments
___ Enrollments
___ Lists of recruits
___ Substitutes
___ Lists of rejected men
___ Wagoners' rolls
___ Casualty lists

Church Records
___ Pew rents
___ Membership lists
___ Rate rolls
___ Collection lists
___ Subscription lists
___ Lists of paupers

School Lists
___ Matriculation lists
___ Attendance lists
___ Examination lists
___ Tuition lists
___ Subscription Lists
___ Pupil lists
___ Teacher lists

Legislative Records
___ Petitions
___ Memorials

Ships' Records
___ Crew lists
___ Register of seamen
___ Seamens' oaths
___ Seamens' certificates
___ Officers' lists
___ Sick rosters
___ Death registers
___ Casualty lists

Miscellaneous Records
___ City directories
___ Register of prisoners
___ Register of slaves
___ Register of free negroes
___ Prisoners of war
___ Manumission lists
___ Register of unmarried persons
___ Orphans' register
___ Lists of physicians
___ Lists of midwives
___ Lists of strangers

reservations) and members of nomad tribes in unsettled territories were not counted. It is safe to say that those enumerations of Native Americans made before 1880 are incomplete and, frequently, inaccurate. Additionally, in many instances, Native American origins are not indicated.

1880 NATIVE AMERICAN CENSUS

In 1880, a special enumeration was taken of Native Americans living near military reservations in the Dakota and Washington territories and the state of California. The census included the name of the tribe, the reservation, the agency, and the nearest post office; the number of people living in the household, with a description of the dwelling; the Native American name with English translation for each family member; relationship to head of household; martial and tribal status; and occupation, health, education, land ownership, and source of sustenance. Some enumerators also added customs and lifestyle data.

The *1880 Census of Indians, Not-Taxed* is in four volumes in National Archives Record Group 29. Volumes 1 and 2 cover Fort Simcoe, Washington, and Tulalip, Washington Territory. Volume 3 covers Fort Yates, Dakota Territory, and volume 4 covers California.

1885–1940 NATIVE AMERICAN CENSUSES

The 1885 to 1940 Indian census rolls are on National Archives microfilm M–595 (692 rolls). Census enumerations were taken regularly, though not annually, by Indian agents on each reservation from 1885 to 1942. Throughout these rolls are scattered letters written by agents describing why returns were not taken with instructions to enumerators on how to take the census. Vital records are noted in the age column or appended in separate lists.

In 1978, E. Kay Kirkham, Field Operations, Genealogical Society of Utah, updated and corrected the National Archives listing of Native American bands and tribes in these 692 microfilm rolls. He compiled an index for all tribes and bands, with Indian agency, National Archives reel number, and Genealogical Society of Utah call number. Tribes are found under several agencies during the period covered by the census, so it is important to study the history of the tribe before beginning research. Copies of this register are available in the Family History Library's American Reference area. Copies can be made on request for use in family history centers to access the lists more easily. There is no master name index to the Native Americans themselves.

Three copies of the census were made: one for the federal government in Washington (now transferred to the National Archives); a second for the Superintendent at Indian Affairs (Bureau of Indian Affairs); and a third for the Indian agency. Many Bureau of Indian Affairs copies were destroyed. Some local copies are still in agencies' possession or have been transferred to National Archives regional archives.

1898–1906 Indian Census Cards Index

The Indian Census Cards Index was compiled by the Dawes Commission to verify individual rights to tribal allotments for the Five Civilized Tribes (Cherokee, Chickasaw, Choctaw, Creek, and Seminole). To search this index, send the name of the tribe, name of the individual, approximate date of birth or death, and location to the Director, National Archives—Southwest Region, Box 6216, Fort Worth, TX 76115. Copies of the index are available from the Five Civilized Tribes Center, Bureau of Indian Affairs, Muskogee Agency, Fourth Floor, Federal Building, Muskogee, OK 74401, and through the Family History Library.

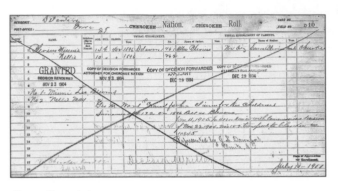

Dawes Commission enrollment card dated 1896

In the 1910 census, a special Indian schedule is sometimes found at the end of regular population schedules for some counties. For example, NV 1910 lists tribe, tribe of father, tribe of mother, proportion of Native American blood, and number of times married.

1910–1939 Indian School Census

The Bureau of Indian Affairs took separate Indian school censuses from 1910 to 1939. These include names of all children between six and eighteen years of age, sex, tribe, degree of Native American blood, distance from home to the school, parent or guardian, and attendance during the year. Some schedules are available on microfilm, but most are still in original form in the Federal Records Center for the region where the tribe was located. Unlike other population census records, these often include the mother's surname.

Native American census records can be used to identify relationships, mothers' full names, aliases, ancestral rights, and inheritances. These census records, however, apply only to Native Americans registered with the Bureau of Indian Affairs. Many Native American families never enrolled with the government. These persons are recorded in the regular census schedules, usually without evidence of their Native American ties.

Other miscellaneous records document Native American populations. Supplementary rolls list births, deaths, and sometimes marriages. Deduction rolls give deaths or removals from the jurisdiction. Additional rolls include arrivals and births. Allotment rolls list those entitled to payment and the payments received. For a more detailed description of these and other Native American sources, see *The Source: A Guidebook to American Genealogy,* chapter 14 (1984. Reprint. Salt Lake City: Ancestry Incorporated, 1997).

NOTES

1. Carmen R. Delle Donne. *Federal Census Schedules, 1850–80: Primary Sources for Historical Research*. Reference Information Paper 67 (1973). Filled with interesting details on why and how the census was taken, 1850 to 1880.

2. U.S. Department of Commerce. *Bureau of the Census. A Century of Population Growth from the First Census of the United States to the Twelfth, 1790–1900*. Washington, D.C.: Government Printing Office, 1909. Reprint. Baltimore: Genealogical Publishing Co., 1967. Includes much information about the 1790 census and a list of common surnames and their distribution in the states.

3. Szucs, Loretto Dennis, and Sandra Hargreaves Luebking. *The Archives: A Guide to the National Archives Field Branches*. Salt Lake City: Ancestry, 1988.

4. Delle Donne, 1973.

5. Ibid.

6. Arlene H. Eakle. "Census Records" in *The Source: A Guidebook of American Genealogy*. Salt Lake City: Ancestry, 1984.

7. Val D. Greenwood. *The Researcher's Guide to American Genealogy*. 2nd ed. Baltimore: Genealogical Publishing Co., 1990.

8. Delle Donne, 1973.

BIBLIOGRAPHY

Anderson, Robert C., et al. "Duplicate Census Enumerations." *The American Genealogist* 62 (2) (April 1987): 97–105; 62 (3) (July 1987): 173–81; 62 (4) (October 1987): 241–44.

Barrows, Robert G. "The Ninth Federal Census of Indianapolis: A Case Study in Civic Chauvinism," *Indiana Magazine of History* 73 (1) (March 1977): 1–16.

Bureau of the Census. *Heads of Families at the First Census of the United States Taken in the Year 1790.* 12 vols. Washington, D.C.: Government Printing Office, 1908.

Bureau of the Census. *Records of State Enumerations, 1782–1785.* 1908. Reprint. Baltimore: Genealogical Publishing Co., 1970.

Burroughs, Tony. *Black Roots: A Beginnier's Guide to Tracing The African American Family Tree.* New York City: Fireside, 2001.

Carpenter, Niles. *Immigrants and Their Children 1920: A Study Based on Census Statistics Relative to the Foreign Born and the Native White of Foreign or Mixed Parentage* Census Monographs VII. Washington, D.C.: Department of Commerce, Bureau of the Census, 1927.

Census Enumeration District Descriptions, 1830–1890 and 1910–1950. National Archives Microfilm Publication T-1224, 146 rolls.

Census Enumeration District Descriptions, 1900. National Archives Microfilm Publication T-1210, 10 rolls.

A Census of Pensioners for Revolutionary or Military Services. 1841, various years. Reprint. Baltimore: Genealogical Publishing Co., 1996.

Conzen, Michael P. "Spatial Data from Nineteenth Century Manuscript Censuses: A Technique for Rural Settlement and Land Use Analysis." *The Professional Geographer* 21 (5): 337–43 (September 1969). A primer on mapping the enumerator's route.

Creekmore, Pollyanna. *Early East Tennessee Tax-Payers.* Easley, S.C.: Southern Historical Press, 1980.

Davenport, David P. "Duration of Residence in the 1855 Census of New York State," *Historical Methods* 18 (1) (Winter 1985): 5–12.

Davidson, Katherine H., and Charlotte M. Ashby, comps. *Preliminary Inventory of the Records of the Bureau of the Census. Preliminary Inventory No. 161.* Washington, D.C.: National Archives and Records Service, 1964.

Department of Commerce, Bureau of the Census. *Fourteenth Census of the United States, January 1, 1920: Instructions to Enumerators.* Washington, D.C.: Government Printing Office, 1919.

deValinger, Leon, Jr. *Reconstructed Census for Delaware. Washington, D.C.:* National Genealogical Society, 1954.

Dubester, Henry J. *State Censuses: An Annotated Bibliography of Censuses of Population Taken After the Year 1790 by States and Territories of the United States. Washington, D.C.:* Bureau of the Census, 1948. Reprint. Knightstown, Ind.: The Bookmark, 1975.

Eichholz, Alice. *Ancestry's Red Book: American State, County and Town Sources.* Rev. ed. Salt Lake City: Ancestry, 1992. Chapters appear alphabetically by state. Within each state chapter is a description of available federal, state, special, and local censuses and their respective finding aids.

_____, and James M. Rose, comps. *Free Black Heads of Households in the New York State Federal Census 1790–1830.* Gale Genealogy and Local History Series, vol. 14. Detroit: Gale Research Co., 1981.

The 1790–1890 Federal Population Censuses: Catalog of National Archives Microfilm. Washington, D.C.: National Archives Trust Fund Board, 1993.

Fishbein, Meyer H. *The Censuses of Manufacturers, 1810–1890.* Reference Information Paper 50 (1973).

Fothergill, Augusta B., and John M. Naugle. *Virginia Tax Payers 1782–1787. Other Than Those Published in the United States Census Bureau.* 1940. Reprint. Baltimore: Genealogical Publishing Co., 1971.

Franklin, W. Neil, comp. *Federal Population and Mortality Census Schedules, 1790–1890 in the National Archives and the States: Outline of a Lecture on Their Availability, Content and Use.* Special List no. 24. Washington, D.C.: National Archives and Records Service, General Services Administration, 1971. The greater part of this work describes the federal censuses and their availability in 1971. However, a discussion of mortality schedules is still valid. The compiler's bibliography cites some relatively obscure but important finding aids.

Frederick, Nancy Gubb. *1880 Illinois Census Index, Soundex Codes O-200 to O240.* Evanston, Ill.: the compiler, 1981.

A General Index to a Census of Pensioners . . . 1840. Baltimore: Genealogical Publishing Co., 1965.

Georgia Department of Archives and History. *Some Early Tax Digests of Georgia.* Atlanta: Department of Archives, 1926.

Giltner, Charlotte L. "Interpreting the 1790 Census." Detroit Society for Genealogical *Research Magazine* 51 (3) (Spring 1988): 110, 112.

Green, Kellee. "The Fourteenth Numbering of the People: The 1920 Federal Census." *Prologue: Quarterly of the National Archives* 23 (2) (Summer 1991): 131–45.

Greenwood, Val D. *The Researcher's Guide to American Genealogy.* 2nd ed. Baltimore: Genealogical Publishing Co., 1990. Particularly pp. 181–253.

Guide to Genealogical Research in the National Archives. Washington, D.C.: National Archives, 1983. Particularly pp. 9–38.

Heinemann, Charles B. *"First Census" of Kentucky, 1790.* 1940. Reprint. Baltimore: Genealogical Publishing Co., 1971.

Hollingsworth, Harry. "History and Availability of United States Census Schedules, 1850–1880," *Genealogical Journal* 7 (3) (September 1978): 143–50.

Indexes to Manufacturers' Census of 1820: An Edited Printing of the Original Indexes and Information. Reprint. Knightstown, Ind.: Bookmark, n.d.

Justesen, Elaine, and Ann Hughes, comps. *New York City 1915 State Census Street Address Index.* Vol. 1, Manhattan. Edited by Raymond G. Matthews. Salt Lake City: Family History Library, 1992.

Lainhart, Ann S. *State Census Records.* Baltimore: Genealogical Publishing Co., 1992.

McLeod, Dean L. "Record Source Failure; Some Implications for Analysis." *Genealogical Journal* 7 (2) (June 1978): 98–105.

Mariner, Mary Lou Craver, and Patricia Roughan Bellows. *A Research Aid for the Massachusetts 1910 Federal Census.* Sudbury, Mass.: Computerized Assistance, 1988. An index by towns and counties of enumeration districts, wards, and precincts and where to locate them on the microfilm. Enables a researcher to find town by roll, volume, and page number. Includes a large foldout street map of 1910 Boston with the wards indicated, plus county maps for the entire commonwealth.

National Archives and Records Administration. *Federal Population and Mortality Schedules, 1790–1910, in the National Archives and the States.* Washington, D.C.: National Archives, 1986. Two microfiche.

_____. *Guide to Genealogical Research in the National Archives.* 3rd. ed. Washington, D.C.: National Archives and Records Administration, 2001.

National Archives and Records Service. Cartographic Records of the Bureau of the Census. Preliminary Inventory No. 103. Washington, D.C.: 1958. Includes a concise administrative history of federal census-taking. Following the inventory is a list showing the availability in the National Archives of maps of enumeration districts for each of the censuses, 1880 to 1940. The list is arranged by state, thereunder by county, and thereunder by locality.

_____. *Geographic Index to Census Microfilm (Major Subdivisions)*. This is the title of National Archives and Records Service Form NAR T56, bound, processed sets of completed copies of which comprise this finding aid. The forms are arranged alphabetically by state and thereunder alphabetically by county and major city. The forms show, for each subdivision, where applicable, the numbers assigned the rolls of microfilm that reproduce the schedules for that subdivision for each of the decennial censuses, 1800 to 1880. Sets of this finding aid are available for use in the Microfilm Reading Room of the National Archives.

_____. *Population Schedules, 1800–1870: Volume Index to Counties and Major Cities*. National Archives and Records Service Lists, No. 8. Washington, D.C.: 1969. Each bound volume of schedules in the National Archives bears an identifying number which is shown in this publication. Its arrangement is alphabetical by name of state and thereunder by name of county.

_____. Records of the Bureau of the Census. Preliminary Inventory No. 161. Washington, D.C.: 1964. Includes an administrative history of census-taking, an outline of preservation problems, and a description of the population schedules (1790 to 1950).

National Archives Trust Fund Board. *Federal Population Censuses, 1790–1890: A Catalog of Microfilm Copies of the Schedules*. Washington, D.C.: National Archives Trust Fund Board, 1979. This catalog is arranged chronologically, thereunder by state or territory, and then by county. Given for each microfilm publication is the series number and the total number of microfilm rolls in the enumeration. The catalog further identifies each microfilm roll by number and contents.

_____. *1900 Federal Population Census: A Catalog of Microfilm Copies of the Schedules*. Washington, D.C.: 1978. This catalog lists the 1,854 rolls of microfilm on which the 1900 population census schedules appear. The census schedules are arranged by state or territory and then by county. Numbers for the 7,846 rolls of 1900 Soundex appear in the second half of the book.

_____. *The 1910 Federal Population Census: A Catalog of Microfilm Copies of the Schedules*. Washington, D.C.: 1982. This catalog lists the 1,784 rolls of microfilm on which the 1910 population census schedules appear. The census schedules are arranged by state or territory and then by county. Numbers for the 4,642 rolls of 1910 Soundex/Miracode appear in the second half of the catalog.

_____. *The 1920 Federal Population Census: Catalog of National Archives Microfilm*. Washington, D.C.: 1991. This catalog lists the 8,585 rolls of 1920 Soundex in the front portion of the book. The catalog lists 2,076 rolls of 1920 census schedules arranged by state or territory and then by county.

Nelson, Ken. *1890 Census Index Register.* Salt Lake City: Genealogical Society of Utah, 1984.

Norton, James S. *New Jersey in 1793.* Distributed by The Everton Publishers, Box 368, Logan UT 84321.

Owen, Lois, and Theodore R. Nelson, comps. *New York City 1915 State Census Street Address Index.* Vol. 2, Brooklyn. Edited by Raymond G. Matthews. Salt Lake City: Family History Library, 1993.

Parker, J. Carlyle. *City, County, Town and Township Index to the 1850 Census Schedules.* Detroit: Gale Research Co., 1979. Designed to identify cities, counties, towns, and townships in every state as they were in 1850, this alphabetically arranged list matches localities with appropriate census microfilm numbers. Its usefulness is not limited to the 1850 census because it can be used as a gazetteer to locate places that no longer exist and places that have been lost due to boundary changes.

Petty, Gerald M. "Virginia 1820 Federal Census: Names Not on the Microfilm Copy." *Virginia Genealogist* 18 (1974): 136–39.

Schedules of the Colorado State Census of 1885. National Archives Microfilm Publication M-158 (eight rolls).

Schedules of the Florida State Census of 1885. National Archives Microfilm Publication M-845 (thirteen rolls).

Schedules of the Nebraska State Census of 1885. National Archives Microfilm Publication M-352 (fifty-six rolls).

Schedules of the New Mexico Territory Census of 1885. National Archives Microfilm Publication M-846 (six rolls).

The schedules of the 1885 Dakota Territory census are divided, the appropriate portions being held by the state historical societies of North and South Dakota. In addition to the federally supported 1885 state censuses, other states took censuses without federal support (see the sources listed above).

Schlesinger, Keith R. "An 'Urban Finding Aid' for the Federal Census," *Prologue* 13 (4): 251–62 (Winter 1981).

_____, and Peggy Tuck Sinko. "Urban Finding Aid for Manuscript Census Searches." *National Genealogical Society Quarterly* 69 (3) (September 1981): 171–80.

Shepard, JoAnne (Bureau of the Census). *Age Search Information.* Washington, D.C.: Government Printing Office, 1990.

Sistler, Byron, and Barbara Sistler. *Index to Early East Tennessee Tax Lists.* Nashville: Byron Sistler & Associates, 1977.

Stephenson, Charles. "The Methodology of Historical Census Record Linkage: A User's Guide to the Soundex," *Journal of Family History* 5 (1) (Spring 1980): 112–15. Reprinted in Prologue 12 (2) (Fall 1980): 151–53.

Steuart, Bradley W. *The Soundex Reference Guide: Soundex Codes to Over 125,000 Surnames*. Bountiful, Utah: Precision Indexing, 1990.

Straney, Shirley Garton. "1800 Census, Cumberland County; A Contribution," The *Genealogical Magazine of New Jersey* 60 (1) (January 1985): 27–34.

Street Indexes to the 39 Largest Cities in the 1910 Census. National Archives Microfiche Publication M-1283.

Stryker-Rodda, Kenn. *Revolutionary Census of New Jersey: An Index, Based on Ratables of the Inhabitants During the Period of the American Revolution*. New Orleans: Polyanthos, 1972.

Swenson, Helen Smothers. *Index to 1890 Census of the United States*. Round Rock, Tex.: the author, 1981.

Thorndale, William. "Census Indexes and Spelling Variants." *APG* [Association of Professional Genealogists] *Newsletter* 4 (5) (May 1982): 6–9. Reprinted in *The Source: A Guidebook of American Genealogy*, edited by Arlene Eakle and Johni Cerny. Salt Lake City: Ancestry, 1984, pp. 17–20.

_____, and William Dollarhide. *Map Guide to the U.S. Federal Censuses, 1790–1920*. Baltimore: Genealogical Publishing Co., 1987.

Thurber, Evangeline. "The 1890 Census Records of the Veterans of the Union Army." *National Genealogical Society Quarterly* 34 (March 1946): 7–9.

U.S. Bureau of the Census. *200 Years of U.S. Census Taking: Population and Housing Questions, 1790–1990*. Washington, D.C.: Government Printing Office, 1989. Earlier editions had different titles: Population and Housing Inquiries in U.S. Decennial Censuses, 1790–1970 (1973) and Twenty Censuses: Population and Housing Questions, 1790–1980 (1979).

U.S. Census Office. *Eighth Census, 1860*. Eighth Census, United States—1860. Act of Congress of Twenty-third May, 1850. Instructions to U.S. Marshals. Instructions to Assistants. Washington, D.C.: G. W. Bowman, 1860. Enumerator's instructions for the 1860 census (omitted from Wright and 200 Years of U.S. Census Taking).

U. S. Congress. Senate. *The History and Growth of the United States Census*. Prepared for the Senate Committee on the Census by Carroll D. Wright. S. Doc. 194,56 Cong., I sess., Serial 385b. Reprint. 1967. In the appendixes are reproduced the schedules of inquiry of each of the decennial censuses from 1790 to 1890 and the instructions for the taking of each of the decennial censuses from 1820 to 1890.

U.S. Library of Congress. *Census Library Project. State Censuses: An Annotated Bibliography of Censuses of Population Taken After the Year 1790 by States and Territories of the United States*. Prepared by Henry J. Dubester. Washington, D.C.: Government Printing Office, 1948.

_____. *Index to the Eleventh Census of the United States, 1890*. National Archives Microfilm Publication M-496 (two rolls).

_____. *Special Schedules of the Eleventh Census (1890) Enumerating Union Veterans and Widows of Union Veterans of the Civil War*. National Archives Microfilm Publication M-123 (118 rolls). The schedules for the states alphabetically from Alabama through Kansas and part of Kentucky were destroyed before the veterans schedules were acquired by the National Archives in 1943. Only the schedules for the states in the latter part of the alphabet are thus available for use. In recent years, state-by-state indexes for the veterans schedules have become available. They must, of course, be used with the same caution as any census indexes.

U.S. National Archives. *Federal Population Censuses, 1790–1890*. Washington, D.C.: National Archives, various dates.

_____. *1900 Federal Population Census*. Washington, D.C.: National Archives, 1978.

_____. *1910 Federal Population Census*. Washington, D.C.: National Archives, 1982.

_____. *1920 Federal Population Census*. Washington, D.C.: National Archives, 1991.

Vallentine, John F. "Effective Use of Census Indexes in Locating People." *Genealogical Journal* 4 (2) (June 1975): 51–58.

_____. "State and Territories Census Records in the United States." *Genealogical Journal* 2 (4) (December 1973): 133–39.

Volkel, Lowell M. *Illinois Mortality Schedule 1850*. 3 vols. Indianapolis: Heritage House, 1972.

_____. *Illinois Mortality Schedule 1860*. 5 vols. Indianapolis: Heritage House, 1979.

_____. *Illinois Mortality Schedule 1870*. 2 vols. Indianapolis: Heritage House, 1985.

Warren, James W. *Minnesota 1900 Census Mortality Schedules*. St. Paul, Minn.: Warren Research & Marketing, 1991–92.

Warren, Mary Bondurant. "Census Enumerations: How Were They Taken? Do Local Copies Exist?," *Family Puzzlers* no. 475 (November 1976): 1–16.

Wright, Carroll D. *The History and Growth of the United States Census*. Washington, D.C.: Government Printing Office, 1900. Reprint. New York: Johnson Reprint, 1966. A basic source for background and details of the census-taking process, 1790 to 1890. There is nothing as detailed for later censuses.

APPENDIX I

Following is a directory of electronic census information providers. All information included in each listing was provided by the individual companies and does not necessarily reflect the views of the authors.

ALLCENSUS

OVERVIEW OF COMPANY/ORGANIZATION

Jon and Teri McInnis founded Allcensus in the July 1998. The Company plans to provide census records for the United States and Canada in an economical and easy-to-use format that will assist those doing genealogy research. Eventually, indexes will be added to the records that will allow researchers to follow a family and its members throughout the census.

CONTACT INFORMATION

ALLCENSUS
P.O. Box 206
Green Creek, NJ 08219
Phone: 609-889-3744
Fax: 609-889-6715
E-Mail: allcensus@snip.net
E-Mail: Comments@allcensus.com
URL: http://www.allcensus.com
President: Jon S. McInnis

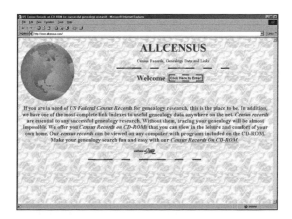

Overview of Census Products/Services

ALLCENSUS offers digital images of the actual pages of the Federal Census records from 1790 to 1920 (1930 when available). The images are on CD-ROM and divided into respective counties or cities. Corrections to page numbering are made when scanning so that researchers are less likely to place family members incorrectly. Each page is compared to the microfilm so that all possible information is obtained and poor quality pages are enhanced to bring out data that may not have been apparent on the film.

ANCESTRY.COM

Overview of Company/Organization

The mission of Ancestry.com and its related site at MyFamily.com is to connect and strengthen families on the World Wide Web. The company is managed by a highly experienced team with years of service in Internet and electronic publishing businesses.

For more than eighteen years, the Ancestry brand has been the recognized leader for quality genealogical publishing and a trusted resource for materials such as *The Source: A Guidebook of American Genealogy*, *The Redbook: American State, County & Town Sources*, *They Became Americans: Finding Naturalization Records*, the *Ancestry Reference Library* CD-ROM and more. Launched in 1996, Ancestry.com was the first family history Web site to publish the Social Security Death Index and other large databases online. Currently, Ancestry.com offers over 1 billion names in over 3,000 unique databases. With a paid subscription base of over 400,000, Ancestry.com is the third largest subscription-based Web site on the Internet.

Contact Information

MyFamily.com, Inc.

360 W. 4800 North, Provo, UT 84064

Phone: 1-800-ANCESTRY

Fax: 801-705-7001

URL: http://www.ancestry.com

E-MAIL: support@ancestry.com

Contact name: NA

Overview of Census Products/Services

Ancestry.com is the leading provider of online census images. Ancestry.com's online census image offerings include a complete set of images for each census year from 1790–1930. At the time of publication, the company had complete heads-of-household indexes linked to images for the 1790-1850 census years, with a partial heads-of-household index linked to images for the 1860 census. Ancestry.com has also started releasing an every-name index linked to images for the 1930 census; this index will be completed by 2003. Ancestry.com offers these census images using a special cleaning and quality process created for this project. Images have been scanned in 256 shades of gray allowing for the best images technology can offer.

Ancestry.com also has indexes created by Accelerated Indexing Systems (AIS) available both online and on CD-ROM. The AIS collection includes Federal Census Indexes, State Census Indexes, and indexes to various Federal non-population schedules (mortality schedules, veterans schedules, slaves schedules) for most of the United States and parts of Canada. The collection contains other non-census records such as colonial records (pre-1790 tax lists, resident's lists, etc.) and censuses from 1790 to 1870. Some census indexes for later years exist for some states (e.g. Hawaii 1910, Colorado 1880, etc.).

Census offerings from Ancestry.com also include the 1890 Census Substitute. When a basement fire in the Commerce Building in Washington, D.C. destroyed most of the 1890 federal census, much needed information for researchers using records in this time period was lost. Ancestry.com has taken great lengths to gather information to help researchers in this time period. The 1890 Census Substitute includes fragments of the original 1890 census that survived the fire (images to be posted), special veterans schedules, several Native American tribe censuses for years surrounding 1890, state censuses (1885 or 1895), city and county directories, alumni directories, and voter registration documents. When completed, this collection will be an unparalleled tool for researchers of American ancestors.

BLUE ROSES PUBLISHING COMPANY

OVERVIEW OF COMPANY/ORGANIZATION

Blue Roses Publishing Company opened for business on 1 January 1995. After transcribing U.S. Census Records for ten years, the company's founder Mary Brooks began publishing her work in books under the name of "1850 CENSUS RECORDS." The books are still being published, along with images of the U.S. Census Records on CD-ROMs. In 1998 the Web site 1850 CENSUS RECORDS was launched with God's Mountain Top Vision, CD-ROM Census Records, World Genealogy Records, World Wedding Bells, World Birth & Death Records and Family Tree Datadex Web sites following.

Blue Roses Publishing Company is continuing the goal of publishing quality material for the public, for researching family histories, and for other purposes.

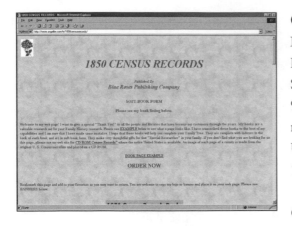

CONTACT INFORMATION

Blue Roses Publishing Company

P.O. Box 60934

San Angelo, TX 76906

915-944-0909

roses.blue@verizon.net

URLs:

1850 CENSUS RECORDS

  http://www.angelfire.com/tx/1850censusrecords/

CD ROM Census Records

  http://members.tripod.com/~sweetblueroses/index.html

CD ROM Census Records (Mirror Site)

  http://www.angelfire.com/tx/1850censusrecords/ cdrom/index.html

OVERVIEW OF CENSUS PRODUCTS/SERVICES

Blue Roses Publishing Company offers over seventy soft-bound books of 1850 Federal Census Records transcribed for various counties. The company also sells U.S. Federal Census Records on CD-ROM for other years and has a large in-stock supply of county CD-ROMs available.

CENSUS VIEW

OVERVIEW OF COMPANY/ORGANIZATION

Gary and Nancy Schlegel of Ripley, OK founded Census View in 1991. The company was bought by Kathy Stokes Hudson in February 2001

Census View will continue to produce the high quality, high-resolution images for family historians and other researchers.

CONTACT INFORMATION

Census View

Rt 3 Box 252-S

Seminole, OK 74868

Phone: 1-800-959-9968

Fax: 1-405-944-5861

E-mail: CensusView@CensusView.org

URL: www.CensusView.org

Contact name: Kathy Hudson

OVERVIEW OF CENSUS PRODUCTS/SERVICES

Census View has census records beginning with 1790 thru 1920 for various states and counties. It also has the 1840 Census of Pensioners for the Revolutionary or Military Census. The company is constantly expanding into new areas.

Census View was the first company to produce high-resolution digital images of census microfilm on CD-ROM. Census View CDs are not installable; they are read directly from the CD so there is no computer memory used to read the census information. With Census View you can lighten, darken, invert colors, and zoom in and out. The CD has its own printing program. You can print a portrait, landscape top and landscape bottom. (Where the printing ends on the landscape top and bottom on the first page, it picks right back up where it left off on the second.)

CENSUS4ALL

OVERVIEW OF COMPANY/ORGANIZATION

Census4all was founded in Arlington, Virginia in 2000 by a group of genealogists, investors, business managers, and marketing specialists. Census4all's mission is to develop an index for those states from the 1910 Federal Census that have never before been indexed, and make them available over the Internet to genealogy researchers around the world.

CONTACT INFORMATION

CENSUS4ALL.COM

PO Box 12015, Arlington, VA 22219

Phone: 703-243-2755

Fax: 703-783-0350

URL: http://www.census4all.com

E-MAIL: census4all@census4all.com

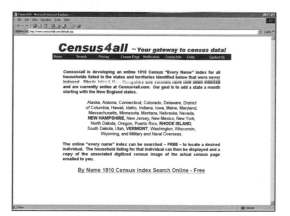

OVERVIEW OF CENSUS PRODUCTS/SERVICES

As of Aug 2001, Census4all had completed three of the twenty-nine states in 1910 that were never indexed by the WPA back in the 1930s: Rhode Island, New Hampshire, and Vermont. The company has also digitized each census page from these three censuses and have the pages and the index available online at its Web site: www.census4all.com. Census4all's indexes are "all-name" indexes. Using all-name indexes, researchers can search for children, spouses, boarders, in-laws, etc. not just the head of the household. It is a much more significant undertaking to complete an all-name index than to just index each head of household. At Census4all.com's Web site, researchers can do individual searches as many times as they need to find their ancestor's census entry free of charge. Once a specific individual of interest has been found in the index, Census4all offers the researcher the opportunity to obtain a listing of all members in that individual's household for a nominal fee. For this fee, the researcher is provided the full name, age, county, and state of residence for all household members. If a researcher is interested in getting a copy of the original census page(s) for this household, Census4all will immediately e-mail a file containing the page(s) for a small fee. The company expects to bring a new 1910 state census online every month or so. If you wish to be notified when certain states become available, sign up at its Web site to receive an e-mail notification.

GENEALOGY.COM

OVERVIEW OF COMPANY/ORGANIZATION

Genealogy.com is a division of A&E Television Networks. The company enriches the lives of its customers by providing the tools, resources, and community that empower them to uncover and share their unique family stories. Headquartered in Fremont, CA, it designs, develops, and markets genealogy software applications and online resources that enable family history enthusiasts to research, organize, and document their heritage at home or away. Developing software since 1984, Genealogy.com continues to be the leader in the genealogy technology space, producing the No. 1 selling family tree software—*Family Tree Maker®*—for more than a decade. The company also provides extensive online genealogy resources, including subscriptions that give researchers continuous, easy access to valuable family history information.

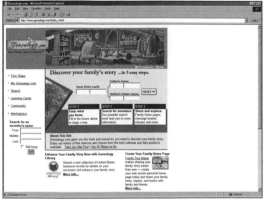

CONTACT INFORMATION

Genealogy.com

P.O. Box 22295

Denver CO 80222

Phone: 1-800-548-1806

Fax: 510-794-9152

URL: http://familytreemaker.genealogy.com/ 1900census.html

E-mail: NA

OVERVIEW OF CENSUS PRODUCTS/SERVICES

The 1900 Census provides family history researchers with access to the entire collection of microfilm images and indexes from the 1900 Census, and is the only database to list every U.S. resident from 1900. Available via monthly or yearly subscriptions, the 1900 Census Collection can be accessed at <http://familytreemaker.genealogy.com/1900census.html>.

Offering quick, easy, and continuous access to 75 million names from across the United States, including the District of Columbia, the Indian territories and the military, the 1900 Census Collection allows new and experienced genealogists alike to discover a wide variety of details from their family's story from a single research destination.

In addition to the 1900 Census, Genealogy.com also offers indexed 1850 census microfilm images for select states as well as Census Indexes for a number of states ranging from 1789–1910 on CD-ROM or through a subscription to Genealogy Library. For more information, visit www.Genealogy.com.

HERITAGE QUEST

OVERVIEW OF COMPANY/ORGANIZATION

Founded in 1983 by Brad and Raeone Steuart, HeritageQuest is the leading source of genealogical data, products, supplies, and equipment for consumers and institutions. In August 2001 Heritage Quest was purchased by ProQuest Information & Learning and became an imprint of that company. HeritageQuest's Source Document holdings have soared to 250,000 titles, ranking it among America's largest genealogical information providers. It is dedicated to producing high-use data, landmark publications, general reference books, and timely, informative periodicals for genealogy enthusiasts at every level. HeritageQuest's team of professional genealogists has designed, implemented, and continue to manage the creation of even more tools and indexes.

With over 400 years of combined experience, the HeritageQuest team is dedicated to its mission: To provide the highest quality data, products, and services fundamental to assisting everyone in the quest for their heritage.

CONTACT INFORMATION

HeritageQuest, ProQuest Information & Learning
669 West 900 North, North Salt Lake, UT 84054
Phone: 1-800-760-2455

Fax: 801-298-5468

URL: http://www.HeritageQuest.com

E-MAIL: Sales@HeritageQuest.com

Contact name: Brad Steuart

OVERVIEW OF CENSUS PRODUCTS/SERVICES

Heritage Quest is the first company to complete the digitization of all 12,555 rolls of microfilm of the U.S. Federal census schedules from 1790 to 1920. These 10+ million images of every page of the census, three terabytes of information, are available to researchers online and on CD-ROM. Researchers can view any roll of census microfilm. The most powerful difference between HeritageQuest Online ™ and other online services is that HeritageQuest provides the actual image of the original document or page where the information came from. Researchers can instantly see and verify the original material. While most researchers do not have a microfilm reader at home, they do have a personal computer. With this new technology HeritageQuest has allowed researchers to quickly view, copy and paste images of the original pages of the census into their genealogical files.

HeritageQuest has not only digitized each page of the census, but it has also enhanced those image frames that were difficult, if not impossible, to read. Images that had become bleached or darkened have been restored using the latest computer techniques. The entire census has been remastered. Frames that could not be read now can be. HeritageQuest is also completely re-indexing every census from 1790 to 1920. The complete indexes and the enhanced image of each page have been mounted on its Web site. HeritageQuest provides these indexes in several formats, in print and electronic formats. The CD-ROM formats are available as indexes only, or indexes linked to the original census page images. Researchers can request the print and CD-ROM editions of the census indexes for an entire state, by surname for the entire country or by a particular group. For example it has produced separate indexes to every Irish, German, English, Scottish, Welsh, and African American household in the United States in 1870. Accurate indexes, linked to original enhanced images are what HeritageQuest is known for.

LDS CHURCH

OVERVIEW OF COMPANY/ORGANIZATION

The Family History Library is operated by The Church of Jesus Christ of Latter-day Saints but is open to the general public. Admission is free but there are nominal charges for book and microfilm copies. The collection includes over 2.2 million rolls of microfilm; 742,000 microfiche; 300,000 books, serials and other formats; and 4,500 periodicals.

CONTACT INFORMATION

Family History Library
35 North West Temple Street
Salt Lake City, Utah 84150-3400
Phone: (801) 240-2331
Fax: 801-240-1584
URL: www.familysearch.org
E-MAIL: fhl@ldschurch.org

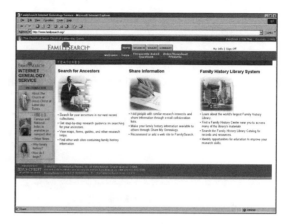

OVERVIEW OF CENSUS PRODUCTS/SERVICES

The Family History Library has all extant United States census records available on microfilm for 1790 through 1920. Book, CD, and microfiche indexes are available for 1790 through 1870 for each state. The 1880, 1900, 1910, and 1920 United States census records were indexed using the Soundex method which takes into account the spelling variations of surnames. The Soundex system is limited in that it is generally a "head of household" index. The 1880 Soundex is also limited in that households are only listed if they have children age ten and under. As of 2001, there is a new compact disc version of the 1880 census which includes an "every name" index. Searches on this new index can be made for individuals on a national or regional basis. Once the individual is identified on the index, his or her family unit can then be displayed. It is also possible to view neighboring families. The 1910 federal census indexed only 22 states, while the 1900 and 1920 censuses are complete.

ROOTSWEB.COM

OVERVIEW OF COMPANY/ORGANIZATION

RootsWeb.com is the Internet's oldest and largest free family research community, sponsoring one of the largest volunteer genealogy projects on the Web. RootsWeb was founded in 1986. The ROOTS-L mailing list was created in 1987, and the RootsWeb Surname List in 1988. Today, hundreds of millions of names can be found in RootsWeb databases, millions of posts have been made on the RootsWeb Message Boards, hundreds of thousands of pedigree files have been uploaded to WordConnect, and thousands of independently authored Web sites are hosted for free on its servers. Among its major hosted sites are USGenWeb, WorldGenWeb, Cyndi's List, Immigrant Ship Transcribers Guild, Obituary Daily Times, and Free Birth Marriage & Death Index (United Kingdom).

The three-part mission of RootsWeb is to educate those that are new to family history, to connect family historians to each other with powerful collaboration tools, and to sponsor other organizations with similar goals.

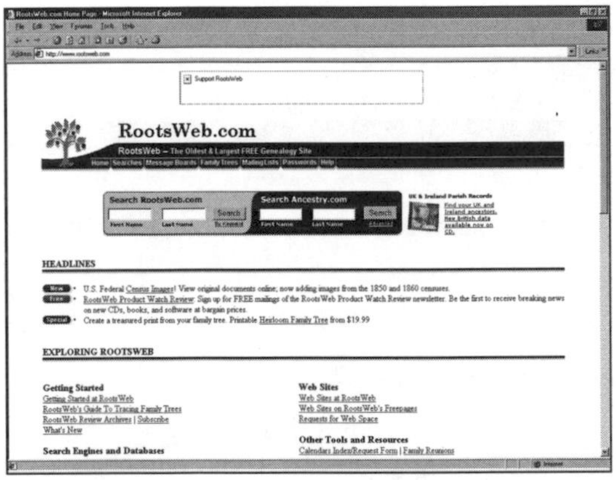

CONTACT INFORMATION

RootsWeb, part of MyFamily.com, Inc.

360 W. 4800 North

Provo, UT 84064

Phone: (801) 705-7000

Fax: 801-705-7001

URL: http://www.rootsweb.com

E-mail: laryn@rootsweb.com

Contact name: Laryn Brown

OVERVIEW OF CENSUS PRODUCTS/SERVICES

RootsWeb is the host server for thousands of privately authored Web pages, archives, and mailing lists, many of which contain census information. Many of the volunteers of the USGenWeb project and the WorldGenWeb project use RootsWeb as host to their pages.

S-K PUBLICATIONS

OVERVIEW OF COMPANY/ORGANIZATION

S-K Publications was founded in 1986 by John Schunk. Its mission is to produce top-quality census images (in books and on CDs) for genealogy researchers.

CONTACT INFORMATION

S-K Publications

PO Box 8173

Wichita, KS 67208-0173

PH 316-685-3201

FAX 316-685-6650

census@SKcensus.com

http://www.SKcensus.com
Contact: John Schunk

OVERVIEW OF CENSUS PRODUCTS/SERVICES

S-K Publications is currently scanning census digital images onto CD-ROMs in high-quality, user-friendly format. Counties being selected for scanning come from all states and all census years for 1790 through 1920. The number of different county/census years currently available in each state are as follows: Alabama (14), Arkansas (9), California (6), Colorado (22), Florida (8), Georgia (28), Illinois (18), Indiana (18), Iowa (9), Kansas (11), Kentucky (28), Louisiana (48), Maine (1), Maryland (18), Massachusetts (1), Michigan (9), Minnesota (10), Mississippi (7), Missouri (38), Nebraska (9), New Jersey (1), New Mexico (4), North Carolina (36), North Dakota (49), Ohio (13), Oklahoma (3), Pennsylvania (9), Rhode Island (4), South Carolina (22), South Dakota (1), Tennessee (31), Texas (100), Virginia (28), Washington (3), West Virginia (25), and Wisconsin (7).

S-K Publications also has census reproductions available in book form for many counties for the years 1800 through 1850. All counties in Arkansas and Mississippi are available in book form for these years, and many counties are available in the following states: Alabama, Georgia, Illinois, Indiana, Iowa, Kentucky, Maryland, Michigan, Missouri, New York, North Carolina, Ohio, Pennsylvania, South Carolina, Tennessee, Texas, Virginia, West Virginia, and Wisconsin.

USGENWEB

OVERVIEW OF COMPANY/ORGANIZATION

In the spring of 1996, a group of genealogists led by Jeff Murphy organized the Kentucky Comprehensive Genealogy Database Project, which evolved into the KyGenWeb Project. The idea was to provide a single entry point for genealogy data and research for all counties in Kentucky. In addition, the information for each county would be indexed and cross-linked to make it easier for researchers to find a name or other data that they sought.

In June 1996, as the KyGenWeb Project was nearing 100 percent county coverage, interested volunteers decided to create a similar set of pages for all states, establishing The USGenWeb Project. Bill Couch wanted to follow in the footsteps of the KY Project with a similar site for Arkansas. Jeff Murphy set up a main page for the states that included a template for volunteers to use. Announcements were made to genealogy mailing lists and newsgroups, and news of this project was spread by e-mail and word of mouth. Volunteers were found who were willing to coordinate the efforts for each state, and additional volunteers were sought to create and maintain Web sites for every county in the United States. By July of 1996, most states were online with state homepages and most had several volunteers.

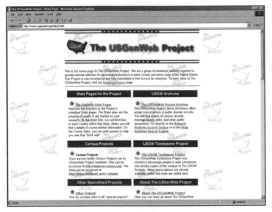

Contact Information

USGenWeb

Address: NA

Phone: NA

Fax: NA

URL: www.usgenweb.org, www.usgenweb.net, and www.usgenweb.com

E-mail: admin@usgenweb.org

Overview of Census Products/Services

There are two valuable census projects run by USGenWeb Project members. One can be accessed at <http://www.rootsweb.com/~census/>. The other can be accessed at <http://www.us-census.org/>. In addition, census transcriptions and indexes can be found in the USGenWeb Archives <http://www.rootsweb.com/~usgenweb/> and on the different county sites.

APPENDIX II

Following is a directory of state and national archives with U.S. census holdings.

ALABAMA
ARCHIVES, STATE & NATIONAL

Alabama Department of Archives & History
624 Washington Avenue
Montgomery, AL
Mail to:
P.O. Box 300100
Montgomery AL 36130-0100
Tel: 334-242-4435
Fax: 334-240-3433
URL: http://www.archives.state.al.us/
index.html

National Archives–Southeast Region
1557 St. Joseph Ave.
East Point, GA 30344-2593
Tel: 404-763-7474
Fax: 404-763-7059
E-mail: center@atlanta.nara.gov
URL: http://www.nara.gov/regional/
atlanta.html

ALASKA
ARCHIVES, STATE & NATIONAL

Alaska State Archives & Records Management Services
141 Willoughby Ave.
Juneau, AK 99801-1720
Tel: 907-465-2270
907-465-2317
Fax: 907-465-2465
E-mail:archives@eed.state.ak.us
URL: http://www.archives.state.ak.us/

National Archives–Pacific Alaska Region
654 W. Third Avenue
Anchorage, AK 99501-2145
Tel: 907-271-2441
Fax: 907-271-2442
Email: archives@alaska.nara.gov
URL: http://www.nara.gov/regional/
anchorag.html

ARIZONA
ARCHIVES, STATE & NATIONAL

Arizona Department of Library, Archives and Public Records Archives Division
State Capitol, Suite 342
1700 W. Washington St.
Phoenix, AZ 85007
Tel: 602-542-4159
Fax: 602-542-4402
Email: archive@lib.az.us
URL: http://www.lib.az.us/archives/index.html

National Archives–Pacific Region (Laguna Niguel)
24000 Avila Rd., First Floor-East Entrance
P.O. Box 6719
Laguna Niguel, CA 92607-6719
Tel: 949-360-2641
Fax: 949-360-2624
E-mail: laguna.archives@nara.gov
URL: http://www.nara.gov/regional/laguna.html

ARKANSAS
ARCHIVES, STATE & NATIONAL

Arkansas History Commission & State Archives
One Capitol Mall
Little Rock, AR 72201
Tel: 501-682-6900
URL: http://www.ark-ives.com/ahc.html

National Archives–Southwest Region
501 W. Felix Street, Building 1
P.O. Box 6216
Fort Worth, TX 76115-0216

Tel: 817-334-5515
Fax: 817-334-5511
E-mail: ftworth.archives@nara.gov
URL: http://www.nara.gov/regional/ftworth.html

Southwest Arkansas Regional Archives
Old Washington Historic State Park
Hempstead County Courthouse
P.O. Box 98
Washington, AR 71862
Tel: 870-983-2684 (Mon-Fri)
870-983-2733 (Sat-Sun)
URL: http://peace.saumag.edu/swark/sara/sara.html

CALIFORNIA
ARCHIVES, STATE & NATIONAL

California State Archives
1020 O Street
Sacramento, CA 95814
Tel: 916-653-2246
Fax: 916-653-7363
Email: ArchivesWeb@ss.ca.gov
URL: http://www.ss.ca.gov/archives/archives_b.htm

National Archives–Pacific Region (Laguna Niguel)
24000 Avila Rd., First Floor-East Entrance
P.O. Box 6719
Laguna Niguel, CA 92607-6719
Tel: 949-360-2626
Fax: 949-360-2624
Email: laguna.archives@nara.gov
URL: http://www.nara.gov/regional/laguna.html

National Archives–Pacific Region (San Francisco)
1000 Commodore Drive

San Bruno, CA 94066
Tel: 650-876-9001
Fax: 650-876-9233
Email: sanbruno.archives@nara.gov
URL: http://www.nara.gov/regional/
sanfranc.html

COLORADO
ARCHIVES, STATE & NATIONAL

Colorado State Archives
1313 Sherman Street - Room 1B-20
Denver, CO 80203
Tel: (303)866-2358
Fax: (303)866-2257
archives@state.co.us
http://www.archives.state.co.us/
index.html

**National Archives—Rocky
Mountain Region (Denver)**
Bldg. 48, Denver Federal Center
West 6th Avenue and Kipling Street
Denver, Colorado 80225-0307
Mailing Address:
P.O. Box 25307
Denver, Colorado 80225-0307
Phone: 303-236-0817
Fax: 303-236-9297
E-mail: denver.archives@nara.gov
http://www.nara.gov/regional/
denver.html

CONNECTICUT
ARCHIVES, STATE & NATIONAL

Connecticut State Archives
Connecticut State Library
231 Capitol Avenue
Hartford, CT 06106
Tel: 860-757-6595
Fax: 860-757-6542
E-mail: MJones@cslib.org

URL: http://www.cslib.org/
archives.htm

**National Archives-Northeast
Region (Boston)**
Frederick C. Murphy Federal Center
380 Trapelo Road
Waltham, MA 02154-8104
Tel: 781-647-8104
Fax: 781-647-8088
Email: waltham.center@nara.gov
URL: http://www.nara.gov/regional/
boston.html

DELAWARE
ARCHIVES, STATE & NATIONAL

Delaware Public Archives
121 Duke of York Street
Dover, DE 19901
(302) 739-5318
Email: archives@state.de.us
URL: http://www.state.de.us/sos/dpa/

**National Archives-Mid Atlantic
Region**
900 Market Street
Philadelphia, Pennsylvania 19107-4292
Tel: 215-597-3000
Fax: 215-597-2303
E-mail: philadelphia.archives@nara.gov
URL: http://www.nara.gov/regional/
philacc.html

DISTRICT OF COLUMBIA
ARCHIVES, STATE & NATIONAL

District of Columbia Archives
1300 Naylor Court, NW
Washington, DC 20001-4225
Tel: 202-727-2054

Maryland State Archives
Hall of Records Building
350 Rowe Blvd.
Annapolis, MD 21401
Tel: (410) 260-6400; (800) 235-4045
Fax: (410) 974-3895
E-mail: archives@mdarchives.state.md.us
URL: www.mdarchives.state.md.us

National Archives and Records
Administration (NARA)
Archives I
700 Pennsylvania Avenue, NW
Washington, DC 20408
Tel: 202-501-5410 (Genealogical Staff)
202-501-5400 (Record Availability)
Fax: 301-713-6905 (Fax-on-Demand
Information)
Email: inquire@arch1.nara.gov
URL: http://www.nara.gov/nara/dc/
Archives1_directions.html

National Archives and Records
Administration (NARA)
Archives II
8601 Adelphi Road
College Park, MD 20740
Tel: 202-501-5400 (Record Availability)
301-713-6800 (General Reference)
301-713-7040 (Cartographic Reference)
Fax: 301-713-6905 (Fax-on-Demand
Information)
E-mail: inquire@arch2.nara.gov
URL: http://www.nara.gov/nara/dc/
Archives2_directions.html

National Archives and Records
Administration (NARA)
Washington National Records
Center
Shipping Address:
4205 Suitland Road
Suitland, MD 20746-8001
Mail:
4205 Suitland Road

Washington, DC 20409-0002
Tel: 301-457-7000
Fax: 301-457-7117
Email: center@suitland.nara.gov
URL: http://www.nara.gov/nara/dc/
wnrc.html

FLORIDA
ARCHIVES, STATE & NATIONAL

Florida State Archives
Bureau of Archives Management
Division of Library & Information
Services
Public Services Section
R.A. Gray Building
500 South Bronough Street
Tallahassee, FL 32399-0250
Tel: (850) 245-6700
URL: http://dlis.dos.state.fl.us/barm/
fsa.html

National Archives-Southeast Region
1557 St. Joseph Avenue
East Point, GA 30344
Tel: 404-763-7474
Fax: 404-763-7059
Email: atlanta.center@nara.gov
URL: http://www.nara.gov/regional/
atlanta.html

GEORGIA
ARCHIVES, STATE & NATIONAL

Georgia Department of Archives
and History
Office of Secretary of State
330 Capitol Avenue, SE
Atlanta, GA 30334
Tel: (404) 656-2350
E-mail: reference@sos.state.ga.us
URL: http://www.sos.state.ga.us/
archives

National Archives-Southeast Region
1557 St. Joseph Avenue
East Point, GA 30344
Tel: 404-763-7474
Fax: 404-763-7059
Email: atlanta.center@nara.gov
URL: http://www.nara.gov/regional/
atlanta.html

HAWAII
ARCHIVES, STATE & NATIONAL

Hawaii State Archives
Iolani Palace Grounds
Kekauluohi Building
King & Richards Streets
Honolulu, HI 96813
Tel: 808-586-0313
808-586-0329
Fax: 808-586-0330
URL: http://www.hawaii.gov/dags/
archives/welcome.html

National Archives-Pacific Region
(San Francisco)
1000 Commodore Drive
San Bruno, CA 94066
Tel: 650-876-9001
Fax: 650-876-0920
Email: sanbruno.archives@nara.gov
URL: http://www.nara.gov/regional/
sanfranc.html

IDAHO
ARCHIVES, STATE & NATIONAL

Idaho State Historical Library &
Archives
325 W. State Street
Boise, ID 83702
Tel: 208-334-2150
Fax: 208-334-4016
URL: http://www.lili.org/isl/

National Archives-Pacific Alaska
Region (Seattle)
6125 Sand Point Way, NE
Seattle, WA 98115-7999
Tel: 206-526-6501
Fax: 206-526-6575
Email: seattle.archives@nara.gov
URL: http://www.nara.gov/regional/
seattle.html

ILLINOIS
ARCHIVES, STATE & NATIONAL

Illinois State Archives
Reference Unit
Margaret Cross Norton Building
Capitol Complex
Springfield, IL 62756
Tel: 217-782-3556
Fax: 217-524-3930
URL:http://www.cyberdriveillinois.com
/departments/archives/serv_sta.html

National Archives-Great Lakes
Region
7358 Pulaski Road
Chicago, IL 60629
Tel: 773-581-7816
Fax: 312-886-7883
E-mail: chicago.archives@nara.gov
URL: http://www.nara.gov/regional/
chicago.html

Illinois Regional Archives Depository
(IRAD)
Illinois State Archives Reference Unit
Margaret Cross Norton Building
Capitol Complex
Springfield, IL 62756
Tel: 217-785-1266
Fax: 217-524-3930
URL: http://www.cyberdriveillinois.
com/departments/archives/irad/irad-
home.html

Eastern Illinois University
Booth Library

600 Lincoln Avenue

Charleston, IL 61920

Telephone: (217) 581-6093

URL: http://www.eiu.edu/~booth/

This library serves the following counties: Clark, Clay, Coles, Crawford, Cumberland, Douglas, Edgar, Edwards, Effingham, Jasper, Lawrence, Moultrie, Richland, Shelby, Wabash, Wayne.

Illinois State University

Williams Hall

Campus Box 5500

Normal, IL 61790-5500

Telephone: (309) 452-6027

This library serves the following counties: Champaign, DeWitt, Ford, Grundy, Iroquois, Kankakee, Livingston, Logan, Marshall, McLean, Piatt, Tazewell, Vermilion, Woodford.

Northeastern Illinois University
Ronald Williams Library

5500 N. St. Louis Avenue

Chicago, IL 60625-4699

Tel: (773) 442-4506

http://www.neiu.edu/~neiulib/

This library serves Cook County.

Northern Illinois University

Swen Parson Hall, Room 155

DeKalb, IL 60115

Tel: 815-753-1807

This library serves the following counties: Boone, Bureau, Carroll, DeKalb, DuPage, Jo Daviess, Kane, Kendall, Lake, LaSalle, Lee, McHenry, Ogle, Putnam, Stephenson, Whiteside, Will, Winnebago.

Southern Illinois University
Morris Library
Special Collections

Carbondale, IL 62901-6632

Tel: 618-453-3040

URL: http://www.lib.siu.edu/

This library serves the following counties: Alexander, Clinton, Franklin, Gallatin, Hamilton, Hardin, Jackson, Jefferson, Johnson, Madison, Marion, Massac, Monroe, Perry, Pope, Pulaski, Randolph, St. Clair, Saline, Union, Washington, White, Williamson.

University of Illinois at Springfield
Brookens Library

P.O. Box 19243

Springfield, IL 62794

Tel: 217- 206-6520

Fax: 217-786-6633

URL: http://www.uis.edu/library/ lib-arch

This library serves the following counties: Bond, Cass, Christian, Fayette, Greene, Jersey, Macon, Macoupin, Mason, Menard, Montgomery, Morgan, Sangamon, Scott.

Western Illinois University
University Library
Archives & Special Collections

1 University Circle

Macomb, IL 61455

Tel: 309-298-2717/8

Email: mfgrl@WIU.edu

URL: http://www.wiu.edu/library/

This library serves the following counties: Adams, Brown, Calhoun, Fulton, Hancock, Henderson, Henry, Knox, McDonough, Mercer, Peoria, Pike, Rock Island, Schuyler, Stark, Warren.

INDIANA
ARCHIVES, STATE & NATIONAL

Indiana State Archives
6440 E. 30th St.
Indianapolis, IN 46219
Telephone: (317) 591-5222
E-mail: arc@icpr.state.in.us
URL: http://www.ai.org/icpr/webfile/
archives/homepage.html

**National Archives-Great Lakes
Region**
7358 Pulaski Road
Chicago, IL 60629-5898
Tel: 773-581-7816
Fax: 312-886-7883
Email: chicago.archives@nara.gov
URL: http://www.nara.gov/regional/
chicago.html

IOWA
ARCHIVES, STATE & NATIONAL

**Iowa State Archives
State Historical Society of Iowa**
Capitol Complex
State of Iowa Historical Building
600 East Locust
Des Moines, IA 50319
Tel: 515-281-6200
URL: http://www.iowahistory.org/

**National Archives-Central Plains
Region**
2312 East Bannister Road
Kansas City, MO 64131
Tel: 816-926-6920
Fax: 816-926-6982
E-mail: kansascity.archives@nara.gov
URL: http://www.nara.gov/regional/
kansas.html

KANSAS
ARCHIVES, STATE & NATIONAL

**Kansas State Archives
Kansas State Historical
Society/Library & Archives
The Kansas History Center**
6425 SW Sixth Street
Topeka, KS 66615-1099
Tel:(785) 272-8681
TTY: (785) 272-8683
FAX: (785) 272-8682
Email: Webmaster@kshs.org
URL: http://www.kshs.org/archives/
index.htm

**National Archives-Central Plains
Region**
2312 East Bannister Road
Kansas City, MO 64131
Tel: 816-926-6920
Fax: 816-926-6982
E-mail: kansascity.archives@nara.gov
URL: http://www.nara.gov/regional/
kansas.html

KENTUCKY
ARCHIVES, STATE & NATIONAL

**Kentucky Department for Libraries
and Archives**
Public Records Division
Archives Research Room
300 Coffee Tree Road
P.O. Box 537
Frankfort, KY 40602-0537
Tel: 502-564-8300
Fax: 502-564-5773
URL: http://www.kdla.state.ky.us/

National Archives-Southeast Region
1557 St. Joseph Avenue
East Point, GA 30344
Tel: 404-763-7474

Fax: 404-763-7059
Email: atlanta.center@nara.gov
URL: http://www.nara.gov/regional/
atlanta.html

LOUISIANA
ARCHIVES, STATE & NATIONAL

Louisiana State Archives
3851 Essen Lane
Baton Rouge, LA 70809-2137
Tel: (225) 922-1000
E-mail: archives@sec.state.la.us
URL: http://www.sec.state.la.us/
archives/archives/archives-index.htm

National Archives-Southwest Region
501 West Felix Street
Building 1, Dock 1
P.O. Box 6216
Fort Worth, TX 76115-0216
Tel: 817-334-5515
Fax: 817-334-5511
E-mail: ftworth.archives@nara.gov
URL: http://www.nara.gov/regional/
ftworth.html

MAINE
ARCHIVES, STATE & NATIONAL

Maine State Archives
84 State House Station
Augusta, ME 04333-0084
Phone: 207-287-5795
FAX: 207-287-5739
URL: http://www.state.me.us/sos/arc/

National Archives-Northeast Region (Boston)
Frederick C. Murphy Federal Center
380 Trapelo Road
Waltham, MA 02154-8104
Tel: 781-647-8104

Fax: 781-647-8088
E-mail: waltham.center@nara.gov
URL: http://www.nara.gov/regional/
boston.html

MARYLAND
ARCHIVES, STATE & NATIONAL

Maryland State Archives
Hall of Records Building
350 Rowe Blvd.
Annapolis, MD 21401
Tel: (410) 260-6400
(800) 235-4045 MD toll free
fax: (410) 974-3895
Email: archives@mdarchives.state.md.us
URL: www.mdarchives.state.md.us

National Archives-Mid Atlantic Region
900 Market Street
Philadelphia, Pennsylvania 19107-4292
Tel: 215-597-3000
Fax: 215-597-2303
Email: philadelphia.archives@nara.gov
URL: http://www.nara.gov/regional/
philacc.html

MASSACHUSETTS
ARCHIVES, STATE & NATIONAL

Massachusetts Archives
Reference Supervisor
220 Morrissey Blvd.
Boston, MA 02125
Tel: 617-727-2816
Fax: (617) 288-8429
Email: archives@sec.state.ma.us
URL: http://www.state.ma.us/sec/arc/
arcidx.htm

National Archives-Northeast Region (Boston)
Frederick C. Murphy Federal Center
380 Trapelo Road
Waltham, MA 02154-8104
Tel: 781-647-8104
Fax: 781-647-8088
Email: waltham.center@nara.gov
URL: http://www.nara.gov/regional/boston.html

MICHIGAN
ARCHIVES, STATE & NATIONAL

Michigan State Archives
Michigan Library and Historical Center
717 West Allegan Street
Lansing MI 48918-1800
(517) 373-3559
TDD 1-800-827-7007
URL: http://www.sos.state.mi.us/history/archive/archive.html

National Archives-Great Lakes Region
7358 Pulaski Road
Chicago, IL 60629
Tel: 773-581-7816
Fax: 312 886 7883
E-mail: chicago.archives@nara.gov
URL: http://www.nara.gov/regional/chicago.html

MINNESOTA
ARCHIVES, STATE & NATIONAL

Minnesota State Archives
Minnesota Historical Society Research Center
345 Kellogg Boulevard
St. Paul, MN 55102
Tel: 651-296-6126
URL: http://www.mnhs.org/index.html

National Archives-Central Plains Region
2312 East Bannister Road
Kansas City, MO 64131
Tel: 816-926-6920
Fax: 816-926-6982
E-mail: kansascity.archives@nara.gov
URL: http://www.nara.gov/regional/kansas.html

National Archives-Great Lakes Region
7358 Pulaski Road
Chicago, IL 60629
Tel: 773-581-7816
Fax: 312-886-7883
Email: chicago.archives@nara.gov
URL: http://www.nara.gov/regional/chicago.html

MISSISSIPPI
ARCHIVES, STATE & NATIONAL

Mississippi Department of Archives and History
War Memorial Building
100 South State Street
Jackson, MS 39201
P.O. Box 571
Jackson, MS 39205-0571
Tel: 601-359-6850
Administration Fax: (601) 359-6975
Archives and Library Division Fax: (601) 359-6964
Historic Preservation Division Fax: (601) 359-6955
E-mail: webmaster@mdah.state.ms.us
URL: http://www.mdah.state.ms.us/

National Archives-Southeast Region
1557 St. Joseph Avenue
East Point, GA 30344
Tel: 404-763-7474
Fax: 404-763-7059

Email: atlanta.center@nara.gov
URL: http://www.nara.gov/regional/
atlanta.html

MISSOURI
ARCHIVES, STATE & NATIONAL

Missouri State Archives
600 W. Main
P.O. Box 1747
Jefferson City, Missouri 65102
Telephone: (573) 751-3280
E-mail:archref@sosmail.state.mo.us
URL: http://mosl.sos.state.mo.us/rec-
man/arch.html

**National Archives-Central Plains
Region**
2312 East Bannister Road
Kansas City, MO 64131
Tel: 816-926-6920
Fax: 816-926-6982
E-mail: kansascity.archives@nara.gov
URL: http://www.nara.gov/regional/
kansas.html

MONTANA
ARCHIVES, STATE & NATIONAL

**Montana State Archives
Montana Historical Society**
Memorial Building
225 N. Roberts St.
PO Box 201201
Helena, MT 59620-1201
Tel: 800-243-9900
406-444-4774/5
Fax: 406-444-5297
Email: archives@state.mt.us
URL: http://www.montanahistorical
society.org/departments/archives/index.
html

**National Archives—Rocky
Mountain Region (Denver)**
Bldg. 48, Denver Federal Center
West 6th Avenue and Kipling Street
Denver, Colorado 80225-0307
Mailing Address:
P.O. Box 25307
Denver, Colorado 80225-0307
Phone: 303-236-0817
Fax: 303-236-9297
E-mail: denver.archives@nara.gov
http://www.nara.gov/regional/
denver.html

NEBRASKA
ARCHIVES, STATE & NATIONAL

**Nebraska State Historical
Society/State Archives Division**
1500 R Street
P.O. Box 82554
Lincoln, NE 68501
Tel: 402-471-3270
402-471-4771 (library)
Fax: 402-471-3100
URL: http://www.nebraskahistory.org/

**National Archives-Central Plains
Region**
2312 East Bannister Road
Kansas City, MO 64131
Tel: 816-926-6920
Fax: 816-926-6982
E-mail: kansascity.archives@nara.gov
URL: http://www.nara.gov/regional/
kansas.html

NEVADA
ARCHIVES, STATE & NATIONAL

**National Archives-Pacific Region
(Laguna Niguel)**
24000 Avila Rd., First Floor-East
Entrance

P.O. Box 6719
Laguna Niguel, CA 92607-6719
Tel: 949-360-2626
Fax: 949-360-2624
E-mail: laguna.archives@nara.gov
URL: http://www.nara.gov/regional/
laguna.html
(Serves Clark County)

National Archives-Pacific Region (San Francisco)

1000 Commodore Drive
San Bruno, CA 94066
Tel: 650-876-9001
Fax: 650-876-9233
Email: sanbruno.archives@nara.gov
URL: http://www.nara.gov/regional/
sanfranc.html
(Serves Nevada, except for Clark County)

Nevada State Library and Archives

100 N. Stewart Street
Carson City, NV 89710
Tel: 702-687-5160 (Library)
702-687-5210 (Archives)
URL: http://dmla.clan.lib.nv.us/docs/
nsla/

NEW HAMPSHIRE

ARCHIVES, STATE & NATIONAL

National Archives-Northeast Region (Boston)

Frederick C. Murphy Federal Center
380 Trapelo Road
Waltham, MA 02154-8104
Tel: 781-647-8104
Fax: 781-647-8088
Email: waltham.center@nara.gov
URL: http://www.nara.gov/regional/
boston.html

New Hampshire Division of Records Management and Archives

71 South Fruit Street
Concord, NH 03301
Tel: 603-271-2236
Fax: 603-271-2272
URL: http://www.state.nh.us/state/
index.html

NEW JERSEY

ARCHIVES, STATE & NATIONAL

National Archives-Northeast Region

201 Varick Street
New York, New York 10014-4811
Phone: 212-337-1300
Fax: 212-337-1306
E-mail: newyork.archives@nara.gov
URL: http://www.nara.gov/regional/
newyork.html

New Jersey State Archives

225 West State Street-Level 2
Department of State Building
P.O. Box 307
Trenton, NJ 08625-0307
Tel: (609) 292-6260 (general information)
    (609) 633-8334 (administrative office)
Fax: (609) 396-2454
Email: info@archive.sos.state.nj.us
URL:
http://www.state.nj.us/state/darm/archives.html

NEW MEXICO

ARCHIVES, STATE & NATIONAL

National Archives—Rocky Mountain Region (Denver)

Bldg. 48, Denver Federal Center
West 6th Avenue and Kipling Street

Denver, Colorado 80225-0307
Mailing Address:
P.O. Box 25307
Denver, Colorado 80225-0307
Phone: 303-236-0817
Fax: 303-236-9297
E-mail: denver.archives@nara.gov
http://www.nara.gov/regional/
denver.html

New Mexico State Records Center & Archives
1209 Camino Carlos Rey
Santa Fe, NM 87505
Mailing address:
1205 Camino Carlos Rey
Santa Fe, New Mexico 87505.
Tel: 505-476-7908
Fax: 505-476-7909
E-mail: archives@rain.state.nm.us
URL: http://www.state.nm.us/cpr/

NEW YORK
ARCHIVES, STATE & NATIONAL

National Archives–Northeast Region
201 Varick Street
New York, New York 10014-4811
Phone: 212-337-1300
Fax: 212-337-1306
E-mail: newyork.archives@nara.gov
URL: http://www.nara.gov/regional/
newyork.html

New York State Archives
Cultural Education Center Room 3043
Albany, NY 12230
Phone 518-474-8955
Email: archref@mail.nysed.gov
URL: http://www.sara.nysed.gov/

NORTH CAROLINA
ARCHIVES, STATE & NATIONAL

National Archives–Southeast Region
1557 St. Joseph Avenue
East Point, GA 30344
Tel: 404-763-7474
Fax: 404-763-7059
E-mail: atlanta.center@nara.gov
URL: http://www.nara.gov/regional/
atlanta.html

North Carolina State Archives
Archives and History/State Library Building
109 East Jones Street
Raleigh, NC 27601-2807
Mailing address:
North Carolina State Archives
Public Services Branch
4614 Mail Service Center
Raleigh, N.C. 27699-4614
Tel: 919-733-3952
Fax: 919-733-1354
Email: archives@ncsl.dcr.state.nc.us
URL: http://www.ah.dcr.state.nc.us/
archives/arch/archhp.htm

NORTH DAKOTA
ARCHIVES, STATE & NATIONAL

National Archives–Central Plains Region
2312 East Bannister Road
Kansas City, MO 64131
Tel: 816-926-6920
Fax: 816-926-6982
E-mail: kansascity.archives@nara.gov
URL: http://www.nara.gov/regional/
kansas.html

National Archives—Rocky Mountain Region (Denver)
Bldg. 48, Denver Federal Center
West 6th Avenue and Kipling Street
Denver, Colorado 80225-0307
Mailing Address:
P.O. Box 25307
Denver, Colorado 80225-0307
Phone: 303-236-0817
Fax: 303-236-9297
E-mail: denver.archives@nara.gov
URL: http://www.nara.gov/regional/denver.html

State Archives and Historical Research Library
State Historical Society of North Dakota
North Dakota Heritage Center
612 East Boulevard Avenue
Bismarck, ND 58505-0830
Tel: 701-328-2091
Email: archives@state.nd.us
URL: http://www.state.nd.us/hist/sal.htm

OHIO

ARCHIVES, STATE & NATIONAL

National Archives Great Lakes Region
7358 Pulaski Road
Chicago, IL 60629
Tel: 773-581-7816
Fax: 312-886-7883
Email: chicago.archives@nara.gov
URL: http://www.nara.gov/regional/chicago.html

Ohio State Archives
Ohio State Historical Society
1982 Velma Avenue
Columbus, OH 43211-2497
Tel: 614-297-2510
Fax: 614-297-2411

Email: ohswww@winslo.ohio.gov
URL: http://www.ohiohistory.org/resource/archlib/

OKLAHOMA

ARCHIVES, STATE & NATIONAL

National Archives-Southwest Region
501 West Felix Street
Building 1, Dock 1
P.O. Box 6216
Fort Worth, TX 76115-0216
Tel: 817-334-5515
Fax: 817-334-5511
Email: ftworth.archives@nara.gov
URL: http://www.nara.gov/regional/ftworth.html

Oklahoma State Archives and Records Management
Allen Wright Memorial Library
200 NE 18th Street
Oklahoma City, OK 73105-3298
Tel: (405) 522-3579
Fax: (405) 522-3583
http://www.odl.state.ok.us/oar/index.htm

OREGON

ARCHIVES, STATE & NATIONAL

National Archives-Pacific Alaska Region (Seattle)
6125 Sand Point Way, NE
Seattle, WA 98115-7999
Tel: 206-526-6501
Fax: 206-526-6575
Email: seattle.archives@nara.gov
URL: http://www.nara.gov/regional/seattle.html

Oregon State Archives
800 Summer Street, NE
Salem, OR 97310
Tel: 503-373-0701
Fax: 503-373-0953
Email: reference.archives@state.or.us
  (Reference requests welcome)
URL: http://arcweb.sos.state.or.us/

PENNSYLVANIA
ARCHIVES, STATE & NATIONAL

National Archives-Mid Atlantic Region
900 Market Street
Philadelphia, Pennsylvania 19107-4292
Tel: 215-597-3000
Fax: 215-597-2303
Email: philadelphia.archives@nara.gov
URL: http://www.nara.gov/regional/
philacc.html

Pennsylvania State Archives
350 North Street
Harrisburg, PA 17120-0090
(717) 783-3281
URL: http://www.phmc.state.pa.us/
bah/dam/overview.htm?secid=31

RHODE ISLAND
ARCHIVES, STATE & NATIONAL

National Archives-Northeast Region (Boston)
Frederick C. Murphy Federal Center
380 Trapelo Road
Waltham, MA 02154-8104
Tel: 781-647-8104
Fax: 781-647-8088
E-mail: waltham.center@nara.gov
URL: http://www.nara.gov/regional/
boston.html

Rhode Island State Archives
337 Westminster Street
Providence, RI 02903
Tel: 401-222-2353
Fax: 401-222-3199
Email: reference@archives.state.ri.us
URL: http://www.state.ri.us/archives/

SOUTH CAROLINA
ARCHIVES, STATE & NATIONAL

National Archives-Southeast Region
1557 St. Joseph Avenue
East Point, GA 30344
Tel: 404-763-7474
Fax: 404-763-7059
E-mail: atlanta.center@nara.gov
URL: http://www.nara.gov/regional/
atlanta.html

South Carolina Department of Archives and History
8301 Parklane Road
Columbia, SC 29223
Tele: (803) 896-6100
Fax: (803) 896-6198
URL:

SOUTH DAKOTA
ARCHIVES, STATE & NATIONAL

National Archives-Central Plains Region
2312 East Bannister Road
Kansas City, MO 64131
Tel: 816-926-6920
Fax: 816-926-6982
E-mail: kansascity.archives@nara.gov
URL: http://www.nara.gov/regional/
kansas.html

National Archives—Rocky Mountain Region (Denver)
Bldg. 48, Denver Federal Center

West 6th Avenue and Kipling Street
Denver, Colorado 80225-0307
Mailing Address:
P.O. Box 25307
Denver, Colorado 80225-0307
Phone: 303-236-0817
Fax: 303-236-9297
E-mail: denver.archives@nara.gov
http://www.nara.gov/regional/
denver.html

South Dakota State Archives

Cultural Heritage Center
900 Governors Drive
Pierre, SD   57501-2217
Tel: 605-773-3804
Fax: 605-773-6041
E-mail: Archref@state.sd.us
URL: http://www.sdhistory.org/
archives.htm

TENNESSEE

ARCHIVES, STATE & NATIONAL

National Archives-Southeast Region

1557 St. Joseph Avenue
East Point, GA   30344
Tel: 404-763-7474
Fax: 404-763-7059
E-mail: atlanta.center@nara.gov
URL: http://www.nara.gov/regional/
atlanta.html

Tennessee State Library and Archives

State Library and Archives Building
403 Seventh Avenue, North
Nashville, TN 37243-0312
Tel: 615-741-2764
   615-741-6471
E-mail: reference@mail.state.tn.us
URL: http://www.state.tn.us/
sos/statelib/tslahome.htm

TEXAS

ARCHIVES, STATE & NATIONAL

National Archives-Southwest Region

501 West Felix Street
Building 1, Dock 1
P.O. Box 6216
Fort Worth, TX   76115-0216
Tel: 817-334-5515
Fax: 817-334-5511
Email: ftworth.archives@nara.gov
URL: http://www.nara.gov/regional/
ftworth.html

Texas State Library and Archives Commission

Lorenzo de Zavala State Archives and
Library Building
1201 Brazos Street
P.O. Box 12927
Austin, TX 78711
Tel: 512-463-5455
512-463-5463 (Genealogy Collection,
Room 110)
512-463-5480 (Archives)
Email: archinfo@tsl.state.tx.us
(archives)
    geninfo@tsl.state.tx.us (genealogy
collection)
URL: http://www.tsl.state.tx.us/

UTAH

ARCHIVES, STATE & NATIONAL

National Archives—Rocky Mountain Region (Denver)

Bldg. 48, Denver Federal Center
West 6th Avenue and Kipling Street
Denver, Colorado 80225-0307
Mailing Address:
P.O. Box 25307
Denver, Colorado 80225-0307
Phone: 303-236-0817

Fax: 303-236-9297
E-mail: denver.archives@nara.gov
http://www.nara.gov/regional/
denver.html

Utah State Archives
Archives Building
P.O. Box 141021
Salt Lake City, UT 84114-1021
Tel: 801-538-3013 (Research Center)
Fax: 801-538-3354
E-mail: research@das.state.ut.us
URL: http://www.archives.state.ut.us/

VERMONT
ARCHIVES, STATE & NATIONAL

National Archives-Northeast Region (Boston)
Frederick C. Murphy Federal Center
380 Trapelo Road
Waltham, MA 02154-8104
Tel: 781-647-8104
Fax: 781-647-8088
E-mail: waltham.center@nara.gov
URL: http://www.nara.gov/regional/
boston.html

Vermont State Archives
Redstone Building
26 Terrace Street
Drawer 09
Montpelier, Vermont   05609-1101
Tel: 802-828-2363
Email: gsanford@sec.state.vt.us
URL: http://vermont-archives.org/

VIRGINIA
ARCHIVES, STATE & NATIONAL

National Archives-Mid Atlantic Region
900 Market Street
Philadelphia, Pennsylvania 19107-4292

Tel: 215-597-3000
Fax: 215-597-2303
Email: philadelphia.archives@nara.gov
URL: http://www.nara.gov/regional/
philacc.html

Library of Virginia, Archives Division
800 E. Broad Street
Richmond, VA 23219
Tel: 804-692-3888
Fax: 804-692-3556
URL: http://www.lva.lib.va.us

WASHINGTON
ARCHIVES, STATE & NATIONAL

National Archives-Pacific Alaska Region (Seattle)
6125 Sand Point Way, NE
Seattle, WA 98115-7999
Tel: 206-526-6501
Fax: 206-526-6575
Email: seattle.archives@nara.gov
URL: http://www.nara.gov/regional/
seattle.html

Washington State Archives
1129 Washington Street, SE
P.O. Box 40238
Olympia, WA 98504-0238
Tel: 360-753-5485 (Administration)
   360-586-1492 (Research)
Email: archives@secstate.wa.gov
URL: http://www.secstate.wa.gov/
archives/

Central Regional Branch
Central Washington University
Bledsow-Washington Archives Building
400 E. 8th Ave., MS-7547
Ellensburg, WA 98926-7547
Tel: 509-963-2136
Fax: 509-963-1753

http://www.cwu.edu/~archives/
home.htm
(Benton, Chelan, Douglas, Franklin,
Grant, Kittitas, Klickitat, Okanogan, and
Yakima Counties)

Eastern Regional Branch
Eastern Washington University
211 Tawanka
Cheney, WA 99004
Tel: 509-359-6900
Fax: (509) 359-6286
Email: era@mail.ewu.edu
http://www.ewu.edu/era/
(Adams, Asotin, Columbia, Ferry,
Garfield, Lincoln, Pend Oreille, Spokane,
Stevens, Walla Walla, and Whitman
Counties)

Northwest Regional Branch
Western Washington University
Goltz-Murray Archives Building
Bellingham, WA 98225-9123
Tel: 360-650-3125
Fax: 360-650-3323
email: state.archives@wwu.edu
(Clallam, Island, Jefferson, San Juan,
Skagit, Snohomish, and Whatcom
Counties)

Puget Sount Regional Branch
Pritchard-Fleming Building
3000 Landerholm Circle SE, MS-N100
Bellevue, WA 98007-6484
Tel: (425) 564-3940
Fax: (425) 564-3945
E-mail: Archives@bcc.ctc.edu
(King, Kitsap and Pierce Counties)

Southwest Regional Branch
1129 Washington Street, SE
P.O. Box 40238
Olympia, WA 98504-0238
Tel: 360-753-1684
Fax: 360-664-8814

(Clark, Cowlitz, Grays Harbor, Lewis,
Mason, Pacific, Skamania, Thurston, and
Wahkiakum Counties)

WEST VIRGINIA
ARCHIVES, STATE & NATIONAL

National Archives-Mid Atlantic
Region
900 Market Street
Philadelphia, Pennsylvania 19107-4292
Tel: 215-597-3000
Fax: 215-597-2303
Email: philadelphia.archives@nara.gov
URL: http://www.nara.gov/regional/
philacc.html

West Virginia State Archives and
History Library
West Virginia Division of Culture and
History
Cultural Center, Capitol Complex
1900 Kanawha Boulevard, East
Charleston, WV 25305-0300
Tel: 304-558-0230
Fax: 304-558-2779
URL: http://www.wvculture.org/his-
tory/index.html

WISCONSIN
ARCHIVES, STATE & NATIONAL

National Archives-Great Lakes
Region
7358 Pulaski Road
Chicago, IL 60629
Tel: 773-581-7816
Fax: 312-886-7883
Email: chicago.archives@nara.gov
URL: http://www.nara.gov/regional/
chicago.html

**State Historical Society of
Wisconsin/Archives Division**
816 State Street
Madison, WI 53706
Tel: 608-264-6460
Email:
Archives.Reference@CCMAIL.ADP.WI
SC.EDU
URL: http://www.shsw.wisc.edu/
archives/

WYOMING

ARCHIVES, STATE & NATIONAL

**National Archives—Rocky
Mountain Region (Denver)**
Bldg. 48, Denver Federal Center
West 6th Avenue and Kipling Street
Denver, Colorado 80225-0307
Mailing Address:
P.O. Box 25307
Denver, Colorado 80225-0307
Phone: 303-236-0817
Fax: 303-236-9297
E-mail: denver.archives@nara.gov
http://www.nara.gov/regional/
denver.html

Wyoming State Archives
Barrett Building
2301 Central Avenue
Cheyenne, WY 82002
Tel: (307) 777-7826
FAX: (307) 777-7044
E-mail:WYARCHIVE@STATE.WY.US
URL: http://spacr.state.wy.us/cr/
archives/ index.htm

APPENDIX III

Following is a collection of census extraction forms for the years 1790 to 1930. The same forms are also available for download (as a .pdf) on the Ancestry.com Web site at <http://www.ancestry.com/save/charts/census.htm>.

Also included is a chart showing what questions were asked in each census, as well as form BC-600 from the U.S. Census Bureau <http://www.census.gov/genealogy/www/agesearch.html>. This form, along with a congressionally mandated fee, is required by the Bureau for a search of confidential records of the Federal population censuses from 1910 to 1990.

1790 United States Federal Census

State: _____   Call Number/URL: _____

Enumeration Date: _____

county	city	page	names of heads of families	free white males of 16 years & upwards, including heads of families	free white males under 16 years	free white females including heads of families	all other free persons	slaves

To search the 1790 census online, visit www.ancestry.com

Ancestry®Census Form 001

1800 United States Federal Census

State: _____ Call Number/URL: _____ Enumeration Date: _____

For more family history charts and forms, visit www.ancestry.com/save/charts/ancchart.htm

Ancestry.com℠

county	city	page	names of heads of families	free white males					free white females					all other free persons	slaves
				under 10	10 thru 15	16 thru 25	26 thru 44	45 and over	under 10	10 thru 15	16 thru 25	26 thru 44	45 and over		

To search the 1800 census online, visit www.ancestry.com

Ancestry® Census Form 002

1810 United States Federal Census

State: _____   Call Number/URL: _____

Enumeration Date: _____

county	city	page	names of heads of families	free white males					free white females					all other free persons	slaves
				under 10	10 thru 15	16 thru 25	26 thru 44	45 and over	under 10	10 thru 15	16 thru 25	26 thru 44	45 and over		

To search the 1810 census online, visit www.ancestry.com

1820 United States Federal Census

Ancestry.com℠

For more family history charts and forms,
visit www.ancestry.com/save/charts/ancchart.htm

Page: _____ State: _____ County: _____ Call Number/URL: _____ Enumeration Date: _____

Name of the county, parish, township, town or city where the family resides	Names of heads of families	Free White Males						Free White Females						Foreigners not naturalized	Numbers of persons engaged in Agriculture	Numbers of persons engaged in Commerce	Numbers of persons engaged in Manufactures	Slaves								Free Colored Persons								All other persons except Indians not taxed
		Free white males under ten years (to 10)	Free white males of ten and under sixteen (10 to 16)	Free white males between sixteen and eighteen (16 to 18)	Free white males of of sixteen and under twenty-six, including heads of families (16 to 26)	Free white males of twenty six and under forty-five, including heads of families (26 to 45)	Free white males of forty five and upwards, including heads of families (45 & c.)	Free white females under ten years (to 10)	Free white females of ten and under sixteen (10 to 16)	Free white females between sixteen and eighteen (16 to 18)	Free white females of twenty six and under forty five, including heads of families (18 to 26)	Free white females of of sixteen and under twenty-six, including heads of families (26 to 45)	Free white females of forty five and upwards, including heads of families (45 & c.)					Males under fourteen (to 14)	Males of fourteen and under twenty-six (to 26)	Males of twenty-six and under forty-five (to 45)	Males of forty-five and upwards (45 & c.)	Females under fourteen (to 14)	Females of fourteen and under twenty-six (to 26)	Females of twenty-six and under forty-five (to 45)	Females of forty-five and upwards (45 & c.)	Males under fourteen (to 14)	Males of fourteen and under twenty-six (to 26)	Males of twenty-six and under forty-five (to 45)	Males of forty-five and upwards (45 & c.)	Females under fourteen (to 14)	Females of fourteen and under twenty-six (to 26)	Females of twenty-six and under forty-five (to 45)	Females of forty-five and upwards (45 & c.)	

copyright © 2001 MyFamily.com, Inc.

To search the 1820 census online, visit www.ancestry.com

Ancestry® Census Form 004

Ancestry.com℠

1830 United States Federal Census

FREE WHITE PERSONS, (INCLUDING HEADS OF FAMILIES).

Names of Heads of Families

Name of the county, city, ward, town, township, parish, precinct, hundred, or district.

LINE NUMBER

Males.

Under five years of age	under 5
Of five and under ten.	5 to 10
Of ten and under fifteen.	10 to 15
Of fifteen and under twenty.	15 to 20
Of twenty and under thirty.	20 to 30
Of thirty and under forty.	30 to 40
Of forty and under fifty.	40 to 50
Of fifty and under sixty.	50 to 60
Of sixty and under seventy.	60 to 70
Of seventy and under eighty.	70 to 80
Of eighty and under ninety.	80 to 90
Of ninety and under one hundred.	90 to 100
Of one hundred and upward.	100, &c.

Females.

Under five years of age	under 5
Of five and under ten.	5 to 10
Of ten and under fifteen.	10 to 15
Of fifteen and under twenty.	15 to 20
Of twenty and under thirty.	20 to 30
Of thirty and under forty.	30 to 40
Of forty and under fifty.	40 to 50
Of fifty and under sixty.	50 to 60
Of sixty and under seventy.	60 to 70
Of seventy and under eighty.	70 to 80
Of eighty and under ninety.	80 to 90
Of ninety and under one hundred.	90 to 100
Of one hundred and upward.	100, &c.

Slaves.

Males.

Age range	
Under ten years of age.	under 10
Of ten and under twenty-four.	10 to 24
Of twenty-four and under thirty-six.	24 to 36
Of thirty-six and under fifty-five.	36 to 55
Of fifty-five and under one hundred.	55 to 100
Of one hundred and upwards.	100 & c.

Females.

Age range	
Under ten years of age.	under 10
Of ten and under twenty-four.	10 to 24
Of twenty-four and under thirty-six.	24 to 36
Of thirty-six and under fifty-five.	36 to 55
Of fifty-five and under one hundred.	55 to 100
Of one hundred and upwards.	100 & c.

Free Colored Persons.

Males.

Age range	
Under ten years of age.	under 10
Of ten and under twenty-four.	10 to 24
Of twenty-four and under thirty-six.	24 to 36
Of thirty-six and under fifty-five.	36 to 55
Of fifty-five and under one hundred.	55 to 100
Of one hundred and upwards.	100 & c.

Females.

Age range	
Under ten years of age.	under 10
Of ten and under twenty-four.	10 to 24
Of twenty-four and under thirty-six.	24 to 36
Of thirty-six and under fifty-five.	36 to 55
Of fifty-five and under one hundred.	55 to 100
Of one hundred and upwards.	100 & c.

LINE NUMBER

TOTAL

WHITE PERSONS included in foregoing.

Category	
Who are Deaf and Dumb, under fourteen years of age.	under 14
Who are Deaf and Dumb, of the age of fourteen and under 25.	14 to 25
Who are Deaf twenty-five and upwards.	25 & c.
Who are blind.	
ALIENS—Foreigners not naturalized.	

SLAVES AND COLORED PERSONS, included in foregoing.

Category	
Who are Deaf and Dumb, under fourteen years of age.	under 14
Who are Deaf and Dumb, of the age of fourteen and under 25.	14 to 25
Who are Deaf twenty-five and upwards.	25 & c.
Who are blind.	

Ancestry.com℠

1840 United States Federal Census

Page: _____

State: _____ County: _____ Call Number/URL: _____ Enumeration Date: _____

FREE WHITE PERSONS, (INCLUDING HEADS OF FAMILIES)

LINE NUMBER	Name of the county, city, ward, town, township, parish, precinct, hundred, or district.	Names of Heads of Families

Males. — Under 5; 5 & under 10; 10 & under 15; 15 & under 20; 20 & under 30; 30 & under 40; 40 & under 50; 50 & under 60; 60 & under 70; 70 & under 80; 80 & under 90; 90 & under 100; 100 & upwards

Females. — Under 5; 5 & under 10; 10 & under 15; 15 & under 20; 20 & under 30; 30 & under 40; 40 & under 50; 50 & under 60; 60 & under 70; 70 & under 80; 80 & under 90; 90 & under 100; 100 & upwards

Free Colored Persons.

Males. — Under 10; 10 & under 24; 24 & under 35; 35 & under 55; 55 & under 100; 100 & upwards

Females. — Under 10; 10 & under 24; 24 & under 35; 35 & under 55; 55 & under 100; 100 & upwards

Slaves.

Males. — Under 10; 10 & under 24; 24 & under 35; 35 & under 55; 55 & under 100; 100 & upwards

Females. — Under 10; 10 & under 24; 24 & under 35; 35 & under 55; 55 & under 100; 100 & upwards

TOTAL

Number of persons in each family employed in

- Mining.
- Agriculure.
- Commerce.
- Manufacture and trade.
- Navigaion of the ocean.
- Navigaion of canals, lakes, rivers.
- Learned professional engineers.

Pensioners for Revolutionary or military services, included in the foregoing.

Names	Ages

Under 14; 14 & under 25; 25 & upwards

Deaf and Dumb, Blind, and Insane White Persons, ncluded in the foregoing.

Deaf and Dumb — Under 14; 14 & under 25; 25 & upwards

Blind and Insane — Blind.; Insane idiots at public charge; Insane and idiots at private charge

Deaf and Dumb, Blind, and Insane Colored Persons, Included in the foregoing.

Deaf, Dumb, and Blind — Deaf & Dumb; Blind; Insane and idiots at private charge

Insane and Idiots — Deaf, Dumb, and Blind; Insane and idiots at public charge

Schools & c.

- Universities or college
- Number of students
- Acadamies & Grammar Schools
- No. of Scholars
- Primary and Common Schools
- No. of Scholars at Public charge
- No. of white persons over 20 years of age in each family who cannot read and write.

1850 United States Federal Census

Ancestry.com℠

Page: _____ State: _____ County: _____ City: _____ Call Number/URL: _____ Enumeration Date: _____

Dwelling - houses numbered in the order of visitation	Families numbered in the order of visitation	The Name of every Person whose usual place of abode on the first day of June, 1850, was in this family	Description			Profession, Occupation, or Trade of each Male Person over 15 years of age	Value of Real Estate owned	Place of Birth Naming the State, Territory, or Country	Married within the year	Attended School within the year	Persons over 20 y'rs of age who cannot read & write	Whether deaf and dumb, blind, insane, idiotic, pauper, or convict
			Age	Sex	Color < White black, or mulatto							
1	2	3	4	5	6	7	8	9	10	11	12	13

1860 United States Federal Census

Ancestry.com℠

For more family history charts and forms,
visit www.ancestry.com/save/charts/ancchart.htm

Page: _____ State: _____ County: _____ City: _____ Call Number/JRL: _____ Enumeration Date: _____

1	2	3	Description			7	8	9	10	11	12	13	14
Dwelling -houses numbered in the order of visitation	Families numbered in the order of visitation	The Name of every Person whose usual place of abode on the first day of June, 1860, was in this family.	Age	Sex	Color< White black, or mulatto	Profession, Occupation, or Trade of each Male Person over 15 years of age.	Value of Real Estate	Value of Personal Estate	Place of Birth Naming the State, Territory, or Country	Married within the year	Attended School within the year	Persons over 20 y'rs of age who cannot read & write	Whether deaf and dumb, blind, insane, idiotic, pauper, or convict
			4	5	6								

To search the 1860 census online, visit www.ancestry.com

copyright © 2001 MyFamily.com, Inc.

Ancestry® Census Form 008

1870 United States Federal Census

For more family history charts and forms,
visit www.ancestry.com/save/charts/ancchart.htm

Page: _____ State: _____ County: _____ City: _____ Call Number/URL: _____ Enumeration Date: _____

1	2	3		Description			7	Value of Real Estate owned		10	Parentage					Edu-cation		Whether	Constitutional Relations	
Dwelling - houses numbered in the order of visitation	Families numbered in the order of visitation	The Name of every Person whose place of abode on the first day of June, 1870, was in this family	Age at last birth-day. If under 1 year, give months in fractions, thus 3/12	Sex—Male (M), Female (F).	Color—White (W); Black (B); Mulatto (M); Chinese, (C); Indian, (I).	Profession, Occupation, or Trade of each Male Person over 15 years of age		Value of Real Estate	Value of Personal Estate	Place of Birth Naming the State, Territory, or Country	Father of Foreign born	Mother of Foreign born	If born within the year, state month (Jan., &c.)	If married within the year, state month (Jan., &c.)	Attended School within the year	Cannot read	Cannot write	Whether deaf and dumb, blind, insane, idiotic, pauper, or convict	Male Citizens of U.S. of 21 years of age and upwards	Male Citizens of U.S. of 21 years of age and upwards where right to vote is denied on other grounds than rebellion or other crime
		3	4	5	6	7		8	9	10	11	12	13	14	15	16	17	18	19	20

To search the 1870 census online, visit www.ancestry.com

Ancestry® Census Form 009

1880 United States Federal Census

Ancestry.com℠

State: _____ County: _____ City: _____ Page: _____ E.D.: _____ Call #/URL: _____ Enumeration Date: _____

For more family history charts and forms, visit www.ancestry.com/save/charts/ancchart.htm

	In Cities				Personal Description					Civil Condition				Occupation		Health					Education			Nativity		
	Name of street	House number	Dwelling houses numbered in order of visitation.	Families numbered in order of visitation.	The Name of each Person whose place of abode on 1st day of June 1880, was in this family.	Color—White, W: Black, B: Mulatto, Mu: Chinese, C: Indian, I.	Sex—Male, M: Female, F.	Age at last birthday prior to June 1, 1880. If under 1 year, give months in fractions, thus: 8/12	If born within the Census year, give the month.	Relationship of each person to the head of this family—whether wife, son, daughter, servant, boarder, or other.	Single	Married	Widowed, divorced	Married during Census year	Profession, Occupation, or Trade of each person, male or female.	Numbers of months this person has been unemployed during the Census year.	Is the person (on the day of the enumerator's visit) sick, or temporarily disabled, so as to be unable to attend to ordinary business or duties? If so, what is the sickness or disability?	Blind	Deaf and dumb	Idiotic	Insane	Maimed, crippled, bedridden, or otherwise disabled	Attended school within the Census year.	Cannot read	Cannot write	Place of Birth of this person, naming State or Territory of United States, or the Country if of foreign birth.	Place of Birth of the father of this person, naming State or Territory of United States, or the Country if of foreign birth.	Place of Birth of the mother of this person, naming State or Territory of United States, or the Country if of foreign birth.
			1	2	3	4	5	6	7	8	9	10	11	12	13	14	15	16	17	18	19	20	21	22	23	24	25	26

To search the 1880 census online, visit www.ancestry.com

Ancestry® Census Form 010

1890 Veterans Schedule

State: _____

County: _____

City, township: _____

Enumeration District: _____

Sheet Number: _____

Enumeration Date: _____

Call Number/URL: _____

Line number	House no.	Family no.	Names of surviving Soldiers, Sailors, Marines, and widows	Rank	Company	Name of regiment or vessel	Date of Enlistment			Date of Discharge			Length of service			Post office address	Disability incurred
	1	2	3	4	5	6	Day	Month	Year	Day	Month	Year	Years	Months	Days	10	11
									7			8			9		

NOTES:

Ancestry.com

For more family history charts and forms, visit www.ancestry.com/save/charts/ancchart.htm

To search the census online, visit www.ancestry.com

copyright © 2001 MyFamily.com, Inc.

Ancestry® Census Form 011

1900 United States Federal Census

State: _____

County: _____

City, township: _____

Call Number/URL: _____

Enumeration District: _____

Sheet Number: _____

Enumeration Date: _____

Location					Name	Relation	Personal Description									Nativity		
In Cities	Street	House number	Number of dwelling house in the order of visitation	Number of family, in the order of visitation	of each person whose place of abode on June 1, 1900, was in this family. Enter surname first, then the given name and middle initial, if any. Include every person living on June 1, 1900. Omit children born since June 1, 1900.	Relationship of each person to the head of the family.	Color or Race	Sex	Date of Birth Month	Date of Birth Year	Age at last birthday	Whether single, married, widowed, or divorced	Number of years of present marriage	Mother of how many children	Number of these children living	Place of birth of this person.	Place of birth of Father of this person.	Place of birth of Mother of this person.
Line number			1	2	3	4	5	6	7	7	8	9	10	11	12	13	14	15

Citizenship			Occupation, Trade, or Profession of each person TEN YEARS of age and over.		Education				Ownership of Home				
Year of immigration to the U.S.	Number of years in the U.S.	Naturalization	Occupation	Months not employed	Attended school (in months)	Can read	Can write	Can speak English	Owned or Rented	Owned free or mortgaged	Farm or house	Number of farm schedule	Line number
16	17	18	19	20	21	22	23	24	25	26	27	28	

NOTES:

1910 United States Federal Census

State: _____

County: _____

City, township: _____

Enumeration District: _____

Sheet Number: _____

Enumeration Date: _____

Call Number/URL: _____

Location				Number of Family, in order of visitation	Name	Relation	Personal Description								Nativity			Citizenship	
Line number	Street, Avenue, Road, etc.	House number or farm	Dwelling Number		Name of each person whose place of abode on April 15, 1910, was in this family.	Relationship of this person to the head of the family.	Sex	Color or Race	Age at last birthday	Whether single, married, widowed, or divorced	Number of years of present marriage	Mother of how many children — Number born / Number now living	Place of birth of this person.	Place of birth of Father of this person.	Place of birth of Mother of this person.	Year of immigration to the U.S.	Whether naturalized or Alien
			1	2	3	4	5	6	7	8	9	10 / 11	12	13	14	15	16

Line number	Occupation			Education			Ownership of Home						Citizenship continued
Whether able to speak English; or, if not, give language spoken.	Trade or profession of, or particular kind of work done by this person.	General nature of industry, business, or establishment in which this person works.	Whether an employer, employee, or working on own account	If an employee— Whether out of work on April 15, 1910 / Number of weeks out of work during 1909	Whether able to read	Whether able to write	Attended school any time since Sept. 1, 1909	Owned or Rented	Owned free or mortgaged	Farm or house	Number of farm schedule	Whether a survivor of the Union or Confederate Army or Navy	Whether blind (both eyes) / Whether deaf and dumb
17	18	19	20	21 / 22	23	24	25	26	27	28	29	30	31 / 32

Ancestry® Census Form 013

To search the 1910 census online, visit www.ancestry.com

1920 United States Federal Census

State: _____

County: _____

City, township: _____

Call Number/URL: _____

Enumeration District: _____

Sheet Number: _____

Enumeration Date: _____

	Place of Abode				Name	Relation.	Tenure.		Personal Description.				Citizenship.			Education.		
Line number	Street, avenue, road, etc.	House number or farm	Dwelling Number	Number of family, in order of visitation	of each person whose place of abode on January 1, 1920, was in this family	Relationship of this person to the head of the family.	Home owned or rented	If owned, free or mortgaged	Sex	Color or Race	Age at last birthday	Single, married, widowed, or divorced	Year of immigration to the United States	Naturalized or alien	If naturalized, year of naturalization	Attended school anytime since Sept. 1, 1919	Able to read	Able to write
	1	2	3	4	5	6	7	8	9	10	11	12	13	14	15	16	17	18

	Nativity and Mother Tongue							Occupation.			
Line number	Place of birth of each person and parents of each person enumerated. If born in United States, give the state or territory. If of foreign birth, give the place of birth, and, in addition, the mother tongue.						Able to speak English	Trade, profession, or particular kind of work done.	Industry, business, or establishment in which at work.	Employer, salary or wage worker, or working on own account	No. of farm schedule
	Person		Father		Mother						
	Place of Birth	Mother Tongue	Place of Birth	Mother Tongue	Place of Birth	Mother Tongue					
	19	20	21	22	23	24	25	26	27	28	29

To search the 1920 census online, visit www.ancestry.com

For more family history charts and forms, visit www.ancestry.com/save/charts/ancchart.htm

1930 United States
Federal Census

State: _____
County: _____
City, township: _____

Enumeration District: _____
Sheet Number: _____
Enumeration Date: _____

Call Number/URL: _____

PLACE OF ABODE				NAME	RELATION	HOME DATA				PERSONAL DESCRIPTION					EDUCATION		PLACE OF BIRTH		

PLACE OF ABODE

Street, avenue, road, etc.	House number (in cities or towns)	Number of dwelling house in order of visitation	Number of family in order of visitation
1	2	3	4

NAME — of each person whose *place of abode* on April 1, 1930, was in this family. Enter surname first, then the given name and middle initial, if any. Include every person living on April 1, 1930. Omit children born since April 1, 1930.
5

RELATION — Relationship of this person to the head of the family.
6

HOME DATA

Home owned or rented	Value of home, if owned, or monthly rental, if rented	Radio set	Does this family live on a farm?
7	8	9	10

PERSONAL DESCRIPTION

Sex	Color or race	Age at last birthday	Marital condition	Age at first marriage
11	12	13	14	15

EDUCATION

Attended school or college any time since Sept. 1, 1929	Whether able to read and write
16	17

PLACE OF BIRTH — Place of birth of each person and parents of each person enumerated. If born in the United States, give the State or Territory. If of foreign birth, give the country of birth. See Instructions for additional entries required for certain countries.

PERSON	FATHER	MOTHER
18	19	20

MOTHER TONGUE (OR NATIVE LANGUAGE) OF FOREIGN BORN — Language spoken in home before coming to the United States
21

CODE (For office use only. Do not write in these columns)

State or M.T	Country	Nativity
A	B	C

CITIZENSHIP

Year of immigration to the United States	Naturalized or alien	Whether able to speak English
22	23	24

OCCUPATION AND INDUSTRY

OCCUPATION — Trade, profession, or particular kind of work, as spinner, salesman, riveter, etc.
25

INDUSTRY — Industry or business, as cottonmill, dry goods store, shipyard, public school etc.
26

CODE (For office use only. Do not write in this column)
D

Class of Worker
27

EMPLOYMENT — Whether actually at work

Yes or No	Line number for unemployed
28	29

VETERANS — Whether a veteran of the U.S. military or naval forces mobilized for any war or expedition

Yes or No	What war or expedition
30	31

No. of farm schedule
32

NOTES:

Comparision of Census Information, 1790-1930

Personal Info on Census	1790	1800	1810	1820	1830	1840	1850	1860	1870	1880	1900	1910	1920	1930
Name of family head only	x	x	x	x	x	x								
Headcount by age, gender, ...	x	x	x	x	x	x								
Standard census form					x	x	x	x	x	x	x	x	x	x
Names of all individuals							x	x	x	x	x	x	x	x
Age							x	x	x	x	x	x	x	x
Sex							x	x	x	x	x	x	x	x
Color							x	x	x	x	x	x	x	x
Profession or occupation							x	x	x	x	x	x	x	x
Place of birth							x	x	x	x	x	x	x	x
Attended school that year							x	x	x	x	x	x	x	x
Married that year							x	x	x	x	x			
Read or write							x	x	x	x	x	x		x
Deaf, blind, insane, idiotic, ...							x	x	x	x		x		
Real estate value							x	x	x					
Personal estate value								x	x					
Separate slave schedule							x	x						
Father of foreign birth									x					
Mother of foreign birth									x					
Month of birth											x			
Month of birth that year									x	x				
Male citizen over 21 years									x					
Male over 21 denied vote									x					
Visitation number of dwelling							x	x	x	x	x	x	x	x
Visitation number of family							x	x	x	x	x	x	x	x
Street name in city										x	x	x	x	x
House number in city										x	x	x	x	x
Relationship to family head										x	x	x	x	x
Marital status										x	x	x	x	x
Month of marriage that year									x					
No. of months unemployed										x	x			
Father's birthplace										x	x	x	x	x
Mother's birthplace										x	x	x	x	x
Sickness on census day										x				
Year of birth											x			
No. of years present marriage											x	x		
Mother how many children											x	x		
Number of children living											x	x		
Year of immigration to US											x	x	x	x
No. of years in US											x			
Naturalization status											x	x	x	x
Months attended school											x			

Personal Info on Census	1790	1800	1810	1820	1830	1840	1850	1860	1870	1880	1900	1910	1920	1930
Can speak English											x	x	x	x
Owned house or rented											x	x	x	x
Home free or mortgaged											x	x	x	
Farm or house											x	x		
Language if not English												x		
Nature of industry												x	x	x
Employer, employee, self												x	x	
Out of work for the day												x		x
Weeks/months unemployed												x		
Civil War veteran												x		
Year of naturalization													x	
Native language													x	
Native language of father													x	
Native language of mother													x	
Value of home if owned														x
Monthly rental if renting														x
Radio set														x
Live on a farm														x
Age at first marriage														x
Language before immigration														x
Class of worker														x
Military veteran														x
Veteran of what war														x

APPLICATION FOR SEARCH OF CENSUS RECORDS

IMPORTANT INFORMATION
PLEASE READ AND FOLLOW CAREFULLY

This application is for use in requesting a search of census records.* Copies of these census records often are accepted as evidence of age, citizenship, and place of birth for employment, social security benefits, insurance, and other purposes.

If the applicant is located, an official transcript will be provided including the following information:

Personal Census Information	Available for census year(s)
• Census Year	1910–1990
• County where taken	1910–1980
• State where taken	1910–1990
• Name	1910–1990
• Relationship to head of household	1910–1990
• Name of person in whose household you were counted	1910–1990
• Age at the time of the census	1910–1950, 1970–1990
• Date of birth	
Year and quarter	1960
Month and year	1970–1980
Year	1990
• Place of birth	1910–1950
• Citizenship if requested or if foreign born	1910–1950
• Occupation (if requested)	1910–1950

The Census Bureau's records with **INDIVIDUAL NAMES ARE NOT ON A COMPUTER.** They are on microfilm, arranged according to the address at the time of the census. Censuses are taken primarily for statistical, not legal, purposes. Attention is called to the possibility that the information shown in the census record may not agree with that given in your application. **The record must be copied exactly as it appears on the census form.** The Census Bureau CANNOT make changes even though it realizes that enumerators may have been misinformed or made mistakes in writing down the data they collected. Those agencies that accept census transcripts as evidence of age, relationship, or place of birth usually overlook minor spelling differences but would be reluctant to consider a record that was changed years later at an applicant's request.

If you authorize the Bureau of the Census to send your record to someone other than yourself, you must provide the name and address, including ZIP Code, of the other person/agency.

Birth certificates, including delayed birth certificates, are **not issued** by the Bureau of the Census. You can obtain the birth certificate from the Health Department or the Department of Vital Statistics of the state in which the applicant was born.

The average time it should take you to fill out the BC-600, "Application for Search of Census Records," including the time spent reading instructions is 12 minutes.

If you have any questions regarding these estimates or any other aspect of this form, please call or write the Associate Director for Finance and Administration, Paperwork Reduction Project 0607-0117, Room 3104, FB 3, Bureau of the Census, Washington, D.C. 20233.

Respondents are not required to respond to any information collection unless it displays a valid approval number from the Office of Management and Budget. This 8-digit number appears in the top right corner of page 3 of this form.

* Information from 1920 and earlier censuses is public information and is available from the National Archives.

The completed application should be mailed to the Bureau of the Census, P.O. Box 1545, Jeffersonville, IN 47131, together with a money order or check payable to "Commerce–Census."

INSTRUCTIONS FOR COMPLETING THIS FORM
PRINT OR TYPE INFORMATION EXCEPT SIGNATURE
PLEASE FOLLOW NUMBERED INSTRUCTIONS

1. Purpose

The purpose for which the information is desired must be shown so that a determination may be made under 13 U.S.C. 8(a) that the record is required for proper use. For proof of age, most agencies require documents closest to date of birth; therefore we suggest you complete information for the EARLIEST CENSUS AFTER DATE OF BIRTH.

2. Signature

Each application requires a signature. The signature should be the same as that shown on the line captioned "full name of person whose census record is requested." When the application is for a census record concerning another person, the requester must sign the application, and the authority of the requester must be furnished as stated in instruction 3 below. If signed by marking (X), please indicate the name of the person whose mark it is and have witnesses sign as instructed. IF SIGNATURE IS PRINTED, please indicate that is the usual signature.

3. Confidential information given to other than person to whom it relates

(a) Census information is confidential and ordinarily will not be furnished to another person unless the person to whom it relates authorizes this in the space provided or if there is other proper authorization as indicated in 3(b), 3(c), and 3(d).

(b) Minor children – Information regarding a child who has at this time not reached the legal age of 18 may be obtained upon the written request of either parent or guardian.

(c) Mentally incompetent persons – Information regarding persons who are mentally incompetent may be obtained upon the written request of the legal representative, supported by a certified copy of the court order naming such legal representative.

(d) **Deceased persons – If the record requested relates to a deceased person, the application MUST be signed by (1) a blood relative in the immediate family (parent, brother, sister, or child), (2) the surviving wife or husband, (3) the administrator or executor of the estate, or (4) a beneficiary by will, or insurance. IN ALL CASES INVOLVING DECEASED PERSONS, a certified copy of the death certificate MUST be furnished, and the relationship to the deceased MUST be stated on the application. Legal representatives MUST also furnish a certified copy of the court order naming such legal representatives; and beneficiaries MUST furnish legal evidence of such beneficiary interest.**

4. Fee required

The $40.00 fee is for a search of one census for one person only. The time required to complete a search depends upon the number of cases on hand at the particular time and the difficulty encountered in searching a particular case. The normal processing time requires 3 to 4 weeks. Since the fee covers return postage, do not send a stamped self-addressed envelope with the application.

No more than one census will be searched and the results furnished for one fee. Should it be necessary to search more than one census to find the record, you will be notified to send another fee before another search is made. Tax monies are not available to furnish the information. **If a search has been made, the fee cannot be returned even if the information is not found.**

5. Full schedules

The full schedule is the complete one-line entry of personal data recorded for that individual ONLY. The names of other persons will not be listed. If the applicant specifies "full schedule," the Census Bureau will furnish, in addition to the regular transcript, whatever other information appears on the named person's record in the original schedule, but only for THAT PERSON. In this case the information is typed on a facsimile of the original census schedule and verified as a true copy. There is an additional charge of $10.00 for EACH full schedule requested.

The Census Bureau also will provide "full schedule" information for those other members of the same household for whom authorizations are furnished. (See Instruction 3 for authorization requirements). A fee of $10.00 is required for each person listed on the full schedule.

LIMITATIONS — Certain information, such as place of birth, citizenship, and occupation, is available only for census years 1910 through 1950. Full schedule information is not available for census years 1970, 1980, and 1990.

6. Census years 1910–1920–1930–1940– 1950– 1960–1970–1980–1990

The potential of finding an individual's census record is increased when the respondent provides thorough and accurate address information FOR THE DAY THESE CENSUSES WERE TAKEN. If residing in a city AT THE TIME THESE CENSUSES WERE TAKEN, it is necessary to furnish the house number, the name of the street, city, county, state, and the name of the parent or other head of household with whom residing at the time of the census. If residing in a rural area, it is VERY IMPORTANT to furnish the township, district, precinct or beat, AND the direction and number of miles from the nearest town.

1990 Request — It is VERY IMPORTANT to provide a house number and street name or rural route and box number. Always include a ZIP Code.

7. Locator Map (optional)

Box 7 is provided for a sketch of the area where the applicant lived at the time of the requested census.

IF YOU NEED HELP FILLING OUT THIS APPLICATION, PLEASE CALL 812-218-3046, MONDAY THROUGH FRIDAY 7:00 A.M. THROUGH 4:30 P.M. EASTERN TIME

FORM BC-600
(9-1-98)

U.S. DEPARTMENT OF COMMERCE
BUREAU OF THE CENSUS

APPLICATION FOR SEARCH OF CENSUS RECORDS

RETURN TO: Bureau of the Census, P.O. Box 1545, Jeffersonville, IN 47131

OMB No. 0607-0117; Approval Expires 07/31/2001

NAME OF APPLICANT ▶

1. Purpose for which record is to be used (See Instruction 1)

☐ Passport
(date required) _____

☐ Proof of age

☐ Genealogy

☐ Other – Please specify _____

I certify that information furnished about anyone other than the applicant will not be used to the detriment of such person or persons by me or by anyone else with my permission.

2. Signature – Do not print (Read instruction 2 carefully before signing)

_____

IF SIGNED BY MARK (X), TWO WITNESSES MUST SIGN HERE

Signature _____ Signature _____

Telephone number (Include area code)

PRESENT MAILING ADDRESS

Number and street

City   State   ZIP Code

NOTICE – Intentionally falsifying this application may result in a fine of $10,000 or 5 years of imprisonment, or both (title 18, U.S. Code, section 1001).

3. If the census information is **to be sent to someone other than the person whose record is requested**, give the name and address, including ZIP Code, of the other person or agency.

This authorizes the Bureau of the Census to send the record to: (See instruction 3)

_____
_____
_____

DO NOT USE THIS SPACE – OFFICIAL USE ONLY

Case number

$ _____ (Fee)

☐ Money Order
☐ Check
☐ Other

Papers received (itemize)

Received by	Date	Returned by	Date	Returned

4. **FEE REQUIRED:** (See instructions 4 and 5) A check or money order (**DO NOT SEND CASH**) payable to "Commerce – Census" must be sent with the application. This fee covers the cost of a search of no more than one census year for one person only.

5. Fee required .... $ **40.00**

_____ extra copies @ $2.00 $ _____

_____ full schedules @ $10.00 $ _____

TOTAL amount enclosed $ _____

FULL NAME OF PERSON WHOSE CENSUS RECORD IS REQUESTED ▶

First name	Middle name	Maiden name (If any)	Present last name	Nicknames

Full name of father (Stepfather, guardian, etc.)

Date of birth (If unknown, estimate)	Place of birth (City, county, State)	Race	Sex	Nicknames

Full maiden name of mother (Stepmother, etc.)

Full name of father (Stepfather, guardian, etc.)   Nicknames

First marriage (Name of husband or wife)	Year married (Approximate)	Second marriage (Name of husband or wife)	Year married (Approximate)

Names of brothers and sisters

Name and relationship of all other persons living in household (Aunts, uncles, grandparents, lodgers, etc.)

PLEASE COMPLETE REVERSE SIDE

GIVE PLACE OF RESIDENCE FOR APPROPRIATE CENSUS DATE (SEE INSTRUCTIONS 1 AND 6)

Census date	Number and street (Read instruction 6 first)	City, town, township (Read instruction 6 first)	County and State	Name of person with whom living (Head of household)	Relationship of head of household
April 15, 1910 (See instruction 6)					
Jan. 1, 1920 (See instruction 6)					
April 1, 1930 (See instruction 6)					
April 1, 1940 (See instruction 6)					
April 1, 1950 (See instruction 6)					
April 1, 1960 (See instruction 6)					
April 1, 1970 (See instruction 6)					
April 1, 1980 (See instruction 6)					
April 1, 1990 (See instruction 6)		ZIP Code			

7. LOCATOR MAP (Optional)
PLEASE DRAW A MAP OF WHERE THE APPLICANT LIVED, SHOWING ANY PHYSICAL FEATURES, LANDMARKS, INTERSECTING ROADS, CLOSEST TOWNS, ETC., THAT MAY AID IN LOCATING THE APPLICANT FOR THE CENSUS YEAR REQUESTED.

HAVE YOU SIGNED THE APPLICATION AND ENCLOSED THE CORRECT FEES?

FORM BC-600 (9-1-98)

INDEX

ABOUT THE AUTHORS

Loretto Dennis Szucs holds a B.A. degree in history from Saint Joseph's College in Indiana and has been involved in genealogical research, teaching, lecturing, and publishing for more than twenty-five years. Lou is the author of several publications, including *The Source: A Guidebook of American Genealogy*. Previously employed as an archives specialist for the National Archives, Lou is currently vice president of publishing for MyFamily.com Inc. She has served on the Illinois State Archives Advisory Board and on the governing boards of the Chicago Genealogical Society, the South Suburban Genealogical and Historical Society (Illinois), and the Illinois State Genealogical Society. Lou was the founding secretary for the Federation of Genealogical Societies and has held various positions in that organization, including that of editor of the FGS Forum.

Matthew James Wright graduated cum laude with a B.A. degree in journalism from Brigham Young University in Provo, Utah. He has participated in family history research, both his own and for others, for over fifteen years. For the past seven years he has worked in magazine and book publishing with an emphasis on sports, business, and family history.